PROSECUTING CRIME IN THE PUBLIC INTEREST

This book provides the first detailed analysis of the decision to prosecute made by the statutory Australian Offices of Director of Prosecutions.

It examines the system of prosecution as part of the executive branch of government, and the role and challenges of the individual prosecutors who make decisions within the system. It explores the tension between prosecutorial independence and prosecutorial accountability, and the paradox that political involvement in prosecutions is necessary for accountability and to uphold the public interest, but can compromise independence.

The book makes a unique contribution to both Australian criminal law scholarship and to the international literature on criminal prosecution, by drawing on the sub-disciplines of criminal law and administrative law. It includes case studies on prosecuting child sexual abuse, rape, and government espionage, and comparisons with common law and civil law countries including the USA, the UK, Italy and South Africa.

Prosecuting Crime in the Public Interest

How Tension between Independence and Accountability Threatens the Rule of Law in Australia

Kellie Toole

•HART•
OXFORD • LONDON • NEW YORK • NEW DELHI • SYDNEY

HART PUBLISHING

Bloomsbury Publishing Plc

Kemp House, Chawley Park, Cumnor Hill, Oxford, OX2 9PH, UK

1385 Broadway, New York, NY 10018, USA

29 Earlsfort Terrace, Dublin 2, Ireland

HART PUBLISHING, the Hart/Stag logo, BLOOMSBURY and the Diana logo are trademarks of Bloomsbury Publishing Plc

First published in Great Britain 2024

A catalogue record for this book is available from the British Library.

A catalogue record for this book is available from the Library of Congress.

Library of Congress Control Number: 2024934316

ISBN: HB: 978-1-50997-320-0
ePDF: 978-1-50997-322-4
ePub: 978-1-50997-321-7

Typeset by Compuscript Ltd, Shannon
Printed and bound in Great Britain

To find out more about our authors and books visit www.hartpublishing.co.uk. Here you will find extracts, author information, details of forthcoming events and the option to sign up for our newsletters.

To my Mum and Dad

TABLE OF CONTENTS

TABLE OF CASES

Australia

United States of America

Canada

United Kingdom

South Africa

TABLE OF LEGISLATION

PART 1

The Problem: The Australian Attorney General

1

The Modern Problem

I. The Decision to Prosecute

As Edwards observed in 1995:

> There are few areas of greater importance in maintaining public confidence in government than the ordinary citizen's respect for the administration of justice. That respect, when accorded, springs from the depth of the ordinary person's basic values and hopes. Violate those values and you quickly begin to see the erosion of society's confidence in those to whom the enormous powers of government have been entrusted. Nowhere is this more evident than in the institution and conduct of criminal prosecutions.[1]

Prosecuting a person for a serious crime is widely understood as a significant contest between the individual and the state. However, criminal prosecutions also represent a contest between priorities within the state. Australia inherited from England a system of prosecution where the Attorney General, in the dual role of senior politician and First Law Officer of the Crown, was responsible for instituting and conducting prosecutions according to the values of public interest, independence, and accountability. The decision to prosecute was made pursuant to a broad discretion to prosecute in the public interest, because not all offences were expected to be prosecuted. Nor would it be possible to resource the investigation and prosecution of every breach of every criminal law. The Australian Attorney General prosecuted in this tradition until the 1970s and 1980s.

In late-twentieth-century Australia, various prosecutorial controversies raised concerns that the politico-legal role of the Attorney General compromised prosecutorial independence, because political motivations could influence the decision to prosecute. The problem was compounded by a lack of transparency in prosecutorial decisions, in an environment where the 'new' administrative law was reflecting an increased expectation of openness and accountability in government decision-making.

However, the implementation of prosecutorial reform presented a challenge for the Australian parliaments. The Attorney General's political role had the potential to compromise prosecutorial independence by having political interest, rather

[1] J Edwards, 'The Office of Attorney General – New Levels of Public Expectations and Accountability' in P Stenning (ed), *Accountability for Criminal Justice: Selected Essays* (Toronto, University of Toronto Press, 1995) 294, 304.

than public interest, determine the decision to prosecute. Yet the same political role was integral to determining the public interest, and providing the ultimate check on the exercise of prosecutorial discretion. The dilemma, as Cox states it, was that the exercise of discretion is both 'necessary to organizational effectiveness and the source of potential abuse of power'.[2] Most Australian parliamentarians, ultimately, acknowledged this tension. They decided that the dual Attorney General role undermined community confidence in the criminal justice system by creating the perception and/or reality of political interference in prosecutions, as well as the independence that drove their establishment.

As a result, statutory Offices of Director of Public Prosecutions (ODPPs) were established in every jurisdiction in Australia, in one of the most comprehensive, planned renewals of a modern prosecution system anywhere in the world. Under Australia's federal system, ODPPs are established under statute passed in each jurisdiction. However, the legislation, policies and guidelines that define the scope of the Directors of Public Prosecutions' (DPPs') role and direct their decisions are similar enough to sustain analysis with a national focus. The primary purpose of the reform was to safeguard the independence of the decision to prosecute by distancing, but not entirely separating, it from a political office. This reform was intended to remove the possibility of Attorneys General exercising the prosecutorial discretion on a partisan basis, in the interest of their government, rather than independently, in the interests of the public. Under this system, ODPPs have responsibility for initiating, conducting and terminating prosecutions, and Attorneys General have ultimate responsibility for prosecutorial decisions and policy. The ODPPs were intended to continue to uphold the values of accountability and public interest in prosecutions as well as independence.

This book considers whether decisions to prosecute made by the ODPPs uphold the values of public interest, independence and accountability that are fundamental to the Anglo-Australian prosecutorial tradition. The ODPPs are not the only Australian prosecuting authorities, nor do they undertake the bulk of prosecution work. The term 'prosecution system' is used throughout this book to refer to the ODPPs, but the actual prosecution system includes police prosecution services,[3]

[2] RW Cox III, 'Accountability and Responsibility in Organizations: The Ethics of Discretion' (2004) 13 *Viešoji Politika Ir Administravimas* 39, 48.

[3] In jurisdictions except the Northern Territory, Western Australia, the Australian Capital Territory and the Commonwealth, police prosecute summary matters in the lower courts. This work accounts for approximately 92% of all criminal prosecution: Australian Bureau of Statistics, 'Criminal Courts, Australia' (3 March 2023) www.abs.gov.au/statistics/people/crime-and-justice/criminal-courts-australia/latest-release. Internationally, summary offences have been overlooked: N Lacey, *In Search of Criminal Responsibility: Ideas, Interests, and Institutions* (Oxford, Oxford University Press, 2016) 43. This limitation is evident in Australia, including in this book; for exceptions, see T Krone, 'Police and Prosecution', Conference Paper, National Outlook Symposium on Crime in Australia: Mapping the Boundaries of Australia's Criminal Justice System, 22–23 March 1999; PH Sweeny, 'The Role of the Police Prosecutor in the Magistrates Court System' in IL Potas (ed), *Prosecutorial Discretion*, Seminar Proceedings No 6 (Australian Institute of Criminology, 7–9 November 1984) 135; C Corns, 'Police Summary Prosecutions in Australia and New Zealand: Some Comparisons' (2000) 19 *University of Tasmania Law Review* 280.

government agencies and regulators that prosecute certain offences under relevant enabling statutes.[4] The police and regulators, unlike DPPs, are frequently both investigators and prosecutors. This dual role raises significant issues for independence in prosecutions. However, the whole system of Australian prosecution is too broad for the scope of a single book. The prosecution of the most serious offences is a central and under-researched part of Australia's prosecution system and so is the sole focus of this book.

This book is also restricted to the prosecution of mentally competent adults, because the prosecution of youth offenders and those raising mental impairment defences must respond to very specific statutory obligations, medical evidence and social attitudes. The conclusions in this book may, nevertheless, raise issues that could usefully be applied to other prosecutorial agencies and other categories of offender.[5]

The purpose of this study is to contribute to the understanding of the Australian criminal justice system, the prosecutorial values underpinning it and the appropriateness of the prosecution system to uphold the stated values. However, it also offers insights into the perennial dilemma of balancing independence and accountability to achieve public interest that may be of interest, across jurisdictions, regarding other statutory officers with discretionary powers.

This book explores the implications of all the Australian ODPPs being, in different ways, independent from, and yet overseen by, the Attorney General. It identifies this relationship as creating an unresolved tension that has the potential to undermine prosecutorial independence, accountability and the public interest in prosecutions. It critically analyses the paradox that the political role that compromised independence also protected public interest and accountability. It contends that the internal tension in the DPP–Attorney General relationship has a direct effect on the rule of law.

Prosecuting a person for a serious crime is one of the most intrusive possible actions by the state against an individual. The decision to prosecute goes 'to the relationship between the citizen and the State and specifically concern[s] the legitimate boundaries of public power'.[6] It has profound legal, social and political importance, because it affects the life and liberty of individual criminal defendants and reflects the values articulated through the criminal law. Equally, the 'inaction' involved in the 'decision not to bring charges, is a central feature of prosecutorial discretion, and this substantial power is often disguised'.[7]

[4] eg Taxation Administration Act 1953 (Cth), Competition and Consumer Act 2010 (Cth), Corporations Act 2001 (Cth). Some regulators refer all prosecutions to the Commonwealth DPP: Civil Aviation Act 1988 (Cth) and Civil Aviation Safety Authority, *Enforcement Manual* (July 2023) s 10.2.

[5] Prosecution non-disclosure and use of forensic evidence affect the decision to prosecute, but are outside the scope of this book. See *Mallard v The Queen* (2005) 224 CLR 125; *Eastman v the Australian Capital Territory* [2019] ACTSC 280; *R v Keogh (No 2)* [2014] SASCFC 136; *R v Jama* [2009] VSCA.

[6] C Corns, *Public Prosecutions in Australia: Law, Policy and Practice* (Pyrmont, Thomson Reuters, 2014) 5.

[7] GL Brandon et al, 'Open Prosecution' (2023) 75 *Stanford Law Review* 1365, 1374.

The ODPP guidelines recognise that the decision to prosecute is 'the most important step in the prosecution process',[8] because an inappropriate prosecution can cause embarrassment and hardship to a person who is innocent or has 'merely committed an inadvertent or minor breach of the law'.[9] The guidelines also acknowledge the broader implication that a 'wrong decision to prosecute or, conversely, a wrong decision not to prosecute, tends to undermine the confidence of the community in the criminal justice system'.[10]

However, the decision to prosecute is made by individuals. In 2003, Queensland's Deputy DPP, Paul Rutledge, responded to criticism of a decision not to prosecute a high-profile person accused of child sexual offences. He stated: 'other than the fact of the individual involved – the name – this was a very ordinary exercise of the discretion to prosecute. That's the brutal reality of this thing'.[11] His frank comment is powerfully evocative of the combination of mundanity and brutality involved in deciding whether or not to prosecute. The decision is not only brutal for complainants. In 2005, Stephen Pallaras, the newly appointed South Australian DPP, told the local Press Club that prosecutors

> see the carnage that we as a society wreak upon each other in the black and white of the statements of witnesses, in the colour of the photographs of the injuries of the victims and in the faces of the families that we deal with every day.[12]

The juxtaposition of a powerful state role and its exercise at a very human level has significant implications for the community.

II. The Prosecutor and the Criminal Justice System

The criminal jury trial is an iconic image in popular culture, and the leading actors' 'dichotomous displays of honorable intentions and moral turpitude, have arrested audiences for nearly a century'.[13] However, 'television drama does not allow for the accurate representation'[14] of the criminal trial, or of the roles of the police, lawyers, judges or juries who work within it. The 'cinematic characters are usually divided

[8] Director of Public Prosecutions (Tasmania), *Prosecution Policy and Guidelines* (2022) 5 (*DPP Policy* (Tas)); Director of Public Prosecutions, South Australia, *Statement of Prosecution Policy & Guidelines* (2014) 5 (*DPP Policy* (SA)); Commonwealth Director of Public Prosecutions, *Prosecution Policy of the Commonwealth* (2021) 4 (*DPP Policy* (Cth)).

[9] Director of Public Prosecutions, *Prosecution Policy of the Australian Capital Territory* (2021) 3.

[10] *DPP Policy* (Tas) (n 8) 5; *DPP Policy* (SA) (n 8) 5; *DPP Policy* (Cth) (n 8) 4.

[11] Crime and Misconduct Commission (Queensland), *The Volkers Case: Examining the Conduct of the Police and Prosecution* (March 2003) 70.

[12] S Pallaras, Speech, SA Press Club, 6 May 2005, 2.

[13] PT Brady, 'The Celluloid Advocate: The Evolution of the Twentieth Century Cinematic Lawyer' (2017) 27 *Southern California Interdisciplinary Law Journal* 165, 165.

[14] KB Nunn, 'The Trial as Text: Allegory, Myth and Symbol in the Adversarial Criminal Process – A Critique of the Role of the Public Defender and a Proposal for Reform' (1995) 32 *American Criminal Law Review* 743, 770.

into specific stereotypical … one-dimensional bit parts'.[15] A more accurate representation of all the actors in the criminal trial is important, but there is special importance to understanding the prosecutor: 'the alter ego of the state'.[16]

Australian and international scholars have identified public prosecutions as 'under-researched' since at least 1929,[17] and as recently as 2012,[18] 2013[19] and 2016.[20] Public prosecutions are certainly under-theorised given their significance, and compared to other actors in the criminal justice system. Scholars tend to overlook public prosecutors in favour of judges,[21] and a 2010 study found 'roughly 18 policing publications for every 1 prosecution publication'.[22]

The focus on police and judges overlooks the pivotal role of the prosecutor. Arrests and charges of serious offences by police are not given effect unless the prosecutor prosecutes, and, unlike decisions of prosecutors, 'individualized sentencing policies of various judges cannot be woven into a single policy of law enforcement'.[23] However, public prosecutions are gradually drawing the attention of international scholars. There is now a body of jurisdiction-specific historical, theoretical and empirical research on prosecutions, and a small body of comparative work.[24] The Australian ODPPs have been subject to limited scholarly scrutiny,[25] and have not been included in any significant international comparative studies.[26]

[15] VS Salzmann and Philip T Dunwoody, 'Prime-Time Lies: Do Portrayals of Lawyers Influence How People Think About the Legal Profession' (2005) 58 *SMU Law Review* 412, 427–28.

[16] Nunn (n 14) 787.

[17] R Moley, *Politics and Criminal Prosecution* (New York, Minton, Balch & Company, 1929) 48; FJ Remington and VG Rosenblum, 'The Criminal Law and the Legislative Process' (1960) *University of Illinois Law Forum* 481, 497; J Kaplan, 'Prosecutorial Discretion – A Comment' (1965) 60 *North Western Law Review* 174, 174; BA Grosman, *The Prosecutor: An Inquiry into the Exercise of Discretion* (Toronto, University of Toronto Press, 1969) 3; J Rozenberg, *The Case for the Crown: The Inside Story of the Director of Public Prosecutions* (Wellingborough, Equation, 1987) 13; DT Johnson, *The Japanese Way of Justice: Prosecuting Crime in Japan* (Oxford, Oxford University Press, 2002) 7–8; J Goethals et al, 'Preface to Special Issue: The Future of the Public Prosecutor's Office in the European Union' (2000) 8 *European Journal of Crime, Criminal Law and Criminal Justice* 149, 150.

[18] K Yang, 'Prosecutorial Discretion: A Balancing Act' (Honours Thesis, Murdoch University, 2012) 1; M Tonry, 'Preface' in M Tonry (ed), *Prosecutors and Politics: A Comparative Perspective* (Chicago, University of Chicago Press, 2013) vii.

[19] Corns (n 6) 4.

[20] I Colvin, 'The Charging Decision: Accountability, Transparency, and Control of the Decision to Prosecute' (PhD Thesis, University of Queensland, 2016) 16.

[21] G Di Federico, 'Prosecutorial Independence and the Democratic Requirement of Accountability in Italy: Analysis of a Deviant Case in a Comparative Perspective' (1998) 38 *British Journal of Criminology* 371, 371.

[22] JL Worrall et al, 'Modeling Prosecutors' Charging Decisions in Domestic Violence Cases' (2006) 52 *Crime & Delinquency* 472, 497.

[23] RL Misner, 'Recasting Prosecutorial Discretion' (1996) 86 *Journal of Criminal Law and Criminology* 717, 718–19.

[24] E Luna and M Wade (eds), *The Prosecutor in Transnational Perspective* (Oxford, Oxford University Press, 2012); Tonry (n 18); M Langer and DA Sklansky (eds), *Prosecutors and Democracy: A Cross-National Study* (Cambridge, Cambridge University Press, 2017).

[25] See Corns (n 6); Colvin (n 20).

[26] But see Yang (n 18), which compares Australia and Singapore, and K Yang, 'Public Accountability of Public Prosecutions' (2013) 20 *Murdoch University Law Review* 28, which compares Australia

The prosecutor must be studied in the context of other criminal justice institutions. As Tarling argued in the 1980s, prosecutorial offices' interdependence with other agencies is critical because actions taken in any branch affect other institutions within the system.[27] In 2002, Johnson agreed that one can no more study prosecutors in isolation from other actors in the criminal justice system than 'one can study Hamlet or Genji[28] exclusive of the other actors on their stage'.[29] In 2006, Stuntz was similarly critical of scholarship that ignores the interrelated aspects of policing, adjudication, crime definition and punishment.[30] Luna and Wade confirmed in 2012 that police, prosecutors, defence lawyers and judges all 'serve their individual functions but still interrelate with each other to form an identifiable whole'.[31] They cautioned that a 'monocular focus on an individual actor … risks losing the broader systemic context'.[32] Brown agreed that prosecutorial powers 'fit within a broader systemic context and can be normatively assessed only in light of the other features of the investigative and adjudicative processes of which they are a part'.[33]

I consider how relationships between prosecutors, the police, courts, the government and the Attorney General are relevant to the decision to prosecute. The book does, however, retain a focus on the ODPP and contributes to the understanding of the whole system through a richer understanding of an under-researched key component.

III. The Intersection of Criminal and Administrative Law

The limited attention prosecutors have attracted has, unsurprisingly, been from criminal law scholars. I am a criminal lawyer and this is a criminal law book. However, prosecutors are located within the executive branch of government. The decision to prosecute is an exercise of executive discretion as well as of prosecutorial discretion. The decision to prosecute is, therefore, governed by administrative law.

and Japan. V Colvin and P Stenning (eds), *The Evolving Role of the Public Prosecutor: Challenges and Innovations* (New York, Routledge, 2019) contextualises Australian prosecutions in the international context but does not focus on comparative studies.

[27] R Tarling, 'Interdependence and the Crown Prosecution Service' in JE Hall Williams (ed), *The Role of the Prosecutor: Report of the International Criminal Justice Seminar Held at the London School of Economics and Political Science in January 1987* (London, Dartmouth Publishing, 1988) 43, 43–50.

[28] M Shikibu, *The Tale of Genji* (c 1008) is considered a classic of Japanese fiction.

[29] Johnson (n 17) 12.

[30] WJ Stuntz, 'The Political Constitution of Criminal Justice' (2006) 119 *Harvard Law Review* 780, 831.

[31] E Luna and M Wade, 'Adversarial and Inquisitorial Systems: Distinctive Aspects and Converging Trends' in Luna and Wade (n 24) 177.

[32] ibid 178.

[33] DK Brown, 'American Prosecutors' Powers and Obligations in the Era of Plea Bargaining' in Luna and Wade (n 24) 203.

This book is, therefore, located at the intersection of criminal and administrative law. It analyses the decision to prosecute according to these areas of law, which are both concerned with the relationship between the individual and the state, albeit in different ways. This approach provides an original perspective on the prosecutorial role. It recognises the decision to prosecute as a fundamental aspect of criminal law. However, administrative law scrutinises executive discretion, and provides insights into the exercise of prosecutorial discretion that have not been fully recognised within criminal law.

Administrative law has also developed mechanisms to protect the individual against excesses of government power, which have not been extended to the decision to prosecute. Administrative law principles enlarge the importance of this study beyond what could be achieved within criminal law alone. Most significantly, they expand the means of analysing the relationship between the decision to prosecute and the rule of law. According to Carothers, under the rule of law, laws are publicly available, 'clear in meaning, and apply equally to everyone. They enshrine and uphold the political and civil liberties that have gained status as universal human rights over the last half-century.'[34] The theme of whether the decision to prosecute is defined and applied in a transparent and consistent enough manner to uphold the rule of law arises throughout this examination of the ODPPs' ability to uphold the prosecutorial values.

The ODPP system has been lauded. During the establishment of the South Australian ODPP in 1991, Greg Crafter MP observed that ODPPs in other jurisdictions were 'successful' because they gave the community confidence that the criminal justice system was 'beyond the influence of any political process'.[35] Later that decade, the Western Australian DPP, John McKechnie, praised the ODPP as 'a prosecution service freed from the shackles of the past and from political and other influences'.[36]

The sense of success was enduring. On its twenty-fifth anniversary in 2009, Attorney General Robert McLelland claimed that the Commonwealth ODPP ensured that prosecutorial decisions 'are made on an objective, professional basis, without the fact or appearance of political involvement, and, literally, without fear of retribution or without hope of favour'.[37] Positive appraisals of the prosecutorial system have not been confined to politicians and prosecutors. In 2014, Christopher Corns published the first comprehensive overview of prosecutions in Australia. He concluded that 'the DPP model has been a successful legal and political experiment' that has 'not been adequately acknowledged'.[38]

[34] T Carothers, 'The Rule of Law Revival' (1998) 77 *Foreign Affairs* 95, 96.

[35] South Australia, *Parliamentary Debates*, House of Assembly, 31 October 1991, 1686 (Greg Crafter).

[36] J McKechnie, 'Directors of Public Prosecutions: Independent and Accountable' (1996) 26 *University of Western Australia Law Review* 266, 270.

[37] R McClelland, 'Remarks at the Commonwealth Director of Public Prosecutions 25th Anniversary Dinner', Speech, Old Parliament House, 5 March 2009, 6.

[38] Corns (n 6) 584.

ODPPs are, axiomatically, successful according to the principles that drove their establishment, because the DPP makes the decision to prosecute in an independent statutory office. However, the DPPs' independence has been significantly tempered by the Attorney General's retention of ultimate responsibility for prosecutions. Paradoxically, though, the Attorney General's ability to uphold prosecutorial accountability and the public interest has been significantly tempered by the DPPs' independence. This is a descriptive claim about tension within the ODPPs, rather than a normative claim about the need for greater independence or accountability. However, the rule of law is threatened where a prosecutorial system does not uphold both independence and accountability, which raises normative questions about how the ODPP system should balance core prosecutorial values.

2

The English Origins

Throughout, English prosecutions have been underpinned by the values of public interest, independence and accountability. Legal commentaries and political memoirs acknowledge that these values were widely understood to be interdependent with each other, and with the legal and political role of the Attorney General, and could only be upheld through the exercise of a broad discretion. When Attorneys General took on responsibility for prosecutions, the broad obligations attached to their dual role as First Law Officer of the Crown and senior politician shaped the expectations regarding the decision to prosecute.

From the political–legal role of the Attorney General, the public interest evolved into the fundamental prosecutorial value, with independence and accountability becoming enduring core values that supported the public interest. However, an unresolved and continuing tension developed between the values and the discretion to interpret and apply them.

I. The Attorney General as Prosecutor

The origins of the role of Attorney General are, to some extent, 'now obscure',[1] and subject to 'conjectural effort'.[2] However, by the thirteenth century, *attornati regis* were kept on retainer to 'watch over the Sovereign's interests and to assert his rights in any matter involving a usurpation' of his privileges. These responsibilities included appearing in various courts on matters including criminal prosecutions.[3] Upon his accession in 1399, Henry IV established 'King's Attorneys', who could appear in all courts on his behalf. By 1461, the term 'Attorney General' was used to describe the 'First Law Officer of the Crown',[4]

[1] P East, 'Life as the Attorney-General: Being in the Right Place at the Right Time' (2017) 23 *Auckland University Law Review* 37, 37.

[2] J Edwards, *The Law Officers of The Crown: A Study of the Offices of Attorney-General and Solicitor-General of England, With an Account of the Office of the Director of Public Prosecutions of England* (London, Sweet & Maxwell, 1964) 12.

[3] ibid 17.

[4] F Hanlon, 'An Analysis of the Office of Attorney General in Australia and Directions for the Future' (PhD Thesis, University of Melbourne, 2007) 17.

whose role was restricted to representing the king in court, and did not involve any political duties or acting as legal counsel for government.[5] From 1461, the position of Attorney General became more formalised, took on a political dimension, and steadily grew in influence and prestige. The role gradually took on certain residual prerogative functions that were once within the personal power of the monarch and had not been taken over by the legislature or the judiciary.[6] From the mid-nineteenth century, the increase in volume and complexity of legislation, and growing obligations to advise the Crown, changed the Attorney General's main role from representative of the Crown in court to 'head of a government department'.[7]

The role of Attorney General thus developed a 'hybrid character'[8] consisting of legal and political responsibilities. In some jurisdictions, in some areas of law, the maintenance of a distinction between law and politics has been deemed 'impossible, and therefore a myth'.[9] However, the English prosecutorial system is predicated on the Attorney General having a dual political–legal role, and exercising political and legal judgement separately, as appropriate. The intersection of law and politics gave strength and prestige to the Attorney General's position, but also placed it in a 'no-man's-land where the boundary between law and politics was never clearly distinguishable'.[10] Woodhouse explains that the political role could conflict with the values that were critical to the prosecutorial role:

> the position of the Attorney General is at best awkward and at times barely sustainable. He is required to serve two masters, the government and the law … he is sometimes expected to exhibit partisanship and to pursue the government's interest and at other times to be independent, impartial, upholding the public interest.[11]

This conflict inherent in the dual political–legal role of the Attorney General has been heightened since the two-party system reached its 'apogee' in the 1950s,[12] and provides the foundation for tension between the values of prosecutorial independence,[13] public interest and accountability.

[5] B Selway, 'The Different Role of an Australian Attorney-General' (2002) 13 *Public Law Review* 263, 264.

[6] Edwards, *Law Officers* (n 2) 34.

[7] ibid 51.

[8] LJ King, 'The Attorney General, Politics and the Judiciary' (2000) 29 *University of Western Australia Law Review* 155, 149.

[9] D Kaib, 'The Mississippi Tobacco Case: Reform and the Boundaries of Law and Politics' (PhD Thesis, American University, 2011) 19.

[10] Edwards, *Law Officers* (n 2) 127.

[11] D Woodhouse, 'The Attorney General' (1997) 50 *Parliamentary Affairs* 97, 97.

[12] R McKibbin, 'A Brief Supremacy: The Fragmentation of the Two-Party System in British Politics, c 1950–2015' (2016) 27 *Twentieth Century British History* 450, 452.

[13] Before the 1970s, the dominant concern about the Attorney General's independence was whether their ability to undertake private legal work affected their political–legal role. This is outside the scope of this book, but see Edwards, *Law Officers* (n 2) 90–118.

II. Tension between Prosecutorial Values

A. Independence

Historically, there was no commitment to independence from political influence in prosecutorial decision-making. In the Stuart period, prosecutions for sedition and criminal libel were instituted by the Attorney General for 'blatantly political objects'.[14] In later centuries, too, Attorneys General were openly directed to prosecute by members of the executive. In 1872, Attorney General John Coleridge defended his conduct of an unsuccessful perjury prosecution thus: 'I had no choice as to accepting the conduct of a prosecution, ordered by the Lord Chief Justice … and directed by the government.'[15] There was also evidence that in prosecutions after World War I 'the Attorney-General was a passive instrument for giving effect to decisions formulated by the executive'.[16] However, opposition to political interference in prosecutions coexisted with political prosecutions, and executive directions to prosecute became 'the subject of violent controversy, as to the proper boundaries of government interference in the conduct of criminal prosecutions'.[17]

In 1793, the Attorney General maintained that he could consult parliamentary colleagues on whether or not to prosecute for sedition over the publication of Thomas Paine's *The Rights of Man*, but that only his own conscience and sense of duty could determine the final decision.[18] This principle was repeated in the same year by Lord Eldon, later Lord Chancellor; in 1873 by Prime Minister Gladstone; in 1896 by Prime Minister Salisbury; and in 1903 by Prime Minister Balfour, who stated, in clear opposition to former practice, that it 'is not in the power of the Government to direct the Attorney General to direct a prosecution. No government would do such a thing; no Attorney General would tolerate its being done.'[19]

At the beginning of the twentieth century, 'the Campbell Affair' resolved that the Attorney General should never be directed by the Prime Minister or Cabinet on the decision to prosecute. In 1924, John Campbell, acting editor of the Communist Party publication, the *Workers Weekly*, was charged under the Incitement to Mutiny Act 1797 (UK). He had exhorted troops that in the event of war or repression of industrial disputes, they should engage in class war against their oppressors within Britain instead of against their 'comrades' from the Continent. The Attorney General in the new MacDonald Labour government, Patrick Hastings, gave, but then withdrew, his consent to the prosecution. Campbell was only acting editor,

[14] ibid 5.
[15] ibid 94.
[16] ibid 195.
[17] ibid 94.
[18] ibid 179.
[19] HC Deb 19 February 1903, vol 118, col 377 (Arthur Balfour, Prime Minister).

and since he had been recognised for gallantry in the field, a prosecution was considered unlikely to succeed but certain to provide unwelcome attention for the Communist Party.[20]

The case generated debate about whether the Prime Minister did, and should, direct the Attorney General to withdraw criminal charges against Campbell.[21] The Prime Minister denied direct involvement in the decision, but a Cabinet minute later disclosed the instruction that 'no public prosecution of a political character should be undertaken without the prior sanction of the Cabinet being obtained'.[22] In 1924, the Conservative Prime Minister who replaced Ramsay, Stanley Baldwin, described the offending Cabinet instruction as 'unconstitutional, subversive of the administration of justice and derogatory to the office of Attorney General'.[23] The following year, the Attorney General, Lord Simon, confirmed that no one is prosecuted 'unless the Attorney-General … is satisfied that the case for prosecution lies against him. He should receive orders from nobody.'[24]

The criticism of the handling of *Campbell* unfairly ignored the previous acceptance of executive involvement in prosecutorial decision-making. Nonetheless, the result was that a 'previously controversial principle was elevated to the level of a binding constitutional convention',[25] and the Attorney General's prosecutorial independence from political influence acquired public and political importance. This orthodoxy was affirmed in 1951, when the Labour Attorney General, Hartley Shawcross, delivered a 'classic pronouncement'[26] after consulting with previous Attorneys General, Directors of Public Prosecutions (DPPs) and other government officials. He stated that, in making the decision to prosecute, the Attorney General may consult with his colleagues, and

> he would in some cases be a fool if he did not. On the other hand, the assistance of his colleagues is confined to informing him of particular considerations which might affect his own decision … The responsibility for the eventual decision rests with the Attorney-General.[27]

As Woodhouse argues, the 'line between listening to colleagues and being influenced by them is a thin one'.[28] However, after several centuries of debate, the English settled on the principle, inherited in Australia, that prosecutorial

[20] Edwards, *Law Officers* (n 2) 201.

[21] R Jackson, *Case for the Prosecution: A Biography of Sir Archibald Bodkin, Director of Public Prosecutions, 1920–1930* (London, Arthur Barker, 1962) 208–10.

[22] British Cabinet Minutes, 6 August 1924, cited in BA MacFarlane, 'Sunlight and Disinfectants: Prosecutorial Accountability and Independence Through Public Transparency' (2001) 45 *Criminal Law Quarterly* 272, 276.

[23] HC Deb 11 December 1924, vol 179, cols 354–55, cited in MacFarlane (n 22) 276.

[24] ibid 276.

[25] ibid.

[26] J Edwards, *The Attorney General, Politics and the Public Interest* (London, Sweet & Maxwell 1984) 318.

[27] HC Deb 29 January 1951, vol 483, cols 683–84 (Hartley Shawcross, Attorney General).

[28] Woodhouse (n 11) 98.

independence required 'insulating' prosecutorial decisions 'from direct political or popular influence'.[29]

In England, this commitment to independence was given effect by excluding the Attorney General from Cabinet.[30] However, the personal integrity of the Attorney General was perceived to be the ultimate safeguard against political interference. In 1953, Shawcross confidently asserted that it

> may seem odd to strangers, but in Britain it is well accepted that a man can be an active party politician and at the same time, but in another capacity, bring an absolutely impartial and honest mind to bear on the problems of a non-political nature.[31]

This opinion extended beyond Shawcross's reference to some essential quality of British maleness. A Law Ministers Conference in Canada in 1977 issued a communiqué that prosecutorial independence 'depended to a large extent upon the unimpeachable integrity of the holder of the office'.[32] The principle that the Attorney General *should* make prosecutorial decisions independently from political influence has been asserted in all Commonwealth countries in the decades since the 1950s.[33] However, confidence in the Attorney General's integrity diminished over time, and the question of whether the Attorney General *would* make prosecutorial decisions independently from political influence is more contentious. It raised the issue in England of 'How to preserve the advantages of political independence without abandoning the fundamental democratic principle of public accountability',[34] which ultimately drove the establishment of the Offices of Director of Public Prosecutions (ODPPs) in Australia.

B. Accountability

McKechnie describes the relationship between accountability and independence as 'One of the least understood areas of law and government'.[35] In principle, at least, vesting the Attorney General with individual responsibility for making prosecutorial decisions protected them from influence by other members of the executive. However, it did not foreclose the possibility of their own political interests affecting

[29] A Duff, 'Discretion and Accountability in a Democratic Criminal Law' in M Langer and DA Sklansky (eds), *Prosecutors and Democracy: A Cross-National Study* (Cambridge, Cambridge University Press, 2017) 9, 33.

[30] Edwards, *Law Officers* (n 2) 160–65.

[31] H Shawcross, 'The Office of the Attorney-General' (1953) 7 *Parliamentary Affairs* 380, 387.

[32] Law Ministers' Meeting, Canada, Communique (August 1977) cited in Commonwealth of Australia, *Parliamentary Debates*, House of Representatives, 6 September 1977, 5–6 (Robert Ellicott).

[33] See, eg Ministry of Justice (New Zealand), *Examining the Prosecution Systems of England and Wales, Canada, Australia and Scotland: A Background Document to the Review of Public Prosecution Services in New Zealand* (September 2011).

[34] G Majone, 'Independence vs Accountability?: Non-majoritarian Institutions and Democratic Government in Europe' (European University Institute, 1994) Working Paper No 94/3, 26.

[35] J McKechnie, 'Directors of Public Prosecutions: Independent and Accountable' (1996) 26 *University of Western Australia Law Review* 266, 273.

the legal judgement required for prosecutorial decisions. While the risk of political influence in prosecutorial decisions was managed informally through the personal integrity of the Attorney General and the commitment to prosecutorial independence, it was buttressed by the formal processes of parliament.

Accountability, in the sense of the 'complex of means which reinforce the responsibility of public actors',[36] is inherent in the nature of parliament. It is critical to 'democratic governance based on the rule of law. In the absence of accountability, elections and the notion of the will of the people lose their meaning, and government has the potential to become arbitrary and self-serving.'[37] Accountability is particularly important to prosecutions, because, as Richman argues, a 'liberal democracy that relies on prosecutors to hold others accountable [must] ensure that prosecutors are themselves held to account'.[38]

Parliament assumed a central role in British government and politics after the English Revolution of 1688. Participation in politics was limited to small numbers of men belonging to the aristocracy and substantial land-owning gentry.[39] However, Parliament came to be viewed as a representative institution that was directly accountable to the people,[40] and which felt 'the pressure of the newly enfranchised masses'.[41] The accountability of the Attorney General was a corollary of the power and prestige by then inherent in the office. During the 1960s and 1980s, John Edwards, barrister and professor of law, undertook pioneering and influential work on the British law officers. He observed that in controversial prosecutions, the Attorney General must 'face the House of Commons, when discharging his public accountability' and 'accept the praise or condemnation that will emerge as public reaction to his decisions becomes known'.[42]

Parliamentary accountability still means that Cabinet ministers are, collectively and individually, accountable to Parliament.[43] Collectively, they are taken to have consented to government policy, so they cannot avoid personal responsibility where decisions of the government face public criticism.[44] Individually, they must account to Parliament, and through it to the public, for their actions and decisions.[45] They are required to scrutinise the conduct of officers within

[36] F Contini and R Mohr, 'Reconciling Independence and Accountability in Judicial Systems' (2007) 3 *Utrecht Law Review* 26, 30.

[37] A Adekunle, 'Prosecutorial Independence and Effectiveness of the Nigerian Criminal Justice System' in V Colvin and P Stenning (eds), *The Evolving Role of the Public Prosecutor: Challenges and Innovations* (New York, Routledge, 2019) 220, 226.

[38] D Richman, 'Accounting for Prosecutors' in Langer and Sklansky (n 29) 40, 43.

[39] S Gordon, *Controlling the State: Constitutionalism From Ancient Athens to Today* (Cambridge, MA, Harvard University Press, 2002) 329.

[40] M Cole, *Democracy in Britain* (Edinburgh, Edinburgh University Press, 2006) 78.

[41] L Lipson, 'The Two-Party System in British Politics' (1953) 47 *American Political Science Review* 337, 348.

[42] Edwards, *Attorney General* (n 26) 57.

[43] HV Emy, *The Politics of Australian Democracy: Fundamentals in Dispute*, 2nd rev edn (Melbourne, Macmillan, 1978) 246.

[44] Cole (n 40) 82–84.

[45] G Marshall, 'The Evolving Practice of Parliamentary Accountability: Writing Down the Rules' (1991) 44 *Parliamentary Affairs* 460, 461–65.

their portfolios, and other members of the executive branch, through reports and measures of performance.[46] They can be asked questions, be required to appear before committees of inquiry, face no-confidence and censure motions, and face pressure to resign. Ultimately, the sovereign and delegated powers of Members of Parliament are 'held on behalf of the community',[47] and so Attorneys General are subject to removal from office by the public through elections.[48]

C. Independence and Accountability

Edwards explained in 1964 that, according to the complementarity doctrine, the principle of accountability to Parliament 'is of no less importance than the principle of independence'.[49] He further explained that the Attorney General was not 'a despot capable of striding indiscriminately across the vast territory covered by the criminal law', because responsibility to Parliament counterbalanced their independence.[50]

However, the reconciliation of independence and accountability has proved so challenging across various areas of law that they have been deemed 'antithetical values',[51] which are generally 'in tension, if not actually clashing'.[52]

D. The Public Interest[53]

According to East in 2017, 'Most people, if they know anything about the Attorney-General, know that the Attorney's name is in some way associated with the public interest'.[54] While this statement may or may not accurately reflect public understanding of the role of the Attorney General, it does accurately reflect the importance of the Attorney General's long-standing responsibility for upholding the public interest.

Edwards observed in the mid-twentieth century that the Attorney General, as the representative of the sovereign, had a 'proven record as the repository of the

[46] R Mulgan, '"Accountability": An Ever-Expanding Concept?' (2000) 78 *Public Administration* 555, 556.

[47] DJ Galligan, *Discretionary Powers: A Legal Study of Official Discretion* (Oxford, Oxford University Press, 1986) 4.

[48] R Creyke, *Control of Government Action: Text, Cases and Commentary*, 5th rev edn (Chatswood, LexisNexis Butterworths, 2018) 28.

[49] Edwards, *Law Officers* (n 2) 225.

[50] ibid 227.

[51] Majone (n 34) 2.

[52] Contini and Mohr (n 36) 28.

[53] Theorising about the nature of public interest is beyond the scope of this book, but see, eg G Schubert, *The Public Interest: A Critique of the Theory of a Political Concept* (Glencoe, The Free Press, 1960).

[54] East (n 1) 38.

public conscience',[55] and Shawcross agreed the Attorney General was referred to as 'the protector of … the public interest'.[56] Carney questions the legitimacy of that 'dangerously vague and onerous' title,[57] and argues that Attorneys General are not the 'guardians of the public interest. That responsibility is shared by all who are vested, directly or indirectly, with the sovereign power of the people: Parliament, the executive and the judiciary'.[58] This technical concern notwithstanding, in the case of *Gouriet* in 1978, the House of Lords found that the 'right of the Attorney-General to represent the public interest' was a 'fundamental principle of English law' that was 'not technical, not procedural, not fictional. It is constitutional … it is also wise'.[59]

The Attorney General's prosecutorial role needed to reflect the general obligation to act in the public interest. However, for centuries, the specific content of the public interest in prosecutions was unclear. The role of the Attorney General in acting in the public interest was placed at a premium, without its scope and nature being defined. Even when the obligation to prosecute in the public interest was enacted in the Prosecution of Offences Regulations 1879 (UK), it only included a 'nebulous and highly flexible criterion' that required a prosecution when 'the offence or the circumstances of its commission is of such a character that a prosecution in respect thereof is required in the public interest'.[60] In 1962, Downs wrote that while the term was widely used, any inquiry into its 'meaning plunges the inquirer into a welter of platitudes, generalities, and philosophic arguments. It soon becomes apparent that no general agreement exists about whether the term has any meaning at all, or, if it has, what the meaning is.'[61] He was, however, able to articulate that various schools of thought had defined it as consisting of 'the will of the people' and was 'the course of action that is best for society as a whole'.[62]

The historical explanations of prosecuting in the public interest are certainly vague. Lord Denham, Attorney General from 1830 to 1832, explained that the decision to prosecute was not based on his personal view, but on his 'feeling of what was due to the security of the public and to the honour of the Crown' and necessary 'for the purpose of protecting the peace of the country'.[63]

A century later, Shawcross agreed that the Attorney General 'must have constant regard to what is politic, in the broad abstract sense of what is in the public interest'.[64] He was also somewhat clearer that the assessment of the public interest involved consideration of social factors such as 'the effect which the

[55] Edwards, *Attorney General* (n 26) 139.
[56] Shawcross (n 31) 389.
[57] G Carney, 'Comment – The Role of the Attorney-General' (1997) 9 *Bond Law Review* 1, 6.
[58] ibid 6.
[59] *Gouriet v Union of Post Office* Workers (1978) AC 435 [5], [8].
[60] Prosecution of Offences Regulations 1879 (UK), s 4, cited in Edwards, *Law Officers* (n 2) 379.
[61] A Downs, 'The Public Interest: Its Meaning in a Democracy' (1962) 29 *Social Research* 1, 1.
[62] ibid 11.
[63] Edwards, *Law Officers* (n 2) 182.
[64] Shawcross (n 31) 383.

prosecution, successful or unsuccessful, would have on public morale and order and international relations'.[65] He also noted that individual features of crime and offenders were relevant to an Attorney General's assessment of the public interest in prosecuting a particular case: 'perhaps the wrongdoer has already suffered enough; perhaps the prosecution would enable him to represent himself as a martyr, perhaps he is too ill to stand his trial without great risk to his health, even risk to his life'.[66]

The nebulous nature of the public interest reflects the need for flexibility on a case-by-case basis. Edwards explained the tension that a simple set of criteria cannot explain the public interest, yet 'society has the right to expect' a consistent and 'objective interpretation' of it when Attorneys General make discretionary decisions.[67] In 1960, Schubert was more accepting that 'Fashions change … including fashions in the use of political concepts; and the verbal formula which denotes the idea of responsible official decision-making for Americans in the twentieth century is "the public interest"'.[68]

According to Burbank, neither independence nor accountability 'is an end in itself but rather a means to an end'.[69] In prosecutions, their role is to protect the public interest. The concepts of prosecutorial independence and public interest are so closely connected that their definitions are essentially circular. As Carney explains, prosecutorial independence 'arises from the fact that the Attorney must exercise the various powers and discretions in the *public interest*'.[70] Shawcross articulated the conceptual intertwining of these values by explaining that, in making the decision to prosecute, the only matter he could not consider was the effect on 'my personal or my party's or the Government's political fortunes'. Beyond that, he could 'have regard to a variety of considerations, all of them leading to the final question: would a prosecution be in the public interest'?[71] Independence in prosecutorial decisions thus means untainted by partisan political interests or the political pressure of colleagues and Cabinet; and the public interest means to the benefit the community, and not partisan political interests.

The concept of parliamentary accountability also encompasses the other prosecutorial values. As Oliver explains, parliament involves 'a system of checks, balances and *accountability* that is weighed in favour of the public interest and not in the interests of politicians',[72] and so ministers must explain their actions to

[65] ibid 386.
[66] ibid 385.
[67] Edwards, *Attorney General* (n 26) 334.
[68] Schubert (n 53) 7.
[69] SB Burbank, 'Judicial Independence, Judicial Accountability and Interbranch Relations' (2007) 95 *Georgetown Law Journal* 909, 912.
[70] Carney (n 57) 3 (emphasis in original).
[71] Shawcross (n 31) 385–86.
[72] D Oliver, 'Accountability and the Foundations of British Democracy – the Public Interest and Public Service Principles' in N Bamforth and P Leyland (eds), *Accountability in the Contemporary Constitution* (Oxford, Oxford University Press, 2013) 289, 303 (emphasis in original).

Parliament according to 'public interest standards'.[73] The prosecutorial values are not only linked to each other, but also to the prosecutorial discretion that is exercised by the Attorney General.

III. Public Interest and Prosecutorial Discretion

The requirement to prosecute in the public interest made the English prosecutorial system one of selective enforcement; thus, the decision to prosecute was discretionary. Shawcross stated in 1951 that 'It has never been the rule in this country – and I hope it never will be – that suspected criminal offences must automatically be the subject of prosecution'.[74] In support of his assertion, he quoted Lord Simon's 1925 observation that

> there is no greater nonsense … than the suggestion that in all cases the Attorney General ought to decide to prosecute merely because he thinks there is what the lawyers call a case. It is not true and no one who has held the office of Attorney General supposes it is.[75]

The Attorney General's discretion to prosecute in the public interest involves a tension because it is exercised in their legal capacity as First Law Officer of the Crown, but requires assessments informed by their political role. Possible prosecutions of unlawful industrial action by union workers in the 1970s, and defence and national security issues in the early twenty-first century, demonstrate the potential for partisan interpretations of contemporary social, economic and political issues to factor into the assessment.

A. Industrial Dispute Cases

The 1978 case of *Gouriet* considered whether courts could review decisions of the Attorney General to refuse consent to the institution of relator proceedings: where a member of the public seeks to enforce a public right. Its findings on the assessment of the public interest are relevant to the decision to prosecute. In 1977, the postal workers' union resolved, unlawfully, to refuse to process mail with South Africa to protest the Apartheid regime. Gouriet, one of the founders of the National Association for Freedom,[76] sought an injunction to prevent the post officers' embargo. The Labour Party Attorney General, Samuel Silkin, refused to grant his fiat on public interest grounds. He determined that an injunction

[73] ibid 289–90.
[74] HC Deb 29 January 1951, vol 483, col 680 (Hartley Shawcross, Attorney General).
[75] *Smedleys Ltd v Breed* [1974] AC 839, 856.
[76] The organisation still exists as a 'non-partisan, centre-right, classically liberal campaign group': Freedom Association, 'About' (2023) www.tfa.net/.

would encourage breaches of the law and cause more public inconvenience than the threatened embargo, especially as the Industrial Relations Act 1971 (UK) had decriminalised industrial action.[77] Edwards notes that Michael Havers, the Conservative Attorney General who succeeded Silkin, would have granted the fiat, which demonstrates 'a predictable divergence in the meaning accorded to "the public interest" by adherents of the major political parties'.[78] An editorial in *The Times* suggested the Attorney General's decision appeared to be a concession to the trade union movement. It claimed that the case showed that an Attorney General's interpretation of the public interest is influenced by a 'political career [spent] in the service of one party', making it seem to the public 'indistinguishable from political convenience'.[79]

Gouriet shows that the Attorney General's unique political–legal role provides the authority and means to determine the public interest in prosecutions according to a complex interaction of factors such as future compliance with the law, harmonisation with other legal changes and priorities, and economic security. It also shows that Attorneys General are susceptible to allegations of being motivated by partisan politics rather than legitimate public interest factors.

B. National Security Cases

The concerns about industrial action in *Gouriet* reflected the political environment during the Thatcher government's sustained effort to repress unlawful industrial action. When issues of public interest in prosecutions arose in later decades, the prevailing concern was national security and terrorism. While the topics and political context were different, the national security cases confirmed that the assessment of the public interest was still tied closely to the political role of the Attorney General.

From the 1980s, BAE Systems (and its predecessor, British Aerospace) was the prime British contractor over agreements with Saudi Arabia for the provision of aircraft and weapons systems in exchange for oil. In 2004, two arrests were made under the Anti-Terrorism, Crime and Security Act 2001 (UK) over allegations that contracts were secured through bribes to members of the Saudi royal family and government. The criminal investigation occurred concurrently with negotiations for a further contract.[80] The Saudi government threatened to stop counter-terrorist

[77] Edwards, *Attorney General* (n 26) 335.

[78] ibid 336.

[79] 'Editorial' *The Times* (28 July 1977) cited in P Radan, 'Law, Politics, and the Attorney-General: The Context and Impact of *Gouriet v Union of Post Office Workers*' (2016) 16 *Macquarie Law Journal* 105, 120–21.

[80] The Serious Fraud Office is an independent prosecution agency, and its Director has the same relationship to the Attorney General as does the DPP. The case is central to the independence of the Attorney General and is relevant to the relationship between the DPP and the Attorney General.

co-operation with Britain, and to refuse to enter further contracts, if the criminal investigations continued. In December 2006, the Director of the Serious Fraud Office informed the Attorney General that 'continuing the Al Yamamah investigation would risk serious harm to the UK's national and international security'.[81] The Attorney General, Lord Goldsmith, announced that the decision reflected 'the need to safeguard national and international security'.[82] The decision to discontinue the investigation and prosecution generated allegations of political influence, which were fuelled by Prime Minister Blair's admission that he personally decided to discontinue the investigation to avoid 'the complete wreckage of a relationship that is of fundamental importance to the security of this country'.[83]

National security cases and the strike cases of the 1970s together demonstrate that the public interest in certain decisions to prosecute must be balanced with broader political and economic considerations. This weighing of factors is an inherently political exercise, which resides firmly within the Attorney General's portfolio and creates problems for the assessment of the public interest when the decision to prosecute is shifted to statutory ODPPs.

IV. Conclusions

The normative prosecutorial value of the public interest, buttressed by the values of independence and accountability, also uncontroversially, emerged as the foundation of the Anglo-Australian prosecutorial tradition. However, the lack of precision in the concept of the public interest and the tension inherent in upholding independence and accountability made the decision to prosecute dependent on the exercise of a very wide discretion that had to be informed by the Attorney General's political role but exercised according to factors outside their direct political interests.

The interconnection between the prosecutorial values and the role of the Attorney General remains a central paradox: the independence of prosecutorial decisions needs to be secured through the separation of politics from the decision to prosecute in a system where the public interest and accountability depend on those politics. For centuries, the public and political confidence in the prosecutorial system rested precariously on political and public confidence in the ability and willingness of Attorneys General to subordinate their own political interests to the public interest when making the decision to prosecute.

[81] *R (on the Application of Corner House Research) v Director of the SFO* [2008] UKHL 60 [22].

[82] HL Deb 14 December 2006, vol 687, col 1712 (Lord Goldsmith, Attorney General).

[83] House of Commons, Constitutional Affairs Committee, *Constitutional Role of the Attorney General* (Fifth Report of Session 2006–07, 17 July 2007) Evidence 42, Chairman Qu 330, quoting Prime Minister Blair.

3

Australian Concerns

The Attorney General's responsibility to prosecute according to the British values of public interest, independence and accountability was transplanted to Australia, and the Australian Courts Act 1828 (Imp) empowered the Australian Attorney General to prosecute criminal offences in the English tradition. However, in the 1970s and 1980s, controversial exercises of the Attorney General's prosecutorial discretion raised questions about the prosecutorial independence evident in England since the seventeenth century. When questions of prosecutorial propriety arose in England, they were dealt with by a renewed commitment to the Attorney General's obligation to act independently. By contrast, Australian discontent with the Attorney General's independence coincided with the rise of the 'new' administrative law, and concerns about prosecutorial independence resulted in demands for a prosecution system with a more robust foundation than the personal and political integrity of the Attorney General. While the Australian response intended to reflect the expectations of the emerging legal environment, it actually adhered to the traditional, English meaning of independence and commitment to upholding the public interest and accountability through the Westminster system. These dual purposes created enduring tensions that affect the ability of the Offices of Director of Public Prosecution (ODPPs) to uphold all the stated prosecutorial values.

I. The Australian Attorney General

The Australian Courts Act 1828 (Imp) provided that until the establishment of the grand jury, criminal offences 'shall be prosecuted by information, in the name of His Majesty's attorney general'.[1] In 1980, the High Court of Australia (HCA) explained in *Barton* that the purpose of the Act 'was to arm the Attorney-General for New South Wales … with a power in all respects similar to that enjoyed by the Attorney-General in England and to extend the exercise of the power to all offences, including felonies'.[2]

While the New South Wales (NSW) Attorney General was intended to have the same prosecutorial powers as the Attorney General for England and Wales

[1] Australian Courts Act 1828 (Imp), s 5.
[2] (1980) 147 CLR 75, 92–93.

(English Attorney General), in practice a number of factors increased their power.[3] The right to private prosecutions was curtailed in England from the nineteenth century, but was still exercised by private individuals and by the police on behalf of private individuals. Grand juries acted as a filter on whether or not matters proceeded to trial, and from 1879 the Director of Public Prosecutions (DPP) had a significant responsibility for prosecutions. Neither the grand jury nor private prosecutions were viable in a penal settlement without a free citizenry. By the time democratic values and institutions were adopted in the colony, and then the state, grand juries and private prosecutions had fallen from favour in England and were barely revived anywhere in Australia. The Governor did appoint prosecutors who were able to initiate, conduct and terminate prosecutions. However, their authority was derived from that of the Attorney General,[4] so they were an expression of the prosecutorial role of the Attorney General, rather than a check upon it. This model evolved into the system of Crown Prosecutors across the colonies, and then the states, territories and the Commonwealth, which survived until the establishment of the ODPPs.[5] The NSW Supreme Court's 1844 judgment that the Attorney General's 'powers and functions … are vested exclusively in one officer, without supervision, limitation, or control', remained true well into the twentieth century.[6]

The non-prosecutorial functions of the Australian Attorney General also enhanced the political status and power of the role relative to its English predecessor. The colonies centralised legal services under the control of the Attorney General, which made them responsible for the provision of legal advice to government departments.[7] The HCA held in 1925 that, by 'virtue of his office', the Attorney General 'is the legal adviser to the Crown in right of the Commonwealth and the proper person to conduct or defend proceedings on behalf of the Crown in that right'.[8] Unlike the English Attorney General, the Australian Attorney General was a member of Cabinet, and did not share responsibilities with a Lord Chancellor or Home Secretary.[9] In the early nineteenth century, the roles of the Attorney General and the Solicitor General overlapped, and they were expected to collaborate on the distribution of responsibilities. However, according to the Colonial Secretary in 1829, where there was disagreement between them, the Attorney General had the right 'of dictating to his Colleague'.[10]

[3] F Hanlon, 'Traditional Notions of the Attorney-General: Time for Some Justice' (2008) 33 *Alternative Law Journal* 15, 15.

[4] RR Kidston, 'The Office of Crown Prosecutor (More Particularly in New South Wales)' (1958) 32 *Australian Law Journal* 148, 151.

[5] *Barton* (1980) 147 CLR 75, 101.

[6] *Reg v McDermott* (1844) 1 Legge 236, 237, cited in *Barton* (1980) 147 CLR 75, 93.

[7] B Selway, 'The Different Role of an Australian Attorney-General' (2002) 13 *Public Law Review* 263, 266–67.

[8] *Kidman v Commonwealth* (1925) 37 CLR 233, 240.

[9] Selway (n 7) 268.

[10] Letter from Colonial Secretary to Governor Darling, 1829, cited in K Mason, 'The Office of Solicitor General for New South Wales' [1988] *Bar News* 22, 23.

By the twentieth century, like its English predecessor, the Australian Attorney General was 'the principal legal adviser to the Crown, its Ministers, departments, agencies and authorities'.[11] According to Bradley Selway, then Solicitor General of South Australia (SA), the expanded portfolio meant that the Australian Attorney General was 'much more powerful than his or her English counterpart'.[12] While the Australian Attorney General had 'ultimate control of criminal proceedings', they were expected to exercise their discretion with 'due regard to the public interest'.[13] However, the combination of extensive political and prosecutorial power gave rise to concerns that political interference undermined prosecutorial independence.

II. The Attorney General and Prosecutorial Independence

The issue of prosecutorial independence first arose in Colonial Australia. As Victorian Solicitor General, Isaac Issacs resolved to institute several prosecutions over the collapse of the Mercantile Bank during the Depression of the 1890s.[14] The Attorney General directed the Solicitor General not to prosecute, and so Isaacs resigned his position owing to what he considered an infringement on his individual responsibility to execute his functions.[15]

Despite the concentration of prosecutorial power in the office of Attorney General, and the warning sounded by the Isaacs case, the Australian Attorney General attracted little controversy while prosecuting criminal matters for two centuries. Justice Benjamin Boothby voiced concern in the nineteenth century about possible political influence on prosecutorial decisions. He feared that prosecutions for treason, sedition or political libel initiated by the Attorney General and Solicitor General, as Cabinet ministers, 'who then conducted the prosecution in court, would imperil the interests of the Crown and the public as to the result of a just and necessary prosecution in defence of the public interest'.[16]

Boothby's concerns were prescient but not influential, because he had many opponents after causing 'legal chaos through engaging in arguments' 'both

[11] South Australia, *Parliamentary Debates*, Legislative Council, 25 August 1988, 513 (Christopher Sumner, Attorney General).

[12] Selway (n 7) 272.

[13] South Australia, *Parliamentary Debates*, Legislative Council, 25 August 1988, 513 (Christopher Sumner, Attorney General).

[14] DT Merrett, 'Australian Banking Practice and the Crisis of 1893' (1989) 29 *Australian Economic History Review* 60, 75.

[15] M Kirby, 'Sir Isaac Isaacs – A Sesquicentenary Reflection' (2005) 29 *Melbourne University Law Review* 880, 884; R Pepper, 'Celebrating 100 Years of the Commonwealth Solicitor-General: Closing Remarks', Speech, Banco Court, Sydney, 24 October 2016, 2.

[16] Memorandum of Justice Benjamin Boothby, 1862, cited in J Edwards, *The Law Officers of the Crown: A Study of the Offices of Attorney-General and Solicitor-General of England With an Account of the Office of the Director of Public Prosecutions of England* (London, Sweet & Maxwell, 1964) 168.

sophisticated and absurd' about the validity of laws.[17] However, in the 1970s and 1980s, a combination of specific controversies and the growth of the 'new' administrative law undermined Australian confidence that the integrity of the Attorney General could protect prosecutorial independence.[18]

III. Accountability and the 'New' Administrative Law

Australian politics in the 1970s was significantly defined by Gough Whitlam's term as Prime Minister. His election ended 23 years of conservative federal government and provided 1071 days of progressive reform.[19] Laws increasing 'access to government information'[20] were one of the 'significant concrete advances in Australian democracy'[21] during that time. The change reflected a growing concern about 'big government in Australia and its impact on the citizen', and a commitment to citizens being able to challenge government decisions that affected them personally and to scrutinise government processes generally.[22] Traditionally, the local Member of Parliament was the 'citizen's first avenue of review' for complaints about decisions made by the Member, or in offices and departments within their portfolio.[23] However, as Gardiner argues, by the mid-twentieth century, the intensity of party politics left 'little room for parliament to fulfil its role as Dicey's bulwark against unjust intrusion upon individual freedom by the increasing threat from the executive'.[24]

The changed attitude to the role of parliament contributed to the emergence of the 'new' administrative law. A body of principles constituting administrative law, which checked the 'actions of persons and bodies which constitute the system of government and administration', has been traced to judicial decisions in the early seventeenth century.[25] However, the reforms were 'designed to regulate the relationship between government and individuals and to reconcile the potential

[17] R Cocks, 'Dewigged, Bothered, and Bewildered: British Colonial Judges on Trial, 1800–1900' (2012) 33 *Journal of Legal History* 243, 244.

[18] Similar controversies arose in England in the early 21st century: House of Commons, Constitutional Affairs Committee, *Constitutional Role of the Attorney General* (Fifth Report of Session 2006–07, 17 July 2007) 3.

[19] B Carroll, *Whitlam* (Kenthurst, Rosenberg Publishing, 2011) 138–39; N Hollier, 'The Whitlam Project' (2002) 169 *Overland* 104, 104.

[20] B Walker, 'Whitlam Oration: The Information that Democracy Needs' (2018) 47 *Law Society of NSW Journal* 76, 78.

[21] C Pollard, 'Whitlam and Democracy' (2014) 133 *Arena Magazine* 5, 5.

[22] J McMillan, 'Parliament and Administrative Law' (Department of the Parliamentary Library, 7 November 2000) Research Paper No 13, 1.

[23] DG Gardiner, 'Policy Review Reviewed: The Pubescent State of the New Administrative Law' (1988) 4 *Queensland University of Technology Law Journal* 123, 123.

[24] ibid 125.

[25] P Bayne, 'Prosecutorial Discretion and Administrative Law' in IL Potas (ed), *Prosecutorial Discretion*, Seminar Proceedings No 6 (Australian Institute of Criminology, 7–9 November 1984) 69, 69.

conflict of interests between providing efficient and effective public administration and safeguarding rights of individual justice'.[26] The 1971 Report of the Commonwealth Administrative Review Committee (the Kerr Committee) recommended increased openness, transparency and accountability through judicial and non-judicial review of executive decisions. The new regime was intended to be more flexible and accessible, and less technical, than the English common law, which enforced the limits of government power through prerogative writs such as certiorari, mandamus and habeas corpus.[27]

Critics who considered administrative law a 'despotism on the ruins' of parliamentary sovereignty[28] were a minority by this time. In 1973, support for the Kerr Committee's recommendations facilitated a comprehensive Commonwealth system of administrative review.[29] The framework included codification of judicial review through the Administrative Decisions (Judicial Review) Act 1977 (Cth) and the establishment of the Federal Court to administer the judicial review jurisdiction, the Administrative Appeals Tribunal to undertake independent merits review of decisions made under Commonwealth legislation and various specialist tribunals that were overseen by the Administrative Review Council. Subsequently, an Ombudsman, statutory rights to reasons for decisions, a Privacy Act 1988 (Cth) and Freedom of Information Act 1982 (Cth) were also introduced.[30] This new emphasis on transparency and accountability fundamentally changed the historical reliance on the personal integrity of officeholders. During this period, Australia experienced a series of incidences of actual or perceived political interference in prosecutorial decisions, and the reaction to them was influenced by the growth of the 'new' administrative law.

IV. Seeds of Discontent

Ironically, concerns about prosecutorial independence first gained attention in 1977, when the Commonwealth Attorney General, in circumstances akin to those of Isaacs a century earlier, dramatically resigned rather than compromise prosecutorial independence. The following section discusses the establishment of the Commonwealth ODPP. While this was not the first independent prosecution

[26] J Griffiths, 'Australian Administrative Law: Institutions, Reforms and Impact' (1985) 63 *Public Administration* 445, 446.

[27] R French, 'Administrative Law in Australia: Themes and Values' in M Groves and HP Lee (eds), *Australian Administrative Law: Fundamentals, Principles and Doctrines* (Cambridge, Cambridge University Press, 2007) 15, 20.

[28] CG Haines, 'Effects of the Growth of Administrative Law Upon Traditional Anglo-American Legal Theories and Practices' (1932) 26 *American Political Science Review* 875, 879.

[29] A Mason, 'The Kerr Report of 1971: Its Continuing Significance', Lecture, Council of Australasian Tribunals NSW Chapter, 19 September 2007, 3–5.

[30] R Creyke, 'Administrative Justice – Towards Integrity in Government' (2007) 31 *Melbourne University Law Review* 705, 707.

service to be established in Australia, Commonwealth prosecutions were the first to attract significant attention. A review by the Law Reform Commission (LRC) in the late 1970s highlighted issues with the exercise of the Attorney General's prosecutorial discretion.[31] The section then examines, chronologically, the key controversies that drove the establishment of each of the state ODPPs during the 1970s, 1980s and 1990s.[32] Each of the controversies are described in some detail to demonstrate the factors that provided the impetus for the individual ODPPs and the trend they collectively represented.

A. Prosecutorial Controversies

(i) The Commonwealth

In 1978, the Commonwealth Attorney General provided a reference to the LRC to review the Commonwealth and the Australian Capital Territory (ACT) laws on punishment for Commonwealth offences and related matters. The inquiry considered the exercise of the Attorney General's prosecutorial discretion, including the case of *Sankey v Whitlam* and its political consequences.[33]

A so-called 'Loans Affair' arose when the Whitlam government attempted to raise a $4 billion loan to fund natural resource and energy projects. Unusually, the negotiations for the loan were conducted through a London-based commodity-trading firm rather than through the Loan Council or Treasury, and the funds were to come from the Middle East rather than Europe. The loan was never secured, but the preliminary arrangements raised the legal question of whether its size necessitated the involvement of the Loans Council.

The publicity over the loan resulted in two ministers departing Parliament, and contributed to Whitlam's dismissal as Prime Minister, because the Liberal Opposition used it to justify 'blocking the budget' and forcing an early election.[34] In the middle of the subsequent election campaign, a Sydney solicitor, Danny Sankey, initiated a private prosecution against Whitlam and his Minister for Minerals and Energy, his Treasurer, and his Attorney General.[35] Consistent with

[31] The LRC was established under the Law Reform Commission Act 1973 (Cth), which was superseded by the Australian Law Reform Commission Act 1996 (Cth).

[32] The DPP Bills were passed without controversy in both territories in 1990. The ACT established its office when it took responsibility for its criminal justice system from the Commonwealth: Australian Capital Territory, *Parliamentary Debates*, Legislative Assembly, 31 May 1990, 1965–66 (Bernard Collaery, Attorney General); the Northern Territory (NT) sought simply to reinforce 'that the administration of justice will remain free from party political bias': Northern Territory, *Parliamentary Debates*, Legislative Assembly, 28 February 1990, 8967 (Daryl Manzie, Attorney General).

[33] (1978) 142 CLR 1.

[34] M Sexton, 'The Whitlam Government in Retrospect: Thirty Years On' (2006) 18 *The Sydney Papers* 133, 134.

[35] *Sankey v Whitlam* (1978) 142 CLR 1.

allegations made by the Liberal Opposition,[36] Sankey alleged that the defendants had conspired to deceive the Governor General into unlawfully approving a loan proposal that contravened the Commonwealth and States Financial Agreement of 1927.[37] After the Liberal Party took power under Malcolm Fraser, Attorney General Robert Ellicott, who served as Solicitor General under Whitlam, was asked by all of the defendants, except Lionel Murphy, by then a justice of the HCA, to take over the private prosecution. To assess the sufficiency of the evidence, Ellicott requested that his own Cabinet provide him with access to relevant Whitlam Cabinet papers. The Cabinet refused access, and advised Ellicott to take over the prosecution and terminate it.[38]

Ellicott adhered to the English principle of prosecutorial independence. He perceived that the Prime Minister and Cabinet had tried 'to direct or control' his discretion,[39] and advised Parliament that he resigned to defend the principle that it is 'vital to our system of government that the Attorney-General's discretion in criminal matters remains completely independent'.[40] Ellicott's actions are a classic demonstration of how prosecutorial independence was supposed to be upheld. In a different political climate, his actions could have reassured the community that prosecutorial reform was not required. However, the reaction to the case, including by the LRC, focused more on the general potential for political interference in criminal prosecutions than on Ellicott's particular resistance to it.

The LRC found that state and Commonwealth prosecutions were 'the most secretive, least understood and most poorly documented aspect of the administration of criminal justice', because the decision to prosecute was 'clouded by uncertainty and controversy [and] largely immune from public or even judicial scrutiny and review'.[41] It accepted that prosecutorial decisions were generally made well, and that prosecutors needed to exercise judgement in particular cases. However, it concluded that the absence of publicly available documents to guide the prosecutorial discretion and the paucity of internal guidelines meant that 'unacceptable secrecy' undermined the openness that should be a 'distinctive feature of our criminal justice system'.[42]

In addition to the LRC inquiry, the 1983 report by the NSW Royal Commission of Inquiry into Drug Trafficking and the Royal Commission on the Activities of the Federated Ship Painters and Dockers Union (the Costigan Commission) also

[36] Commonwealth of Australia, *Parliamentary Debates*, House of Representatives, 6 September 1977, 1 (Robert Ellicott).

[37] The Agreement defined the terms and conditions of government borrowing: BS Grewal, 'Australian Loan Council: Arrangements and Experience with Bailouts; (Latin American Research Network, 2000) Research Network Working Paper 397, 4.

[38] Commonwealth of Australia, *Parliamentary Debates*, House of Representatives, 6 September 1977 (Robert Ellicott) 2–5.

[39] ibid 1.

[40] ibid.

[41] The Law Reform Commission, *Sentencing of Federal Offenders: Interim*, Report No 15 (Australian Government Publishing Service, 1980) 63–64.

[42] ibid 70.

identified problems with Commonwealth prosecutions.[43] Both reports noted that states and territories had Crown Prosecutors properly trained and resourced to deal with criminal matters, yet Commonwealth prosecutions were undertaken by government departments and by the Crown Solicitor, who also bore heavy responsibilities for civil advice and litigation.[44] All three inquiries found unacceptable delays, complications and lack of coordination in the prosecution of Commonwealth offences, which demonstrated the need for a specialist prosecution office.[45] An ODPP was established for the Commonwealth in 1984, but it is the only jurisdiction where the Attorney General both has the same prosecutorial powers as the DPP[46] and can direct the DPP on policy matters and in specific cases.[47] The DPPs in the other jurisdictions have only one of these powers. The series of state controversies that contemporaneously raised issues with prosecutorial independence suggested that other Attorneys General might not take Ellicott's principled stance against political pressure.

(ii) Tasmania

The first notable concerns about prosecutorial independence arose in Tasmania over political dealings with the corporation British Tobacco. In the 1960s, arrangements with the Labor government enabled British Tobacco to cultivate extensive land holdings. This arrangement breached the Crown Lands Act 1935 (Tas), which was intended to help small companies by limiting land use by large companies. In 1971, charges of conspiracy to 'obstruct, prevent, pervert, or defeat the administration of the law' or to 'cheat or defraud the public' were laid against two British Tobacco executives and a former Labor minister. Charges were withdrawn the following year, and concerns arose that the decision not to proceed was politically motivated. Suspicions were heightened when, in 1972, Kevin Lyons of the Centre Party, formerly of the Liberal Party, resigned his parliamentary positions and withdrew his support for the government. He held the balance of power in the Tasmanian Parliament and his resignation forced the dissolution of Parliament, and an election that Labor won.[48] In the same year, British Tobacco paid Lyons the equivalent of almost four years of his parliamentary salary for his memoirs, which were never published. The large advance, for

[43] *Royal Commission of Inquiry into Drug Trafficking: Final Report* (Australian Government Publishing Service, February 1983).

[44] Commonwealth of Australia, *Parliamentary Debates*, Senate, 16 November 1983, 2671 (Peter Durack); Commonwealth of Australia, *Parliamentary Debates*, Senate, 16 November 1983, 2672 (Gareth Evans, Attorney General).

[45] Department of the Parliamentary Library, Legislative Research Service, *Short Digest of Bill, Director of Public Prosecutions Bill 1983* (29 November 1983).

[46] Director of Public Prosecutions Act 1983 (Cth), s 10(1)(a).

[47] ibid s 8(1)–(2).

[48] F Madill, 'Love and Hate Under Hare Clark – Impact of Minority Government in Tasmania' (1997) 11 *Legislative Studies* 68, 69; EM Bingham, 'A Political Memoir' (2003) *Tasmanian Historical Research Association* 143, 147, 153–54.

the memoir of an 'unremarkable local politician who had never demonstrated any literary capacity',[49] created speculation that Lyons had, in effect, accepted a bribe to resign so that British Tobacco could oust the Liberal government in retaliation for the criminal charges.[50]

Later in 1972, the Tasmanian Parliament passed the North East Land Development Act 1972 (Tas) to validate retrospectively the actions of British Tobacco and the former government, and indemnify those involved against prosecution or civil penalty. Agitation for a Royal Commission was unsuccessful, and no public inquiry was ever held, although police cleared Lyons of any wrongdoing.[51] The following year, further concerns arose about political corruption and its implications for the independence of prosecutions. The allegations, again, focused on Lyons and his resignation. The former private secretary of the Labor Premier alleged a conspiracy between Lyons, the Labor Party and powerful hoteliers and bookmakers over plans to establish a casino and a government-run TAB (Totalisator Agency Board) that would compete with existing local businesses. The allegations were never subject to a public inquiry. Instead, the police investigated and reported to the Attorney General, who was 'alleged to have been central to the conspiracy' and yet was responsible for any prosecutions resulting from it. The whole situation was associated with a further 'perception of corruption and cover-up'.[52] The Crown Advocate Act 1973 (Tas) was passed to create an independent, statutory office that would professionalise criminal prosecutions and signal to the electorate that prosecutions were independent. As Corns stated, the significance of the establishment of the first fully independent, statutory Australian prosecution service, almost a decade before the establishment of the first Australian ODPP, has been overlooked and underestimated.[53] However, the efficacy of the prosecution service was limited. The enabling legislation did not clarify the relationships between the Attorney General, the Solicitor General and the Crown Advocate, or authorise the publication of guidelines.[54] The Director of Public Prosecutions Act 1973 (Tas), which was passed later the same year, addressed the problematic issues with the Crown Advocate Act 1973 (Tas). However, the Tasmanian Attorney General now has the same prosecutorial powers as the DPP,[55] and can direct the DPP to act as counsel for the Crown or any other person.[56]

[49] J Boyce, *Losing Streak: How Tasmania Was Gamed by the Gambling Industry* (Carlton, Redback, 2017) 14b.

[50] K Barnsley, 'Crony Capitalism or Corruption?: The Curious Case of British Tobacco and a Tasmanian Government' (2011) 58 *Tasmanian Historical Research Association* 173, 179–80.

[51] ibid 181.

[52] Boyce (n 49) 14b.

[53] C Corns, *Public Prosecutions in Australia: Law, Policy and Practice* (Pyrmont, Thomson Reuters, 2014) 74.

[54] D Bugg, 'The Role of the DPP in the 20th Century', Speech, Judicial Conference of Australia, 13 November 1999.

[55] Director of Public Prosecutions Act 1973 (Tas), s 12(2).

[56] ibid s 12(1)(e).

(iii) Victoria

Victoria was the first jurisdiction in Australia to establish a formal ODPP. Crown Prosecutor Richard Read claimed in 1984 that in 'Victoria the machinery of criminal justice has never been allowed to become a pawn in party politics or subject to parliamentary pressure'.[57] However, Labor Party members complained of 'instances of selective prosecution', and advocated separating prosecutions from the 'day-to-day political control of the Attorney-General'[58] to 'remove any suggestion that prosecutions … can be the subject of political pressure'.[59] The Labor Party's commitment to an independent prosecuting authority arose, in part, from the 1982 interim report of the Costigan Commission.[60] The inquiry uncovered decades of union-related criminal activities involving violence, dishonesty, drug trafficking and other organised crime.[61] The offences had proved difficult to police and prosecute, for reasons including the suspected involvement of politicians, police, lawyers, judges, public servants and the business community.[62] The Victorian ODPP was established in 1982, and Victoria is the only jurisdiction where the Attorney General has neither the same prosecutorial powers as the DPP nor the authority to direct the DPP in specific cases.

(iv) Queensland

In 1984, Queensland DPP legislation passed with little opposition, even though it was prompted by a single investigation of a police officer for offences of child pornography and sodomy (then illegal in Queensland).[63] The real debate about the Attorney General's prosecutorial role occurred three years later. Joh Bjelke-Petersen's Country (then National) Party premiership from 1968 to 1987 was dogged by persistent rumours of political and police corruption. In 1987, Tony Fitzgerald KC led the Commission of Inquiry into Possible Illegal Activities and Associated Police Misconduct.[64] After the Inquiry resulted in the imprisonment of the Commissioner of Police for bribery, its scope was expanded, and

[57] RM Read, 'Prosecutorial Discretion in Victoria' in Potas (n 25) 91, 92.

[58] Victoria, *Parliamentary Debates*, Legislative Council, 29 June 1982, 1944 (James Kennan).

[59] ibid 18 November 1982, 2096 (Ian Cathie).

[60] *Royal Commission on the Activities of the Federated Ship Painters and Dockers Union, Interim Report, No 4*, vol 1 (Government of the Commonwealth of Australia and Government of the State of Victoria, 1982). The final report was *Royal Commission on the Activities of the Federated Ship Painters and Dockers Union, Final Report, No 4*, vol 1 (Government of the Commonwealth of Australia and Government of the State of Victoria, 1984).

[61] Victoria, *Parliamentary Debates*, Legislative Council, 14 December 1982, 1415 (William Landeryou).

[62] R Williams, 'Democracy, Development and Anti-Corruption Strategies: Learning from the Australian Experience' (1999) 37 *Journal of Commonwealth and Comparative Politics* 135, 137.

[63] Queensland, *Parliamentary Debates*, Legislative Assembly, 28 November 1984, 3171 (John Innes).

[64] GE Fitzgerald, *Commission of Inquiry into Possible Illegal Activities and Associated Police Misconduct* (3 July 1989).

it uncovered evidence of systemic political corruption.[65] Bjelke-Petersen was deposed by his party, and tried for perjury over his evidence at the Inquiry. The jury could not reach a decision and he was not retried, but three former government ministers were imprisoned and a later civil case found that Bjelke-Petersen had accepted bribes 'numerous times'.[66] The Labor Party took power in 1989, but the reputation of the political and criminal justice system had suffered immense damage.

Fitzgerald recommended the separation of the office of the Attorney General from the Ministry of Justice, because their earlier amalgamation had compromised the independence of the Attorney General.[67] The separation was effected in 1989, reversed in 1992 and reviewed in 1993 by the Parliamentary Committee for Electoral and Administrative Review (PCEAR). Parliament declined to accept PCEAR's recommendation to legislate the powers of the Attorney General to achieve independence and accountability. However, in 1996, the National Party was returned to minority government and allegations quickly arose of an unlawful deal with the Police Union for support in a crucial by-election. The matter was referred to the Criminal Justice Commission (CJC),[68] and in an apparently retaliatory act, the government ordered an inquiry into the CJC.[69] As a political strategy, it was spectacularly unsuccessful. It 'enjoyed no broad political or community support, and was not widely regarded as independent'.[70] As an inquiry, it was equally unsuccessful. On application of the CJC, the Supreme Court apprehended bias on the parts of the inquirers, and disqualified them from conducting further proceedings.[71]

The ruling and the associated scathing media commentary were all damaging to the government, especially to Denver Beanland, the Attorney General. Beanland survived two unsuccessful votes of no-confidence in the Parliament, which revived calls for regulation of the Attorney General.[72] The entrenched corruption throughout Queensland undermined the perception of the integrity of all arms of the criminal justice system, including prosecutions by the Attorney General. The Attorney-General Act 1999 (Qld) was passed to define the scope of, although not codify, prosecutorial powers, and mandate reporting to Parliament whenever

[65] The Inquiry was extended to cover 'any other matter or thing appertaining to the aforesaid matters': Crime and Corruption Commission (Queensland), 'The Fitzgerald Inquiry' (2019) www.ccc.qld.gov.au/about-us/our-history/fitzgerald-inquiry.

[66] J Ransley and R Johnstone, 'The Fitzgerald Symposium' (2009) 18 *Griffith Law Review* 531, 534.

[67] Fitzgerald (n 64) 371.

[68] D Hamer, 'Keating v Morris; Leck v Morris: Politics and Procedure in the "Dr Death" Inquiry' (2006) 25 *University of Queensland Law Review* 131, 139–41.

[69] Criminal Justice Commission (Queensland), *The Impact of the Connolly–Ryan Inquiry on the Criminal Justice Commission* (September 1997) 1.

[70] J Wanna, 'Queensland' (1997) 44 *Australian Journal of Politics and History* 261, 263.

[71] *Re Carruthers v Connolly, Ryan and A-G* [1997] QSC 132.

[72] Wanna (n 70) 264. For the implications of a no-confidence vote, see D Blunt, 'Responsible Government: Ministerial Responsibility and Motions of "Censure"/"No Confidence"' (2004) 19 *Australasian Parliamentary Review* 71.

the Attorney General exercised those powers.[73] The Queensland Attorney General continues to exercise common law and statutory prosecutorial powers, but cannot direct the DPP on specific cases.[74]

(v) New South Wales

In 1986, the NSW Attorney General, Terence Sheahan, described the Australian Courts Act 1828 (Imp) governing prosecutions as an anachronism due for replacement.[75] The bid for reform gained urgency after some unfavourable reports on the justice system. The 'Vinson Report' found improprieties in the investigation, prosecution and adjudication of drug cases, and criticised the 'no bill process' through which prosecutions were discontinued.[76] The report was consistent with the 1985 Annual Report of the Ombudsman, which claimed that a recent investigation revealed inadequacies in the decision to prosecute. The Attorney General quoted in Parliament the Ombudsman's concerns that 'a major prosecution had been no-billed in scandalous circumstances [when] amply strong evidence supported the committal for trial'.[77] The NSW ODPP was established in 1986, but the Attorney General has the equivalent prosecutorial powers[78] and can direct the DPP on policy matters, though not on specific cases.[79]

(vi) Western Australia

In Western Australia (WA), the DPP Bill was first introduced by the Liberal Opposition in 1988 after the 'WA Inc' scandal, where Labor government business dealings lost millions of dollars and resulted in findings of improper conduct by public officers and politicians. The scandal itself, and several consequential, unsuccessful prosecutions of offences of corruption and abuse of office, created concerns 'Australia-wide; indeed, even overseas – of favouritism, cronyism and corruption in Western Australia'.[80] The call for an independent ODPP received impetus after the 1988 homicide of Peter Tan, a Chinese taxi driver who was racially abused and then fatally beaten. The offender was tried for wilful murder, but medical documentation and several witnesses favourable to the prosecution case were not called at trial, and he was convicted of manslaughter and sentenced to two years and

[73] Attorney-General Bill 1998 – Explanatory Notes (Qld), 2–4.

[74] Attorney-General Act 1999 (Qld), ss 7(2) and 8.

[75] New South Wales, *Parliamentary Debates*, Legislative Assembly, 1 December 1986, 7340 (Terence Sheahan).

[76] T Vinson et al, *Accountability and the Legal System: Drug Cases Terminating in the District Court 1980–1982* (Criminology Research Council, 1986) 25–33.

[77] New South Wales, *Parliamentary Debates*, Legislative Assembly, 21 November 1985, 10334 (Terence Sheahan).

[78] Director of Public Prosecutions Act 1986 (NSW), ss 27(1) and 28(1).

[79] ibid ss 26(1) and (3).

[80] Western Australia, *Parliamentary Debates*, Legislative Assembly, 15 June 1988, 1167 (Andrew Mensaros).

five months' imprisonment. Despite media and public outrage, the Attorney General declined to appeal the sentence.[81]

When the successful Bill was introduced in 1991, the Labor government distanced itself from past concerns by arguing that the other Australian ODPPs had been created 'after serious deficiencies had developed in the existing arrangements. We are not in that position in this State.'[82] The Attorney General merely argued that an ODPP 'will make it absolutely clear that the director will act with complete independence from the Attorney General and the Government of the day'.[83] The WA DPP can be directed by the Attorney General on policy matters but not on specific cases,[84] and cannot act inconsistently with the action of the Attorney General.[85]

(vii) South Australia

South Australia established the final Australian ODPP in 1991. The establishment of an office had been discussed for many years,[86] but was opposed by the Attorney General, Christopher Sumner. In his opinion, prosecutions were more effectively conducted by an elected official who could be questioned in Parliament.[87]

However, in 1991, the National Crime Authority (NCA) reported on 'Operation Hydra'. The inquiry into organised crime involved allegations that the Attorney General had improper criminal associations that caused him to act improperly during an illegal drug and prostitution prosecution. The NCA found no evidence to support the allegations against the Attorney General,[88] but recommended the establishment of a statutory ODPP because 'when cases become politicised, the public will find it difficult to distinguish between the role of the Attorney-General as a minister in the Government operating in a political environment, and his role in the conduct of criminal prosecutions'.[89] The Attorney General abandoned his previous opposition and supported the proposal.[90] The SA Attorney General can now direct the DPP on policy matters and on specific cases, but does not have concurrent prosecutorial powers.[91]

[81] ibid 4 April 1989, 158–63 (William Hassell).

[82] Western Australia, *Parliamentary Debates*, Legislative Council, 30 April 1991, 704 (Joseph Berinson, Attorney General).

[83] ibid 699.

[84] Director of Public Prosecutions Act 1991 (WA), ss 27(1) and (2).

[85] ibid s 28.

[86] South Australia, *Parliamentary Debates*, House of Assembly, 31 October 1991, 1686 (Gregory Crafter).

[87] South Australia, *Parliamentary Debates*, Legislative Council, 25 August 1988, 513–14 (Christopher Sumner, Attorney General).

[88] National Crime Authority, *Operation Hydra*, South Australian Reference No 2 (February 1991) 128.

[89] ibid 194.

[90] South Australia, *Parliamentary Debates*, Legislative Council, 21 August 1991, 359 (Christopher Sumner, Attorney General).

[91] Director of Public Prosecutions Act 1991 (SA), s 9; *Nemer v Holloway and Others* (2003) 87 SASR 147, 153–57.

The growth of the 'new' administrative law, and the public and political mood it reflected, meant all Australian governments ultimately determined that enhancing the independence of the prosecution system was necessary to address both particular controversies and a national trend toward open government.

B. Crisis of Confidence

The modern Australian prosecutorial controversies replicated controversies about prosecutorial independence that had arisen in England for centuries. They offended established constitutional principles and prosecutorial traditions as much as emerging administrative law. The number of confirmed or suspected incidences of political interference was small, and failed to demonstrate that political incursions into prosecutorial decision-making were widespread. The decision of Robert Ellicott to resign rather than acquiesce to interference from ministerial colleagues demonstrated principled resistance to political pressures. Nonetheless, the controversies created a crisis of confidence in the ability of the Attorney General to withstand the pressure of modern governments and uphold prosecutorial independence.

In 1988, SA Attorney General Sumner opposed the establishment of an ODPP and delivered a Ministerial Statement to educate the community on the independence of the Attorney General's legal role from the political influence of the executive.[92] However, the growth of administrative law reflected changed expectations about transparency and accountability. Doubts persisted that Attorneys General possessed the personal and political integrity that was, historically, regarded as the only necessary protection of prosecutorial independence. Shawcross reflected this loss of confidence when he resiled from his defence of the integrity of the Attorney General's office delivered in the 1950s. By 1977, his view had been altered by a combination of changed political conditions, nostalgia for his time in office and the circumstances of *Gouriet*. He recommended that 'the once great office of Attorney General' be relocated 'wholly outside the political arena', so that the

> enforcement of the rights of the public and the rule of law would … be given not only the reality (which I hope it still has) but also the appearance (which it now lacks) of complete detachment from party politics.[93]

The concern about the pressure of party politics on the Attorney General was not limited to Shawcross or to England. In 1999, Robert Dean told the Victorian Parliament that the 'sad consequence of modern politics becoming so aggressive

[92] South Australia, *Parliamentary Debates*, Legislative Council, 25 August 1988, 512 (Christopher Sumner, Attorney General).

[93] Letter from H Shawcross, *The Times* (3 August 1977), cited in J Edwards, *The Attorney General, Politics and the Public Interest* (London, Sweet & Maxwell, 1984) 65.

and party-orientated is that the role of the Attorney-General appears to have become incredibly politicised', when it 'should be neutral to political influences in conducting legal affairs'.[94]

The reaction to the possibility of political influence on criminal prosecutions was more pronounced than it had been in the past, and parliaments decided that substantial reform was necessary to uphold prosecutorial independence, meet community standards and uphold confidence in the criminal justice system. However, the following section argues that the type of prosecutorial independence that the ODPPs were intended to achieve conflicted with the Anglo-Australian tradition of prosecutorial accountability, and constrained prosecutorial reform.

V. Politics and the Public Interest

The balancing of prosecutorial independence and prosecutorial accountability involves normative decisions about the appropriate level of political involvement in criminal prosecutions. According to Tonry, common law countries 'differ over the legitimacy of political influence on prosecutorial decisions: Australia and Canada celebrate its absence, the English allow it, and the Americans celebrate it'.[95] His observation acknowledges prosecutorial independence as the foundation of the ODPPs, but ignores that DPPs were also intended to uphold prosecutorial accountability and public interest. The pursuit of prosecutorial independence is common to many jurisdictions, but it is understood differently according to local political contexts. As MacFarlane observes,

> there are many paths to prosecutorial independence [and] each nation needs to develop an approach to independence that makes sense in the context of its own legislative and constitutional framework, as well as the traditions, practices and history of its legal system.[96]

The English concept of prosecutorial independence, as freedom from political interference, drove the reform of the Australian prosecutorial system, and has consistently been its bedrock. Parliamentary debates in the 1980s made it 'absolutely clear' that the DPP would 'act with complete independence from the Attorney General and the Government'.[97] The removal of prosecutorial decisions from political influence was intended to ensure that the prosecutor could and would make decisions without pressure or fear of reprisal. Parliamentarians

[94] Victoria, *Parliamentary Debates*, Legislative Assembly, 9 December 1999, 1025 (Robert Dean).

[95] M Tonry, 'Prosecutors and Politics in Comparative Perspective' in M Tonry (ed), *Prosecutors and Politics: A Comparative Perspective* (Chicago, University of Chicago Press, 2013) 1, 8.

[96] BA MacFarlane, 'Sunlight and Disinfectants: Prosecutorial Accountability and Independence Through Public Transparency' (2001) 45 *Criminal Law Quarterly* 272, 274.

[97] Western Australia, *Parliamentary Debates*, Legislative Council, 23 November 1989, 5196–97 (Joseph Berinson, Attorney General).

considered this reform necessary to ensure 'that the community perceive the law to operate equally against and for all citizens'.[98] They recognised that prosecutorial decisions made by politicians could be 'subject to distortion or misconstruction' and could cause 'public confidence in the administration of the criminal law [to] be eroded'.[99]

Kirby J, on the NSW Court of Appeal in 1994, confirmed that the ODPPs were established 'to ensure a high degree of independence in the vital task of making prosecution decisions', to dispel 'the suspicion that important prosecutorial discretions will be exercised otherwise than on neutral grounds … and to answer the occasional allegation, that the prosecution may not be conducted with appropriate vigour'.[100]

The ODPPs adopted publicly available guidelines and policies as the key instruments directing their daily work, including the decision to prosecute. The guidelines have been modified over time and some regional differences have emerged, but they remain relatively uniform across the country.[101] The guidelines describe prosecutorial independence in terms such as removed from 'the political arena',[102] 'free from political interference'[103] and 'protected against arbitrary action by governments'.[104] Some guidelines do not single out independence from government or political interfence, but make clear that the DPP is independent of all influences, including political ones. They include statements including: 'Prosecutors must: act independently. Prosecutors represent the DPP, not the government, the police, the victim, or any other person';[105] the ODPP 'is independent and represents the community and not any private or sectional interest';[106] and the DPP 'acts independently of inappropriate or sectional interests in the community and of inappropriate influence by the media'.[107] Some guidelines also describe independence as meaning separate from investigative functions, particularly those

[98] Victoria, *Parliamentary Debates*, Legislative Assembly, 18 November 1982, 2096 (Ian Cathie).

[99] Northern Territory, *Parliamentary Debates*, Legislative Assembly, 28 February 1990, 8967 (Daryl Manzie, Attorney General).

[100] *Price v Ferris* (1994) 34 NSWLR 704, 707–08. Kirby J was distinguishing ODPP prosecutions from private prosecutions rather than from prosecutions by the Attorney General.

[101] Director of Public Prosecutions (Tasmania), *Prosecution Policy and Guidelines* (2022) (*DPP Policy* (Tas)); Director of Public Prosecutions for Western Australia, *Statement of Prosecution Policy and Guidelines* (2022) (*DPP Policy* (WA)); Office of the Director of Public Prosecutions, New South Wales, *Prosecution Guidelines* (2021) (*DPP Policy* (NSW)); Department of Justice and Attorney-General (Queensland), *Director's Guidelines* (2016); Director of Public Prosecutions (Victoria) *Policy of the Director of Public Prosecutions for Victoria* (2022) (*DPP Policy* (Vic)); Director of Public Prosecutions, South Australia, *Statement of Prosecution Policy & Guidelines* (2014); Director of Public Prosecutions, *Prosecution Policy of the Australian Capital Territory* (2021) (*DPP Policy* (ACT)); *Guidelines of the Director of Public Prosecutions* (Northern Territory) (2016) (*DPP Policy* (NT)); Commonwealth Director of Public Prosecutions, *Prosecution Policy of the Commonwealth* (*DPP Policy* (Cth)).

[102] *DPP Policy* (Cth) (n 101) 3; *DPP Policy* (ACT) (n 101) 1.

[103] *DPP Policy* (WA) (n 101) 2.1; *DPP Policy* (NT) (n 101) s 2.1.

[104] *DPP Policy* (WA) (n 101) s 6.

[105] *DPP Policy* (Vic) (n 101) s 14.

[106] *DPP Policy* (NT) (n 101) s 1.1.

[107] *DPP Policy* (Tas) (n 101) 1.

conducted by police,[108] and independent of the courts, which only intervene in criminal proceedings to prevent an abuse of process or uphold the right to a fair trial.[109] However, the description of independence as meaning untainted by political interests ignores the commitment to the Westminster system, and the Attorney General's traditional role of upholding prosecutorial accountability and the public interest within it.

VI. Conflict with Other Prosecutorial Values

The tension between the concurrent commitment to public interest, independence and accountability in the English tradition was exacerbated within the ODPP system. The cases that drove the establishment of the ODPPs demonstrated that the political oversight that was the key check on the exercise of prosecutorial discretion had the potential to corrupt its use. A conflict arose between the concerns about political influence undermining independence and commitment to the Attorney General's role in upholding public interest and accountability.

Schubert observed in 1960 that the 'supreme virtue of a democratic system of government is the multiplicity of points of access that it affords for the manifold conflicting interests which necessarily arise in a pluralistic society'.[110] Under the Westminster system, the assessment of the public interest was an inherently political undertaking and only the Attorney General had the resources and the mandate to undertake it. In 1987, before he opted to support the introduction of the ODPP, SA Attorney General Sumner argued that parliamentarians 'are in the business of democracy and debate … of determining the public interest', and so they should make prosecutorial decisions 'rather than having them sloughed off to unelected officials in the bureaucracy'.[111]

The following year, he complained that the trend toward statutory prosecutorial offices reflected a 'most unfortunate development' wherein the characterisation of anything as 'political … denigrates that idea in our community'.[112] Four years later, he relied on the examples of 'harmonious relations with other countries and [between] different groups within the community' to confirm that an elected 'Attorney-General, properly applying his mind to public interest considerations, using the precedents and conventions of the role of the Attorney-General, is a desirable fail-safe provision'.[113] His view received support in 2004, when Bradley

[108] *DPP Policy* (Cth) (n 101); *DPP Policy* (WA) (n 101) s 4; *DPP Policy* (ACT) (n 101) 1; *DPP Policy* (Tas) (n 101) 1.

[109] *DPP Policy* (Tas) (n 101) 1; *DPP Policy* (ACT) (n 101) 1.

[110] G Schubert, *The Public Interest: A Critique of the Theory of a Political Concept* (Glencoe, The Free Press, 1960) 136.

[111] South Australia, *Parliamentary Debates*, Legislative Council, 12 August 1987, 111 (Christopher Sumner, Attorney General).

[112] ibid.

[113] ibid 9 October 1991, 988 (Christopher Sumner, Attorney General).

Selway, by then a Federal Court judge, explained his opposition to the SA ODPP, which had, by then, existed for over a decade. He argued that where the decision to prosecute 'involved public interest considerations I could not see that a public officer had any means of discharging them – nor could I see any democratic mandate that would justify' prosecutorial decisions being made by a non-elected public officer.[114]

Other parliamentarians advocated for political involvement in the assessment of particular cases, such as terrorism, where 'the Government has more ready access to other Governments and to information on matters of national security or international concern'.[115] In 1993, the Queensland DPP, Royce Miller, explained that in Commonwealth prosecutions involving national security issues, the Attorney General might 'know secrets' that mean it is not in 'the public benefit' to proceed to trial.[116] There may also be areas of state and territory criminal law, such as organised crime, where the Attorney General has information relevant to prosecutions that cannot be disseminated. Although, the reasons that justify political involvement also create heightened potential for inappropriate political influence.

Support for the Attorney General being involved in prosecutions presumed their ability to determine the public interest. In Canada, Bruce MacFarlane was Assistant Deputy Attorney General at national level and then Deputy Attorney General at provincial level between the late 1980s and early 2000s, and his insight discloses a weak process for assessing the public interest. He reflected that consultation between Cabinet colleagues 'may take place privately at the Cabinet table, or through an exchange of correspondence with the affected Minister; less commonly, it may occur quite informally over lunch or in the hallways of the Legislature'.[117] He recognised that this 'lack of transparency may, if made public, have the effect of tainting the prosecution decision'.[118] The practical difficulty of the Attorney General actually determining the public interest notwithstanding, the commitment to the democratic role of the elected Attorney General in determining the public interest in prosecuting challenged prosecutorial independence. This tension between values was enhanced by the commitment to the Attorney General upholding prosecutorial accountability.

The commitment to accountability created further potential for conflict in upholding the prosecutorial values. Parliamentary debates on the Attorney General

[114] B Selway, 'Nemer: Ethics and the DPP', Lecture, Selected Issues in Criminal Law & Procedure, University of Adelaide, 7 July 2004, 4.

[115] Western Australia, *Parliamentary Debates*, Legislative Council, 28 March 1991, 702 (Joseph Berinson, Attorney General); Northern Territory, *Parliamentary Debates*, Legislative Assembly, 28 February 1990, 8968 (Daryl Manzie, Attorney General).

[116] Parliamentary Committee for Electoral and Administrative Review, *The Independence of the Attorney-General, Review of an Electoral and Administrative Review Commission Report: Transcript of Proceedings* (Legislative Assembly of Queensland, 27 October 1993) 13 (Royce Miller, Director of Public Prosecutions).

[117] MacFarlane (n 96) 281–82.

[118] ibid 282.

and prosecutorial accountability raised issues almost identical to those concerning the Attorney General and the public interest. In 1986, Attorney General for NSW Terence Sheahan stressed that Attorneys General are preselected by party supporters, elected by constituents to Parliament and elected by parliamentary colleagues as Attorney General.[119] He maintained that it

> would defy the principles of responsible, democratic government if the Attorney General were to abdicate totally his responsibility for such an important area of government, in favour of a person who is not elected, and thus not answerable to Parliament or the community.[120]

Sumner's reservations about the ODPP reflected his views on prosecutorial accountability as well as the public interest. He implicitly recognised that a depoliticised prosecution system presented, in effect, 'a democratic sovereignty problem'.[121] He was 'surprised' that parliamentarians were prepared to 'divest themselves' of 'very important principles of democracy. Democracy is really about elected officials making and taking responsibility for decisions.'[122]

The defence of the prosecutorial role of the Attorney General involved scepticism about the necessity and effectiveness of alternative accountability mechanisms and administrative law principles. Even after the outcome of Operation Hydra, Sumner questioned the value of statutory officers. He observed that 'independent people are not gods. They bring their own prejudices and their own value judgments to things.'[123] In the WA Parliament, Phillip Pendal similarly complained about the trend to 'create whole new structures in order to supervise existing structures'.[124] He pondered 'how long it will be before we are back in this Parliament being asked to discuss a new Bill which will place a check and a balance on the Director of Public Prosecutions'.[125]

The concurrent commitment to public interest, independence and accountability created the paradoxical concerns about the dangers of the Attorney General being too involved in, and too isolated from, prosecutorial decisions.

VII. Conclusions

The Attorney General had been an occasionally troubling, but broadly accepted, prosecutorial model for centuries. This traditional system of prosecutions by

[119] New South Wales, *Parliamentary Debates*, Legislative Assembly, 23 September 1986, 3731 (Terence Sheahan).

[120] ibid 7340.

[121] RM Gold, 'Promoting Democracy in Prosecution' (2011) 86 *Washington Law Review* 69, 84.

[122] South Australia, *Parliamentary Debates*, Legislative Council, 9 October 1991, 988 (Christopher Sumner, Attorney General).

[123] ibid.

[124] Western Australia, *Parliamentary Debates*, Legislative Council, 19 October 1989, 3461–62 (Phillip Pendal).

[125] ibid 24 October 1989, 3594 (Phillip Pendal).

Attorney General and the new administrative law principles that emerged from the 1970s were both committed to upholding public interest, independence and accountability. However, the potential for improper political influence on the decision to prosecute and a lack of transparency about how the decision was made were incompatible with late-twentieth-century expectations of accountability in government decision-making, and with cynicism about the integrity of elected political figures.

The ODPPs were established in response to the perceived misuse of the prosecutorial discretion by the Attorney General and driven by the commitment to a prosecutorial system free from political influence. However, the values of accountability and public interest could only be upheld through the political system. The ODPP system ultimately reflected an uneasy compromise between isolating prosecutorial decisions from appropriate political oversight and protecting prosecutorial decisions from inappropriate political influence. The approach to upholding prosecutorial values adopted in Australia contained an inherent problem that is not yet resolved.

PART 2

The Problematic Solution: The Australian Director of Public Prosecutions

4

The Continuing English Legacy

Once the Australian governments agreed on the need for statutory offices to achieve prosecutorial independence, they had to determine the structure of the Offices of Director of Public Prosecutions (ODPPs). The commitment to the English tradition prevented them from seriously considering original ways of upholding prosecutorial independence. Instead, they each adopted variations of the model of the Director of Public Prosecutions for England and Wales (the English DPP).

The debates on the Australian enabling legislation included arguments that were superficially appealing and ultimately persuasive, although spurious, that the English DPP is independent of the Attorney General. In fact, throughout the twentieth century, an expectation of the independence of the English DPP grew, but it was not accompanied by any corresponding legal authority for the independence of the DPP. Australian jurisdictions therefore created problems for the upholding of all the prosecutorial values by using the English ODPP, which was not independent from the Attorney General, as the model for the Australian ODPPs, which were explicitly intended to be independent from political influence.

I. Reform Possibilities

Broad consensus was reached in Australia during the 1970s–1990s that the Attorney General could no longer take primary responsibility for prosecutions because of the risk of actual or perceived political interference in the decision to prosecute. However, identifying the problem was easier than deciding on a solution. A minority of parliamentarians proposed novel approaches to achieve prosecutorial independence that involved disaggregating or substantially altering the relationship between prosecutorial and political roles.

The dissatisfaction with political involvement in prosecutions leads, logically, to calls for a depoliticised prosecutorial system, where the 'political character of decision-making is displaced'.[1] Some parliamentarians decided that the Attorney General did not need to be involved in prosecutions at all. In 1983, Liberal Opposition Senator Frederick Chaney suggested Australia adopt India's model of 'non-political law officers' to resolve the appearance of conflict between

[1] P Fawcett et al, 'Anti-Politics, Depoliticization, and Governance' in P Fawcett et al (eds), *Anti-Politics, Depoliticization, and Governance* (Oxford, Oxford Scholarship Online, 2017) 1, 7.

'the Attorney-General's essential independence' and 'character as a political animal and … member of the Government'.[2] He implicitly accepted Pettit's view that the 'democratic society which leaves the exercise of power to popular majorities and political elites may easily become the worst of despotisms'.[3] The suggestion of total depoliticisation of the prosecutorial system attracted no support.

There were less extreme proposals to limit the influence of political factors. In 1986, the New South Wales (NSW) Opposition proposed a DPP who was 'totally free and independent of government' but to whom the Attorney General could make submissions for consideration.[4] In 1991, the Western Australian National Party proposed that the DPP report directly to Parliament in the manner of the Ombudsman and the Auditor General.[5] The suggestion was rapidly dismissed simply because it was unprecedented in the prosecutorial context,[6] and has not been revisited in any jurisdiction.

The voices advocating radical models of prosecutorial reform failed to influence the debate. Depoliticisation and representative democracy are not entirely compatible. For the majority of parliamentarians, despite the concerns about prosecutorial independence, the prosecutorial role of the Attorney General was fundamental to good government and representative democracy. Every Australian jurisdiction decided to adopt some variant on the English DPP model, which was by then a century old. The combination of an Attorney General with ultimate responsibility for prosecutions and a statutory DPP with daily, operational responsibility for prosecutions was expected to provide prosecutorial independence and uphold the commitment to the Westminster system. However, the rationale for the adoption of the English system was unsound.

II. Resort to the English Model

From the seventeenth century, the sovereign was considered the *parens patriae*, or parent and legal protector of the nation.[7] They were the criminal prosecutor, but could not sue in their own tribunals or appear before judges.[8] This combination of responsibility for prosecutions but inability to appear in court led to a bifurcated prosecutorial system comprising a centralised public component headed by the

[2] Commonwealth of Australia, *Parliamentary Debates*, Senate, 10 November 1983, 2524 (Frederick Chaney).

[3] P Pettit, 'Deliberative Democracy and the Case for Depoliticising Government' (2001) 24 *University of New South Wales Law Journal* 724, 736.

[4] New South Wales, *Parliamentary Debates*, Legislative Assembly, 1 October 1986, 4320 (John Dowd).

[5] Western Australia, *Parliamentary Debates*, Legislative Council, 14 May 1991, 1745 (John Caldwell).

[6] ibid 1747 (Joseph Berinson, Attorney General).

[7] LB Custer, 'The Origins of the Doctrine of Parens Patriae' (1978) 27 *Emory Law Journal* 195, 201.

[8] *The Attorney General (at the Relation of William Izard) v James Brown, John Hall and Others* [1816] 1 Swans 265, 295, cited in F Hanlon, 'An Analysis of the Office of Attorney General in Australia and Directions for the Future' (PhD Thesis, University of Melbourne, 2007) 59.

Attorney General and a diffuse, democratic, private system of citizen prosecutors. The prosecutorial system trifurcated in the late nineteenth century, when private prosecutions and prosecutions by the Attorney General were bridged by the creation of the DPP. However, a coherent system of public prosecutions did not exist until the Crown Prosecution Service (CPS), headed by the DPP, was established in 1986.

A. Origins in Private Prosecutions

From the time of the Saxon kings, it had been considered the right and duty 'of the private citizen to preserve the King's peace and to bring malefactors to justice'.[9] As Lacey explains, until the nineteenth century, there was no identifiable criminal justice system, 'so great was the measure of decentralized governance … with significant power residing in the hands of local land owners'.[10] As a result of the regionalised social–political–legal system, private prosecutions persisted in England long after public systems were introduced in Scotland, across Continental Europe[11] and in the USA.[12]

However, private prosecutions constituted an unwieldy system that poorly served both victims and defendants. Victims or their families were required to prosecute at their own expense,[13] which could result in their declining to prosecute, conducting a prosecution poorly or being susceptible to 'bribery, collusion and illegal compromises'.[14] Privately prosecuting complex fraud cases with multiple victims was virtually impossible in the developing commercial environment.[15] The most pressing concern, however, was that private prosecutions could be motivated by 'purely partisan, malicious or even corrupt motives'.[16] Despite indictments requiring the endorsement of a grand jury,[17] private prosecutions were frequently

[9] T Mathew DPP, Lecture, London University, 1950, cited in R Jackson, *Case for the Prosecution: A Biography of Sir Archibald Bodkin, Director of Public Prosecutions, 1920–1930* (London, Arthur Barker, 1962) 170.

[10] N Lacey, *In Search of Criminal Responsibility: Ideas, Interests, and Institutions* (Oxford, Oxford University Press, 2016) 109.

[11] *R (Nicklinson) v Ministry of Justice* [2014] UKSC 38 [268].

[12] I Temby, 'Prosecution Discretions and the Director of Public Prosecutions Act 1983' (1985) 59 *Australian Law Journal* 197, 197; J Barth, 'Criminal Prosecution in American History: Private or Public?' (2022) 67 *South Dakota Law Review* 119.

[13] J Hand, 'Primitive Justice: Private Prosecutions in Municipal Court Under New Jersey Rule 7: 4-4 (b)' (1991) 44 *Rutgers Law Review* 205, 211–12.

[14] Commission on Criminal Law, *Eighth Report of Her Majesty's Commissioners on Criminal Law* (5 July 1845), cited in J Edwards, *The Law Officers of The Crown: A Study of the Offices of Attorney-General and Solicitor-General of England, with an Account of the Office of the Director of Public Prosecutions of England* (London, Sweet & Maxwell, 1964) 340.

[15] ibid 384–85.

[16] D Plater, 'The Changing Role of the Modern Prosecutor: Has the Notion of the "Minister of Justice" Outlived its Usefulness?' (PhD Thesis, University of Tasmania, 2011) 68.

[17] B Selway, 'The Different Role of an Australian Attorney-General' (2002) 13 *Public Law Review* 263, 266.

'carried out with a zeal that turned the law into a tool for private vengeance'.[18] The problems with private prosecutions were compounded after the establishment of a professional, paid police force in 1829.[19] While police did not have any statutory prosecutorial powers, they exercised the right of private prosecution on behalf of the community, which created new possibilities for corruption.[20]

The shortcomings of English private prosecutions attracted attention during the 1700s and 1800s. Jeremy Bentham, a leading but not solitary campaigner for reform, argued that a 'fixed establishment of a set of official prosecutors [was] a necessary appendage to every judicial establishment'.[21] Bentham's views had support from Chief Justices of the Court of King's Bench and the Commissioners on the Criminal Law in 1845. In 1870, 1871 and 1873, Bills were unsuccessfully introduced in Parliament proposing the establishment of a public prosecution service.[22] Finally, the Prosecution of Offences Act 1879 (UK) created the position of DPP, and began a more principled, public system of prosecutions. Private prosecutions arose in an organic and somewhat haphazard manner, without a strong sense of principle underpinning them. The 1879 Act adopted the principle, explained by Edwards, 'that efficacious enforcement of the criminal law demands the services of state-appointed prosecutors under central governmental control'.[23] It rejected the previous practice that Lord Denman, a future Chief Justice of the Court of King's Bench, described as a 'strange abandonment of the public interests to chance'.[24]

The movement away from private prosecutions marked a commitment to a more organised and orderly prosecution system that was not open to abuse by individuals. However, it did not establish principles for making prosecutorial decisions. The following section considers the development of the prosecutorial role of the Attorney General and the way that the broader responsibilities of the position created the prosecutorial values that still guide Anglo-Australian prosecutions.

B. Relationship between DPP and Attorney General

The Prosecution of Offences Act 1879 (UK) was an important statement of support for public over private prosecutions, but not of independence from political interference in public prosecutions. The ODPP was established to remedy the deficits in

[18] BA Grosman, *The Prosecutor: An Inquiry into the Exercise of Discretion* (Toronto, University of Toronto Press, 1969) 10.

[19] C Corns, 'Police Summary Prosecutions in Australia and New Zealand: Some Comparisons' (2000) 19 *University of Tasmania Law Review* 280, 282–84.

[20] J Rozenberg, *The Case for the Crown: The Inside Story of the Director of Public Prosecutions* (Wellingborough, Equation, 1987) 83.

[21] J Bentham, *Works*, vol 4 (London, William Tait, 1843) 391.

[22] J Edwards, *The Attorney General, Politics and the Public Interest* (London, Sweet & Maxwell 1984) 2.

[23] Edwards, *Law Officers* (n 14) 9.

[24] Lord Denman, *The Edinburgh Review* (1824) vol xl, 191, cited in ibid 341.

private prosecutions, not in prosecutions by the Attorney General. The legislation specified that the duties of the DPP were to be undertaken 'under the superintendence of the Attorney General', and that the DPP may be 'directed in a special case by the Attorney General'.[25] According to Edwards, the provisions suggested that 'intervention would be exceptional' and not 'exercisable as a normal ingredient in the Attorney General's functions'.[26] However, he also argued that the 'expansive and unequivocal' language of the regulations was that the DPP 'shall in all matters … be subject to the directions of the Attorney General', whose power would be 'unrestricted' and not contingent upon 'any predetermined conditions'.[27] These provisions applied until the Prosecution of Offences Act 1985 (UK). However, there has never been agreement on the meaning of the terms 'supervision' and 'direction' that purport to define the DPP–Attorney General relationship. The disagreement over fundamental terminology is not a semantic issue, and has resulted in continuing disagreement in England over the independence of the DPP.

C. Growing Expectations of Independence

In an address to the Law Society in 1952, the DPP, Theobald Mathew, described the DPP as 'the proud servant' of the public, Parliament and the executive.[28] The statement indicates that commitment to parliamentary sovereignty and the Attorney General's role within Parliament meant that the independence of the DPP was neither expected nor demanded. This mid-twentieth-century attitude reflected the statutory relationship of subservience of the DPP to the Attorney General, established almost 100 years earlier. In the second half of the twentieth century, the actual relationship between the Attorney General and the DPP, and the political expectations of that relationship, began to diverge. DPPs and Attorneys General both began referring to the existence and appropriateness of DPP independence but still acknowledged the formal supervisory role of the Attorney General, which included the ability to give directions to the DPP.

In 1978, former Attorney General Samuel Silkin argued that 'Some seem to think that the director is a mere creature of the Attorney General. They are mistaken. The director is essentially an independent, non-political figure … his decisions are his own', and the Attorney General 'should leave the director to carry out his functions'.[29] However, Silkin qualified his statement by admitting that the Attorney General could interfere in prosecutions to the extent 'necessitated by the

[25] Prosecution of Offences Act 1879 (UK), s 2.
[26] Edwards, *Attorney General* (n 22) 46–47.
[27] ibid 46 (emphasis in original).
[28] T Mathew, address to the Law Society, 1952, cited in Edwards, *Law Officers* (n 14) 390.
[29] *The Parliamentarian* (July 1978), cited in BA MacFarlane, 'Sunlight and Disinfectants: Prosecutorial Accountability and Independence Through Public Transparency' (2001) 45 *Criminal Law Quarterly* 272, 284.

duty of "general superintendence"'.[30] The following year, the Attorney General, Michael Havers, told solicitor and legal commentator Joshua Rozenberg that he was 'not responsible for the individual decisions of the DPP or his officers. The DPP, although being an officer under the Crown, is thus completely independent and non-political.'[31] However, in 1979, Havers recognised the constitutional position that while the 'Director makes many decisions in the course of his duties … I am in the position to exercise my ultimate power of direction'.[32] While the DPP position did not become independent over the years, the comments of two Attorneys General show that a political expectation emerged that the DPP should be independent, at least to some degree.

In 1978, the DPP, Thomas Hetherington, also reflected the change in attitude to the relationship between the Attorney General and the DPP. He did not echo the unabashed expression of subordination to the Attorney General that Mathew endorsed two decades earlier. After Edwards analysed Hetherington's written evidence to the Royal Commission on Criminal Procedure, he concluded that Hetherington offered a 'strong assertion of … *de facto* independence' when he explained that the Attorney General knew of few cases handled by his office.[33] A decade later, Hetherington was still in the role of DPP, and confirmed in an interview with Rozenberg that Attorneys General generally 'felt it right to leave decisions to the Director'.[34] However, he acknowledged that if the Attorney General insisted on a prosecution, as DPP, 'he would ultimately feel bound to comply with the Attorney's wishes'.[35] Rozenberg's summary of the system at the end of the 1980s captured the difficult balance in the relationship between the DPP and the Attorney General. He concluded that Parliament wanted a DPP:

> with enough independence of the government to avoid being subservient to it; and enough supervision by the government to ensure that he is ultimately answerable, through the Attorney, to Parliament … a DPP who was not prepared to be pushed around by the government – unless the government had decided to push him around.[36]

D. The Crown Prosecution Service

The 1986 establishment of the CPS marked a new phase in the relationship between the Attorney General and the DPP. It was preceded by the 1981 report of the Royal Commission on Criminal Procedure (Phillips Commission), which

[30] ibid 272, 284.
[31] Interview with Michael Havers (Joshua Rozenberg), cited in Rozenberg (n 20) 182.
[32] M Havers in the House of Commons, 1979, cited in ibid 182.
[33] T Hetherington, written evidence submitted to the Royal Commission on Criminal Procedure, 1978, cited in Edwards, *Attorney General* (n 22) 46.
[34] Interview with Thomas Hetherington (Joshua Rozenberg), cited in Rozenberg (n 20) 189.
[35] ibid.
[36] ibid.

was mostly concerned with the problems arising from police exercising the right of private prosecution on behalf of the community. The Phillips Commission confirmed suspicions that unwinnable cases were proceeding to trial because police investigators/prosecutors were 'psychologically committed to a belief in the guilt of the subject', and could not take an objective view of the evidence.[37] This proposition was supported by later Canadian inquiries that found police became overly attached to initial theories of cases, which restricted the scope and accuracy of investigations.[38] English police prosecutions were resulting in a 'frighteningly high' rate of directed acquittals,[39] which wasted resources and undermined public confidence in the criminal justice system. The Prosecution of Offences Act 1985 (UK) separated investigatory and prosecutorial functions by removing police from prosecutions and making the DPP, through the CPS, responsible for prosecuting all offences, whether serious or minor.[40]

The Phillips Commission's focus on police prosecutions restricted the attention given to the relationship between the DPP and the Attorney General. However, the CPS changed that relationship in ways relevant to prosecutorial independence. The Prosecution of Offences Act 1985 (UK) removed reference to the possibility of 'direction' by the Attorney General, and retained only the provision that the DPP be under their 'superintendence'.[41] However, the change was one of form, not substance. An international meeting of Attorney Generals' advisers in 1987 agreed that the power to superintend had always included the power to direct, and both the Attorney General and the DPP reported that the new legislation 'went largely unnoticed in their respective offices'.[42]

The failure to clarify the relationship between the Attorney General and the DPP, in the light of growing social and political expectations of DPP independence, supports Sanders's grim assessment in 1987 that the 'CPS merely has been grafted on to a system which has been developing haphazardly for centuries'.[43] His assertion was at least partly vindicated by evidence that confusion about the relationship between the Attorney General and the DPP, and about prosecutorial independence, persisted into the twenty-first century.

[37] *Royal Commission on Criminal Procedure 1978–1981* (Command Report, 1981), cited in Edwards, *Attorney General* (n 22) 86.

[38] BA MacFarlane and SM Cordner, *Wrongful Convictions: The Effect of Tunnel Vision and Predisposing Circumstances in the Criminal Justice System* (Government of Ontario, 2008) 23–25; A Lamer, *The Lamer Commission of Inquiry Pertaining to the Cases of: Ronald Dalton, Gregory Parsons, Randy Druken: Report and Annexes* (St John's Government of Newfoundland and Labrador, 2006) 71.

[39] Interview with Thomas Hetherington (Joshua Rozenberg), cited in Rozenberg (n 20) 82.

[40] ibid 83.

[41] Prosecution of Offences Act 1985 (UK), s 3(1).

[42] Interviews with Thomas Hetherington and Michael Havers (Joshua Rozenberg), cited in Rozenberg (n 20) 181.

[43] A Sanders, 'Incorporating the "Public Interest" in the Decision to Prosecute' in J Williams (ed), *The Role of the Prosecutor: Report of the International Criminal Justice Seminar Held at the London School of Economics and Political Science in January 1987* (London, Dartmouth Publishing, 1988) 30, 38.

E. Twenty-first Century Confusion in England

Issues with prosecutorial independence continued to arise in England in the twenty-first century. In addition to the BAE Systems prosecutorial controversy described in chapter two, the Labour Party faced allegations that, before the 2005 General Election, it offered peerages in exchange for political donations.[44] Preliminary investigations were undertaken into possible breaches of the Honours (Prevention of Abuses) Act 1925 (UK) and the Political Parties Elections and Referendums Act 2000 (UK). In 2007, Scotland Yard arrested Lord Levy, Labour's major fundraiser, but released him without charge. No other investigations or prosecutions proceeded.[45] The Attorney General's responsibility for determining whether government colleagues faced criminal charges again raised allegations that conflict between the Attorney General's legal and political roles compromised the independence of prosecutorial decision-making.

In response to the concerns about the BAE Systems and 'cash for peerages' controversies, the House of Commons' Constitutional Affairs Committee and the Attorney General's office both inquired into the constitutional role of the Attorney General, including the relationship with the DPP. The Attorney General's office concluded in July 2007 that the ability of the Attorney General to direct the DPP 'has never been settled definitively'.[46] The Attorney General, Lord Goldsmith, had testified in the previous month that in the event of 'a difference of view between an Attorney General and a Director then the Attorney General's view should prevail'.[47] Lord Mayhew, Attorney General from 1987 to 1992, defended the pre-eminence of the Attorney General's prosecutorial role more colourfully. He asked:

> If accountability to Parliament is essential, how can some official, however immaculately untainted by political interest, achieve it? To explain any controversial decision the presence of a Minister will always be demanded in the Chamber … If all the wretched Minister could say had to be prefaced with, 'I am informed that it was because of this, that or the other', he would be eaten alive. There would be talk of organ-grinders, monkeys and so forth.[48]

Neither of these comments by Attorneys General are controversial from a constitutional perspective, as both reflect the formal DPP–Attorney General relationship that has existed since 1879. However, attitudes had changed over the following

[44] A number of less prominent cases between *Campbell* and BAE Systems raised similar issues. On the *Khalid* and *Rhodesia Oil Sanctions* cases, see, eg Edwards, *Attorney General* (n 22) 324–34.

[45] B Hourigan, 'Who Pays? Political Donations and Democratic Accountability' (2006) 58 *Institute of Public Affairs Review: A Quarterly Review of Politics and Public Affairs* 12, 12.

[46] Attorney General's Office, *The Governance of Britain: A Consultation on the Role of the Attorney General* (26 July 2007) 8.

[47] House of Commons, Constitutional Affairs Committee, *Constitutional Role of the Attorney General* (Fifth Report of Session 2006–07, 17 July 2007) Evidence 46, Qu 355 (Lord Goldsmith). Patricia Scotland QC commenced as Attorney General in June 2007.

[48] HL Deb 1 February 2007, vol 689, col 350 (Lord Mayhew of Twysden).

century. As discussed in chapter two, concerns about the independence of the Attorney General's prosecutorial decisions were, historically, met with confidence that the Attorney General's personal integrity would ensure prosecutorial decisions were made in the public, not the political, interest. This confidence avoided the need for systemic reform. By the twenty-first century, the concerns about political intrusions into prosecutorial decisions that led to the establishment of the Australian ODPPs several decades earlier also resulted in calls for reforms to protect prosecutorial independence in England.

The Constitutional Affairs Committee concluded that 'inherent tensions' in the Attorney General role were undermining public faith in the criminal justice system. It recommended that the Attorney General's legal and ministerial functions be divided between separate offices, and prosecutorial and other functions be conducted on a non-political basis.[49] Parliament declined to support that suggestion, and also failed to pass a 2009 draft Bill prohibiting the Attorney General from giving directions to the DPP in individual cases (except in defence of national security).[50] Instead, a non-binding protocol between the Attorney General and the DPP, and other prosecuting departments, was adopted to specify that the 'Attorney General will not seek to give a direction in an individual case save very exceptionally where necessary to safeguard national security'.[51]

The disparity between the actual relationship between the Attorney General and the DPP in England and the expectations of the relationship was still evident in oral submissions to the Australian Royal Commission into Institutional Responses to Child Sexual Abuse (Royal Commission) in 2016. The DPP, Alison Saunders, submitted that, in 'theory', the Attorney General can 'direct the DPP, but that's never ever happened and I think would lead to some constitutional issues, if it ever did'.[52] In fact, such a direction would likely be constitutionally sound, and only in breach of the non-binding protocol. The Chief Inspector of the then Her Majesty's Crown Prosecution Service Inspectorate tried to articulate the concept of supervision of the DPP by the Attorney General for the Royal Commission.[53] He could only offer that the 'rather curious concept' is 'very difficult to explain' but

[49] House of Commons (n 47) 41. There were also concerns about the independence of the Attorney General's advice on the legality of the Iraq War that are outside the scope of this book. See J Chilcot, *The Report of the Iraq Inquiry: Report of a Committee of Privy Counsellors* (House of Commons, 6 July 2016).

[50] Constitutional Renewal Bill 2009 (UK), s 5; Constitutional Reform and Governance Act 2010 (UK); M Ryan, 'The Constitutional Reform and Governance Act 2010: The Evolution and Development of a Constitutional Act' (2014) 35 *Liverpool Law Review* 233, 236.

[51] *Protocol Between the Attorney General and the Prosecuting Departments* (Attorney General's Office, Crown Prosecution Service, Serious Fraud Office, Revenue and Customs Prosecutions Office, July 2009) 5.

[52] Evidence to Royal Commission into Institutional Responses into Child Sexual Abuse, Sydney, 29 April 2016, 6 (Alison Saunders).

[53] The independent Crown Prosecution Service Inspectorate inspects the work of the CPS and other prosecuting agencies. See His Majesty's Crown Prosecution Service Inspectorate, 'About HMCPS' (2023) www.justiceinspectorates.gov.uk/hmcpsi/about-hmcpsi/.

most closely resembles 'a parent's relationship with a rather independent-minded 17-year-old child. The Attorney cannot, and does not, interfere with individual decisions … Superintendence is very much based on personal relationships between the Attorney and the Director.'[54]

The misstatements and vagueness of two very highly placed officials in the prosecutorial system highlight the continuing lack of clarity in the English DPP–Attorney General relationship. They focus almost exclusively on personal associations, and 'gentleman's agreements' negotiated between them. Their approach denies the need to understand and articulate the formal relationship and to acknowledge that the Attorney General can, subject to political consequences, direct the DPP on prosecutorial matters. The Constitutional Affairs Committee's criticism of the Attorney General's prosecutorial role in the early 2000s resulted in only a protocol to define the relationship between prosecutorial agencies. Political incentives for the Attorney General to refrain from interfering in prosecutorial matters may generally be effective. However, their ability to intervene for political reasons threatens the de facto independence of the DPP and, through it, the prosecutorial process. The inherent tensions and confusions within the English system cast significant doubt on it as a model for independence in the Australian system.

F. Australian Confusion about English Prosecutorial Independence

The enduring confusion in the English prosecutorial system was never recognised by the Australian reformers who advocated the adoption of that model. The leader of the Victorian Labor Party, John Cain, visited the ODPP in London in the 1970s and had been impressed with the structure that purportedly separated party politics and prosecutions.[55] When he occupied the dual position of Premier and Attorney General of Victoria in 1982, he successfully advocated for the introduction of a comparable office,[56] and started a national trend towards independent statutory prosecution offices based on the English model. Cain maintained that, with the exception of the *Campbell* case discussed in chapter two,[57] there 'has never been the least doubt about the independence of the English DPP'.[58] His assertion was incorrect, however, because the *Campbell* case concerned the independence of the Attorney General, not the DPP, and, more fundamentally, the English DPP was never intended to be, and has never been, independent of the Attorney General.

[54] Evidence to Royal Commission (n 52) 42 (Kevin McGinty).

[55] Victoria, *Parliamentary Debates*, Legislative Assembly, 9 December 1982, 2678 (John Cain, Premier and Attorney General).

[56] The dual role gave rise to frequent criticisms that only his position as 'part time Attorney General' necessitated the devolution of the prosecutorial role. See, eg ibid 2669 (Robert Maclellan).

[57] R Jackson, *Case for the Prosecution: A Biography of Sir Archibald Bodkin, Director of Public Prosecutions, 1920–1930* (London, Arthur Barker, 1962) 208–210.

[58] Victoria, *Parliamentary Debates*, Legislative Assembly, 15 December 1982, 2924 (John Cain, Premier and Attorney General).

Raymond Groom recognised in the Commonwealth Parliament that regulations in England made the DPP 'subject to the directions of the Attorney General'. However, he perpetuated the fiction of the DPP's prosecutorial independence, and downplayed the reality of the Attorney General's ability to direct, by adding that 'in practice the Director in the United Kingdom says that the decisions he makes are his own. Conventions have developed since the office was first established in 1879'.[59] These misunderstandings of the English system continue to resonate within the Australian ODPP system.

III. Conclusions

The relationship between the English Attorney General and DPP remains, largely, as it was instituted in 1879. Over the last half century, the belief in the independence of the DPP has not always matched formal constitutional arrangements. Social and legal attitudes have exerted sufficient pressure for some Attorneys General and DPPs to exaggerate, deliberately or inadvertently, the level of the DPP's de facto independence, and invoke a persistent and powerful myth of de jure independence. The involvement of Attorneys General in prosecutorial decisions is not necessarily undesirable or improper, and by some estimations is necessary. However, in Australia, the entire premise of the ODPP system was independence from political interference of the Attorney General, and yet parliaments essentially transplanted into every jurisdiction in Australia, with the possible exception of Victoria, a system that neither intended nor actually achieved such independence. The misunderstanding of the nature of the DPP–Attorney General relationship in England made that an unsuitable model to solve the prosecutorial problems identified in Australia.

[59] Commonwealth of Australia, *Parliamentary Debates*, House of Representatives, 30 November 1983, 3046 (Raymond Groom).

5

Prosecutorial and Executive Discretion

The Anglo-Australian prosecutorial tradition ostensibly resolves an inherent tension between discretion and the rule of law that has been recognised for centuries. However, the extent of the discretion exercised by the Offices of Director of Public Prosecutions (ODPPs), as a statutory office within the executive branch of government, has unrecognised potential to undermine the rule of law.

A broad discretion was conferred on the ODPPs, with little recognition that, while the exercise of discretion is necessary to achieve individualised justice, it can undermine the rule of law through abuse of power. The potential for the misuse of discretion is particularly open when exercised by a statutory office within the executive branch of government. Prosecutorial discretion, in particular, can undermine the conventional separation of powers doctrine. It allows prosecutors to encroach into the spheres of the other branches of government, especially because the statutes conferring their power place few constraints on their discretion. All of the statutory provisions that create the ODPPs preserve the risk of political interference in prosecutorial decisions.

I. Discretion and the Rule of Law

The dilemma for all democratic countries is, as expressed by Adekunle for Nigeria, to balance 'the ability of the prosecution to accomplish legitimate, publicly desirable goals and objectives, while effectively resisting improper interferences'.[1] The resolution of the dilemma requires the formation of a normative position on the exercise of discretion. In 1960, Pound described discretion as 'an authority conferred by law to act in certain conditions or situations in accordance with an official's … own considered judgment and conscience'.[2] According to Abrams, the level of discretion to confer on prosecutorial decision-makers involves a choice between 'certainty, consistency, and an absence of arbitrariness', which weigh against discretion in prosecutorial decision-making, and 'flexibility, sensitivity,

[1] A Adekunle, 'Prosecutorial Independence and Effectiveness of the Nigerian Criminal Justice System' in V Colvin and P Stenning (eds), *The Evolving Role of the Public Prosecutor: Challenges and Innovations* (New York, Routledge, 2019) 220, 226.

[2] R Pound, 'Discretion, Dispensation and Mitigation: The Problem of the Individual Special Case' (1960) 35 *New York Law Review* 925, 926.

and adaptability', which require open conferral of discretion.[3] This choice has a profound effect not only on the administration of criminal justice, but also on the rule of law.

Tamanaha describes the rule of law as the 'single political ideal [that] has ever achieved global endorsement',[4] and Lino argues that the use of the term is so pervasive that it has become an 'unavoidable cliché'.[5] However, a precise definition has always been elusive,[6] and in 2007 French CJ admitted that a 'rather numinous concept'[7] of the rule of law underpins the Australian legal system.

In the sixteenth century, Sir William Wade, clerk of the Privy Council, was adamant that 'unfettered discretion cannot exist where the rule of law reigns'.[8] In 1885, the English legal theorist AV Dicey built on this tradition. He articulated that the rule of law demanded 'absolute supremacy or predominance of regular law as opposed to the existence of arbitrary power, and … wide discretionary authority on the part of the government'.[9] In his view, 'wherever there is discretion there is room for arbitrariness', which creates insecurity and undermines legal freedom.[10] While this remains the authoritative exposition of the rule of law, alternative definitions have been posited that affect the reconciliation of the rule of law with the exercise of discretion. In 2009, Raz provided an influential explanation that, at its broadest, the rule of law

> means that people should obey the law and be ruled by it. But in political and legal theory it has come to be read in a narrower sense, that the government shall be ruled by the law and subject to it.[11]

Raz later criticised his own formulation,[12] but it remains compatible with the 'unifying thread' of Australian administrative law. Groves and Lee confirm that the 'over-arching core value of the rule of law [is that] those who exercise power do so within and under the law, not above it'.[13] Burton Crawford elaborated in 2017

[3] N Abrams, 'Internal Policy: Guiding the Exercise of Prosecutorial Discretion' (1971) 19 *UCLA Law Review* 1, 3.

[4] BZ Tamanaha, *On the Rule of Law: History, Politics, Theory* (Cambridge, Cambridge University Press, 2004) 3.

[5] D Lino, 'The Rule of Law and the Rule of Empire: AV Dicey in Imperial Context' (2018) 81 *MLR* 739, 739.

[6] See, eg MJ Trebilcock and RJ Daniels, *Rule of Law Reform and Development: Charting the Fragile Path of Progress* (Cheltenham, Edward Elgar Publishing, 2009) 12–14; Tamanaha (n 4) 1–6.

[7] R French, 'Administrative Law in Australia: Themes and Values' in M Groves and HP Lee (eds), *Australian Administrative Law: Fundamentals, Principles and Doctrines* (Cambridge, Cambridge University Press, 2007) 15, 17.

[8] Sir William Wade, cited in J Rozenberg, *Trial of Strength: The Battle Between Ministers and Judges Over Who Makes the Law* (London, Richard Cohen Books, 1997) 103.

[9] AV Dicey, *Introduction to the Study of the Law of the Constitution*, 8th rev edn (Carmel, Liberty Fund, 1915) 120.

[10] ibid 110.

[11] J Raz, *The Authority of Law: Essays on Law and Morality* (Oxford, Oxford Scholarship Online, 2012) 212.

[12] ibid 212.

[13] M Groves and HP Lee, 'Australian Administrative Law: The Constitutional and Legal Matrix' in Groves and Lee (n 7) 1, 14.

that, fundamentally, the concept 'captures a potent belief, rooted in antiquity: that those who hold public power should not be able to do whatever they want', but rather their actions should be constrained by law so 'that there is a government of laws and not men'.[14]

Discretionary decision-making can sit uneasily with the various formulations of the rule of law, which all promote constraints on public power and certainty in the application of law. A fundamental element of the rule of law is that government authority should be exercised in accordance with rules. Discretion can appear to be exercised according to the caprice of the decision-maker rather than according to rules of law. However, as discussed below, there is no binary choice between discretion and constrained public power, because discretions are themselves constrained, in different ways and with different enforcement mechanisms. Jurisdictions, internationally, determine whether to grant discretion to prosecutors according to widely differing interpretations of the rule of law.

The rule of law in the inquisitorial, civil law systems of Continental Europe has, historically, rejected prosecutorial discretion in favour of the legality principle: the principle of mandatory prosecution.[15] Under this system, prosecutors must prosecute every case for which there is sufficient evidence in order to achieve equality before the law and prevent actual or perceived bias, political interference and corruption.[16] Mandatory prosecution is so central to some European prosecutorial systems that breaches of the obligation to prosecute are subject to criminal sanction.[17] This system privileges certainty ahead of flexibility and, as a result, Luna and Wade argue that 'discretion has a very bad name … implying negative concepts such as arbitrariness, abuse of power, and inequality'.[18] According to Boyne, even countries with strong traditions of adherence to the legality principle, like Germany, have found it impossible to maintain mandatory prosecutions given the prevalence and complexity of modern criminal offences.[19] However, while tacit or concealed discretion exists within inquisitorial systems,

[14] L Burton Crawford, *The Rule of Law and the Australian Constitution* (Alexandria, Federation Press, 2017) 10.

[15] This concept of the legality principle differs from the concept in Australian law that as far as possible statutes should be interpreted in a way that does not interfere with fundamental rights: B Walker and D Hume, 'Broadly Framed Powers and the Constitution' in N Williams (ed), *Key Issues in Public Law* (Alexandria, The Federation Press, 2018) 144, 147.

[16] J Iontcheva Turner, 'Prosecutors and Bargaining in Weak Cases: A Comparative View' in E Luna and M Wade (eds), *The Prosecutor on Transnational Perspective* (Oxford, Oxford University Press, 2012) 102, 107; J Herrmann, 'The Rule of Compulsory Prosecution and the Scope of Prosecutorial Discretion in Germany' (1974) 41 *University of Chicago Law Review* 468, 470.

[17] JH Langbein, 'Controlling Prosecutorial Discretion in Germany' (1974) 41 *University of Chicago Law Review* 439, 450.

[18] E Luna and M Wade, 'Looking Back and at the Challenges Ahead' in Luna and Wade, *The Prosecutor* (n 16) 424, 427.

[19] S Boyne, 'Is the Journey From the In-Box to the Out-Box a Straight Line? The Drive for Efficiency and the Prosecution of Low-Level Criminality in Germany' in Luna and Wade, *The Prosecutor* (n 16) 37, 37.

so does the hostility to discretion that underpins the principle of mandatory prosecution.[20]

The Anglo-Australian common law prosecutorial tradition, by contrast, privileges flexibility ahead of certainty because it 'recognizes that a mechanistic application of the law can be inadequate and unjust'.[21] As discussed in chapter one, the exercise of prosecutorial discretion is central to the tradition, and prosecutors are empowered not only to initiate and conduct prosecutions to bring wrongdoers to justice, but to decline to proceed where prosecutions would not be in the public interest. Commentary on this prosecutorial discretion has rarely reflected centuries of debate about whether discretion and the rule of law can be reconciled.

Dicey's strict view of discretion and the rule of law has moderated over time. In the 1891 case of *Sharp v Wakefield*, Lord Halsbury explained that discretion was not arbitrary if it was exercised 'according to the rules of reason and justice, not according to private opinion; according to law', and is 'not arbitrary, vague, and fanciful, but legal and regular'.[22] The Australian barrister and legal scholar Edward Sykes similarly argued in 1935 that the exercise of 'some discretionary power is implied in all government activities', and that discretionary is not the same as arbitrary.[23]

However, common law countries have not experienced inexorable progress toward reconciling discretion and the rule of law. During the mid-twentieth century, Hart and Dworkin engaged in several decades of debate[24] arising from 'America's obsessive fear that discretion and the rule of law are natural antagonists'.[25] Dworkin argued that in all but 'extremely rare' cases, right answers exist for every legal question,[26] and according to Shaw, he engaged in a 'quest … to eliminate discretion'.[27] By contrast, Hart argued that legal rules did not 'yield a unique answer in specific cases'.[28] Shaw explained that Hart maintained that discretion was 'fully compatible with the rule of law as long as the method used to resolve indeterminate cases comports with the rational standards that distinguish discretion from arbitrary choice'.[29]

[20] GC Shaw, 'HLA Hart's Lost Essay: Discretion and the Legal Process School' (2013) 127 *Harvard Law Review* 666, 697.

[21] SI Lezak and M Leonard, 'Prosecutor's Discretion: Out of the Closet – Not Out of Control' (1984) 63 *Oregon Law Review* 247, 257.

[22] *Sharp v Wakefield* [1891] AC 173, 180.

[23] EI Sykes, 'The "Rule of Law" in the Modern World: W Ivor Jennings, "The Law and the Constitution"' (1935) 1 *Res Judicatae* 56, 57.

[24] N Lacey, 'The Path Not Taken: HLA Hart's Harvard Essay on Discretion' (2013) 127 *Harvard Law Review* 636, 641.

[25] Shaw (n 20) 726.

[26] R Dworkin, 'No Right Answer' (1978) 53 *New York University Law Review* 1, 32.

[27] Shaw (n 20) 727; R Dworkin, 'The Model of Rules' (1967) 35 *University of Chicago Law Review* 14, 46.

[28] HLA Hart, 'Discretion' (2013) 127 *Harvard Law Review* 652, 656.

[29] Shaw (n 20) 669.

Despite Dworkin's mission to eliminate discretion, the twenty-first-century concept of the rule of law contemplates its existence with various degrees of enthusiasm. Ramsay reflects Hart's position by arguing that 'discretion can never be completely formulaic. Holes will exist even in the tightest net of legal and ethical rules' and need to be filled by a decision-maker's own judgement.[30] Groves and Lee confirm that modern Australian administrative law is 'mostly about power and discretion'.[31] Bowers actively celebrates that 'the human element of discretion is no unfortunate or inevitable by-product of law's application', rather discretion 'serves to perfect law'.[32]

Discretion is acceptable because it is subject to limits implied from the subject matter, scope and purpose of the relevant legislation, and generally, although not in the case of prosecutions, enforceable by judicial review. Nonetheless, the restraint of government discretion as a bulwark against the arbitrary exercise of power continues to be an essential component of the rule of law. As the civil law tradition recognises, prosecutorial discretion can create uncertainty regarding what matters will be prosecuted, and can enable selective prosecution designed to harass, or protect, certain individuals or groups.[33] Despite these risks, discretion was unquestioningly accepted in English and then Australian law, and the implications of its exercise were ignored during the establishment of the Australian DPPs.

II. The ODPPs and Discretion

The ODPPs were established amid the concurrent commitment to, and suspicions about, discretion. However, the voluminous parliamentary debates across the country and across decades largely ignored the significance and even existence of prosecutorial discretion. Two rare references to prosecutorial discretion in the debates demonstrate an unexamined acceptance of its continued role in Australian prosecutions, and no awareness of the well-established controversies regarding discretion. In Victoria in 1982, Cain simply explained that the DPP would exercise 'discretion in the prosecution process without … the day-to-day political pressures that are upon an Attorney-General'.[34] The Commonwealth Attorney General, Gareth Evans, similarly explained in 1983 that the 'main functions' of the DPP would be 'conducting Commonwealth prosecutions and exercising discretions in

[30] CB Ramsey, 'The Discretionary Power of "Public" Prosecutors in Historical Perspective' (2002) 39 *American Criminal Law Review* 1309, 1318.

[31] Groves and Lee (n 13) 2.

[32] J Bowers, 'Legal Guilt, Normative Innocence, and the Equitable Decision Not to Prosecute' (2010) 110 *Columbia Law Review* 1655, 1672.

[33] Lezak and Leonard (n 21) 255–56.

[34] Victoria, *Parliamentary Debates*, Legislative Assembly, 9 December 1982, 2678 (John Cain, Premier and Attorney General).

relation to prosecutions'.[35] Despite the limited attention, discretion and the rule of law are ostensibly reconciled in the ODPP system. The prosecution policy for Western Australia (WA) articulates that criminal prosecutions 'need to maintain the rule of law'.[36] However, the breadth of provisions in the DPP Acts create a discretion broad enough to raise questions about their compatibility with the rule-of-law principle of non-arbitrary, rule-based exercise of government authority.

III. Restraint by Statutory Powers

Under Australian administrative law, the statute conferring power on executive decision-makers defines the limits of their power.[37] Decision-makers have the 'exclusive right to determine' how to fulfil their functions within the limits set by the relevant statute.[38] The power to prosecute serious criminal offences is conferred through the DPP Act in each jurisdiction. The legislation creates a very broad discretionary power by simply providing that the function of the DPP is to lay charges of indictable offences and to institute, conduct or discontinue criminal proceedings on behalf of the Crown.[39] The extent of this power is revealed in the state DPP Acts that authorise the DPP 'to do all things that are necessary or convenient to be done' for fulfilling their functions,[40] and to conduct prosecutions where it is 'desirable to do so'.[41] The legislation additionally provides, in some circumstances, that the DPP can institute prosecutions where a matter has not been subject to a committal process.[42]

The independence of the office and the conditions of tenure discussed in the following chapter seek to ensure that the decision to prosecute is made in the public interest and not according to the interests of any part of the executive branch of government or the decision-makers within it. However, the direct legislative constraints on the exercise of this power are few and weak. For example, the

[35] Commonwealth of Australia, *Parliamentary Debates*, Senate, 10 November 1983, 2496 (Gareth Evans, Attorney General).

[36] Director of Public Prosecutions for Western Australia, *Statement of Prosecution Policy and Guidelines* (2022) s 32(a).

[37] Burton Crawford (n 14) 112.

[38] JNE Varuhas, 'The Public Interest Conception of Public Law: Its Procedural Origins and Substantive Implications' in J Bell et al (ed), *Public Law Adjudication in Common Law Systems: Process and Substance* (Oxford, Hart Publishing, 2016) 45, 64 referencing *HTV v Price Commission* [1976] ICR 170, 185 and *Home Office v Dorset Yacht Co Ltd* [1970] AC 1004, 1067.

[39] Director of Public Prosecutions Act 1991 (SA), s 7(1); Director of Public Prosecutions Act 1991 (ACT), s 6(1); Director of Public Prosecutions Act 1983 (Cth), s 9(1); Director of Public Prosecutions Act 1984 (Qld), s 10(1); Director of Public Prosecutions Act 1986 (NSW), s 7(1); Public Prosecutions Act 1994 (Vic), s 22(1).

[40] Director of Public Prosecutions Act 1991 (NT), s 21; Director of Public Prosecutions Act 1991 (WA), s 20.

[41] Director of Public Prosecutions Act 1973 (Tas), s 12(1)(a).

[42] See, eg Director of Public Prosecutions Act 1983 (Cth), ss 6(2A)–(2F).

New South Wales (NSW) DPP Act requires that the 'Director shall, if requested to do so by the Attorney General, consult with the Attorney General with respect to matters concerning the exercise of the Director's functions'.[43] The DPP Acts provide little of the restraint that would reconcile the prosecutorial discretion, and its significant implications for individual defendants and the administration of justice, with the rule of law.

Bowers's observation that in the USA, 'Laws are shells, and prosecutors retain almost unfettered discretion to decide how to fill the void within',[44] applies to the Australian prosecutorial system. However, Groves and Lee argue that in Australia, where the rule of law 'buttresses' the Constitution, it is axiomatic that public officials are required to 'remain within the scope of [their] authority',[45] and that even 'the most discretionary powers are not taken to be arbitrary powers'.[46] In 2007, French CJ was satisfied that every 'statutory power is confined, under its inherent logic, by the subject matter, scope and purpose of the legislation by which it is conferred', and that established 'interpretive principle[s]' fetter discretions.[47] However, Walker and Hume doubt the ability of statutes to constrain discretion where powers are drafted in broad terms. They argue that while courts are required to interpret 'broadly framed powers' narrowly, their indeterminate scope can undermine the rule of law, because it is difficult to determine how the laws will be interpreted, or if they have been appropriately exercised.[48] These concerns apply to ODPP decisions. The enabling legislation is extremely broad and does not require the DPP to initiate prosecutions in any particular situations, and prosecutorial decisions are not judiciable. The following section demonstrates the extent of the discretion by describing the multiple points between arrest and trial where the prosecutor can exercise discretion that affects the prosecution of a defendant.[49]

After the police arrest and charge a suspect, the ODPP must determine whether to proceed with the charge, substitute a different charge or charges, or decline to proceed at all. This decision is based, primarily, on the assessment of the evidence the police have collected and/or are likely to collect throughout the investigation.[50] However, it also has to take into account obstacles to prosecution, including immunities,[51] time and jurisdictional limits,[52] and public interest factors. Former NSW DPP, Nicholas Cowdery, observed during a 2015 review of the prosecution

[43] Director of Public Prosecutions Act 1986 (NSW), s 25(1).

[44] Bowers (n 32) 1659–60.

[45] Groves and Lee (n 13) 2.

[46] ibid 3.

[47] French (n 7) 19.

[48] Walker and Hume (n 15) 144, 144–46, 170–71.

[49] Philosophical approaches to the exercise of discretion are beyond the scope of this book, but see, eg I Colvin, 'The Charging Decision: Accountability, Transparency, and Control of the Decision to Prosecute' (PhD Thesis, University of Queensland, 2016).

[50] Police discretion is outside the scope of this book, but see, eg SH Bronitt and P Stenning, 'Understanding Discretion in Modern Policing' (2011) 35 *Criminal Law Journal* 319.

[51] *R v P, GA* (2010) 109 SASR 1; *PGA v The Queen* (2012) 245 CLR 355.

[52] *Angre v Chief of Navy* (No 1) [2016] ADFDAT 1; *Thompson v Chief of Navy* [2015] ADFDAT 1.

of Constable Hoy, discussed in chapter seven, that the 'decision to prosecute arises at all stages of a criminal prosecution – at the laying of a charge, the continuation of a prosecution, the commencement of a trial, even in the course of a trial'.[53] As Chair of the Australian Capital Territory's Board of Inquiry into the Criminal Justice System in 2023, Walter Sofronoff confirmed that the 'decision to prosecute is not static. There is an ongoing duty for prosecutors to consider whether there are reasonable prospects, and it is in the public interest, to continue a prosecution.'[54] The ODPP policies confirm that prosecutors have 'a continuing obligation to assess the evidence as the matter proceeds'.[55] The decision to prosecute 'must be constantly reviewed as circumstances change',[56] such as police investigations yielding more or less evidence than expected, witnesses being unable or unwilling to assist the prosecution as anticipated, plausible defences being presented or plea agreements being reached.

If a charge proceeds through committal or preliminary proceedings in the lower court, the matter is committed to a superior court for sentencing or trial. However, as stated in the Queensland prosecutorial guidelines, committal

> does not absolve the prosecution from its responsibility to independently evaluate the evidence. The test for the Magistrate is limited to whether there is a bare prima facie case. The prosecutor must go further to assess the quality and persuasive strength of the evidence.[57]

If a prosecutor decides not to proceed with a prosecution that has commenced, they must decide how and when to end it. They can either exercise a statutory power not to proceed with a prosecution before the defendant has been arraigned[58] or enter a *nolle prosequi* during trial, but before a verdict is returned.[59] A *nolle prosequi*, meaning 'unwilling to pursue', is a declaration of intention not to pursue a particular prosecution. It halts proceedings without a determination of guilt, and significant defendant rights are affected by its use, especially because it is not justiciable.[60] Unlike the process of 'tendering no evidence', which results in a directed verdict of acquittal, a *nolle prosequi* does not bar the subsequent prosecution of the

[53] Memorandum from Nicholas Cowdery to Police Association of South Australia, 27 April 2015, 2.

[54] W Sofronoff, *Australian Capital Territory, Board of Inquiry: Criminal Justice System, Final Report* (31 July 2023) 51.

[55] Director of Public Prosecutions, South Australia, *Statement of Prosecution Policy & Guidelines* (2014) 5.

[56] Memorandum from Nicholas Cowdery to Police Association of South Australia, 27 April 2015, 2.

[57] Department of Justice and Attorney-General (Queensland), *Director's Guidelines* (2016) 2–3.

[58] See, eg Judiciary Act 1903 (Cth), s 71; Criminal Procedure Act 2004 (WA), s 87(3); Director of Public Prosecutions Act 1990 (ACT), s 7(6) and (7).

[59] The authority for the *nolle prosequi* differs across the jurisdictions. In SA, for example, common law principles apply, but the power is regulated by statute in some jurisdictions, eg the Criminal Code Act 1899 (Qld), s 563, Criminal Code Act 1983 (NT), s 302 and Criminal Code Act 1924 (Tas), s 350. The *nolle prosequi* can be issued in any court except a court of summary jurisdiction: *Question of Law Reserved on Acquittal (No 3 of 1995)* (1996) 66 SASR 450, 455.

[60] LJ King, 'The Attorney General, Politics and the Judiciary' (2000) 29 *University of Western Australia Law Review* 155, 167–69.

defendant on the same charge; that is, double jeopardy does not attach.[61] For this reason, the *nolle prosequi* can be an instrument to either protect a defendant from or subject a defendant to an oppressive process. It can cease a private prosecution that lacks merit, but, alternatively, can cause injustice if entered to forestall a trial that is progressing poorly for the prosecution. It denies the defendant an acquittal and preserves the right of the Crown to initiate a fresh proceeding.[62]

The effects of the failure to recognise the extent and significance of prosecutorial discretion have been compounded by the failure of Australian parliaments to recognise that the location of the ODPPs within the executive undermines the separation of powers that is essential to the rule of law.

IV. Executive Discretion

The existence of prosecutorial discretion in any form or structure, within or outside of government, raises the possibility of its improper use. The establishment of the ODPPs recognised that prosecutorial discretion within the executive provides motivation and opportunity for political influence. This risk is reduced where the prosecutor forms part of an independent judiciary, as in Italy, Colombia and Costa Rica, or exists outside both the judiciary and the executive, as in Chile, Guatemala and Switzerland.[63] However, the Australian parliaments were focused on the misuse of the prosecutorial discretion by the Attorney General. They overlooked the paradox that, like Attorneys General, the ODPPs are part of the executive and open to the opportunities for abuse of power inherent within that branch, but they are also statutory authorities deliberately removed from the controls that operate on the executive.

A. Separation of Powers

The Australian parliamentary system is a variant of the English Westminster system, and so, unlike in the USA, there is an overlap of personnel between the executive and legislative branches, although there is no overlap of function between the branches.[64] The concept of the separation of powers referred to in this book is the normative principle that governmental functions should be divided

[61] *Beckett v New South Wales* (2013) 248 CLR 432, 439. Double jeopardy is now modified by statute in some jurisdictions to allow certain finalised matters to be reopened where there is 'fresh and compelling evidence'. See, eg Criminal Code Act 1899 (Qld), s 678D; Criminal Procedure Act 1921 (SA), ss 145–48.

[62] H Shawcross, 'The Office of the Attorney-General' (1953) 7 *Parliamentary Affairs* 380, 384–85.

[63] V Michel, 'The Role of Prosecutorial Independence and Prosecutorial Accountability in Domestic Human Rights Trials' (2016) *Journal of Human Rights* 1, 5.

[64] E Thompson, 'The Constitution and the Australian System of Limited Government, Responsible Government and Representative Democracy: Revisiting the Washminster Mutation' (2001) 24 *University of New South Wales Law Journal* 657, 663–64.

between three branches of government, each of which is best suited to exercising certain functions. It does not encompass the principle of constitutional separation of judicial power known as the *Boilermakers' principle*.[65]

The original NSW Constitution reflected the British system of a separation of powers observed by convention rather than 'compelled by any constitutional mandate'.[66] Modern state constitutions 'trace their ancestry to colonial constitutions predating Federation',[67] and the High Court of Australia (HCA) has not recognised a formal separation of powers at state level.[68] The Australian Constitution does not expressly mandate a separation of powers. However, the HCA has interpreted 'the compartmentalisation of the legislative, executive and judicial powers' to mean 'that Australia's constitutional framework dictated a separation of powers'.[69] While the Commonwealth separation of powers is only strictly recognised with regard to judicial power,[70] a tradition of practice and common law doctrine means that separation of powers is also 'applied by way of convention' at the federal level.[71] The 'three-way division of functions' that characterises the separation of powers, 'avoids the undue concentration of power in any one branch of government [and] enables each branch to counterbalance the others'.[72] Alvey describes its ultimate role as to safeguard 'freedom from "tyranny" of absolute power in government' and protect 'citizens from the abuse of government power'.[73]

The formal division of responsibility for the prosecution of serious crimes in Australia reflects the conventional adherence to the separation of powers doctrine. The Commonwealth, state and territory parliaments pass criminal laws for their jurisdiction; police investigate crimes and charge suspected criminals; the ODPPs prosecute serious crimes; and the court determines whether or not charges are proven, and imposes penalty on defendants who are found guilty. Through this division of prosecutorial roles, the legislative, executive and judicial branches purport to fulfil distinct functions, check and balance power,[74] and prevent any branch of government 'holding a monopoly of power and, in effect, being judge, jury and executioner'.[75]

[65] *R v Kirby; Ex parte Boilermakers' Society of Australia* (1956) 94 CLR 254. For commentary on the separation of powers doctrine relevant to this case, see, eg G Appleby, 'Imperfection and Inconvenience: *Boilermakers*' and the Separation of Judicial Power in Australia' (2012) 31 *University of Queensland Law Journal* 265; M Gaudron, 'Some Reflections on the Boilermakers Case' (1995) *Journal of Industrial Relations* 306.

[66] *Kable v DPP (NSW)* (1996) 189 CLR 51, 79.

[67] French (n 7) 20.

[68] *Kable* (n 66) 79.

[69] Groves and Lee (n 13) 6.

[70] *Kirby* (n 65).

[71] French (n 7) 18.

[72] J McMillan, 'Rethinking the Separation of Powers' (2010) 38 *Federal Law Review* 423, 423.

[73] J Alvey, 'The Separation of Powers Between the Executive and the Judiciary', Conference Paper, Australasian Study of Parliament Conference, 27–29 September 2017, 2.

[74] M McHugh, 'Tensions Between the Executive and the Judiciary' (2002) 6 *The Judicial Review* 111, 114.

[75] R Sarre, 'The Criminal Process' in M Marmo et al (eds), *Crime and Justice: A Guide to Criminology*, 4th rev edn (Pyrmont, Thomson Reuters, 2012) 435, 437.

However, because legislation specifies only that proscribed conduct is a criminal offence and does not require that all breaches be prosecuted, prosecutors are gatekeepers mediating the interpretation and enforcement of the criminal law.[76] Their exercise of discretion extends beyond their role as part of the executive and crosses the boundaries between the other branches of government. Prosecutors can decline, in individual cases or routinely for certain offences or types of conduct, to prosecute particular cases on public interest grounds. Parliament confers discretions on the executive so that a power can be exercised flexibly with regard to the circumstances of each case. However, the prosecutorial discretion can also be used to subvert the will of the legislature and the public that elected it,[77] through the non-prosecution of criminal offences that the democratically elected parliament has created.[78]

Decisions not to prosecute can also encroach on the role of the courts, because a discretionary decision not to prosecute prevents the court from determining whether a defendant is criminally liable and deserving of punishment. Even in Europe, where prosecutorial discretion is restricted by the legality principle, Weigand argues that the prosecutor's influence on the progress of criminal proceedings makes them 'a judge by another name'.[79] The blurring of boundaries between branches of government reflects, in part, the nature of the decision to prosecute. However, it also reflects the nature of statutory offices, which has the potential to further undermine the separation of powers and the rule of law in the prosecutorial setting.

B. Statutory Offices

Statutory bodies have existed in Australia since at least the 1890s, when railway corporations were 'born of a desire that some public operations … should be free from day-to-day political pressures'.[80] However, statutory offices have faced national and international criticism for their potential to undermine the separation of powers. McMillan explains that the development of administrative law in Australia was characterised by the growth of statutory authorities that bridge the three branches of government. These offices were expected to be 'independent of routine government control', and yet 'compatible with the implementation of a

[76] J Tombs, 'Prosecution – In the Public Interest?' in IL Potas (ed), *Prosecutorial Discretion*, Seminar Proceedings No 6 (Australian Institute of Criminology, 7–9 November 1984) 11, 13.

[77] DJ Givelber, 'The Application of Equal Protection Principles to Selective Enforcement of the Criminal Law' (1973) *University of Illinois Law Forum* 88, 96–98.

[78] K Toole, 'The Making of Prosecutorial Decisions in Australia' (2014) 39 *Alternative Law Journal* 268, 269.

[79] T Weigend, 'A Judge by Another Name? Comparative Perspectives on the Role of the Public Prosecutor' in Luna and Wade, *The Prosecutor* (n 16) 377, 389.

[80] J Goldring and R Wettenhall, 'Three Perspectives on the Responsibility of Statutory Authorities' (1980) 15 *Politics* 136, 136.

government's mandate'.[81] Since the 1970s, the independence that limits the control of statutory offices by ministers has been cited as evidence of 'breakdown in the Westminster system of government responsible to parliament'.[82] Miller criticises such agencies in the USA as being 'a strange amalgam of executive, legislative, and judicial powers, combining functions of all three branches yet the creature of none'.[83] Foote agrees that these characteristics leave independent offices without 'clear lines of authority … politically unaccountable, and therefore vulnerable to regulatory inefficiency and external manipulation'.[84] Similarly, in the European context, Majone observes that independent agencies are 'a serious threat to the rule of law, to parliamentary sovereignty, and to the hallowed principle that governmental policy ought to be subject to control only by persons accountable to the electorate'.[85]

Despite the challenges presented by statutory offices, there has been no recognition that statutory ODPPs, with broad discretion, challenge the separation of powers that is central to the rule of law. In fact, a report of the NSW Parliamentary Library Research Service in 2001 lauded that the 'independent status of the Director reflects the principle of the separation of powers between the executive, parliament and the judiciary, a crucial doctrine of the Westminster system of government'.[86] The Labor MP for Victoria, Joanne Duncan, observed in a 1999 debate about prosecutions that the separation of powers was 'sacrosanct, and never to be compromised'.[87] However, parliamentary debates disclose the persistent misapprehension that ODPPs moved the decision to prosecute from the executive branch. In WA in 1991, the Liberal Party's Peter Foss advocated for a DPP because 'a person who is separate from the Executive' is better placed to make decisions about the administration of justice.[88] In 1994, and again in 1999, the Victorian Parliament engaged in protracted debate over changes to the DPP legislation that shifted prosecutorial responsibility between the DPP, the Attorney General and a committee for public prosecutions. Labor members repeatedly claimed that any restriction on the power of the DPP 'impinges on the doctrine of the separation of powers'.[89] One of the most controversial debates related to a 1994 statutory provision that conferred on the Attorney General sole responsibility for prosecuting contempt of court charges.[90]

[81] J McMillan, 'Parliament and Administrative Law' (Department of the Parliamentary Library, 7 November 2000) Research Paper No 13, 19.

[82] Goldring and Wettenhall (n 80) 139.

[83] GP Miller, 'Independent Agencies' (1986) 1986 *Supreme Court Review* 41, 41.

[84] S Bartlett Foote, 'Independent Agencies Under Attack: A Skeptical View of the Importance of the Debate' (1988) *Duke Law Journal* 223, 223.

[85] G Majone, 'Independence vs Accountability?: Non-majoritarian Institutions and Democratic Government in Europe' (European University Institute, 1994) Working Paper No 94/3, 21.

[86] R Johns, 'Independence and Accountability of the Director of Public Prosecutions: A Comparative Survey' (July 2001) NSW Parliamentary Library Research Service Briefing Paper No 9/2001, 1.

[87] Victoria, *Parliamentary Debates*, Legislative Assembly, 9 December 1999, 1034 (Joanne Duncan).

[88] Western Australia, *Parliamentary Debates*, Legislative Council, 7 June 1990, 2015 (Peter Foss).

[89] Victoria, *Parliamentary Debates*, Legislative Council, 27 May 1994, 992 (Jean McLean).

[90] Public Prosecutions (Amendment) Bill 1999 (Vic), cl 7.

In 1994, independent Member of Parliament Donato Nardella complained that this provision 'affects the separation of powers in a detrimental way'.[91] Carlo Furletti, of the Liberal government, provided a tepid rejoinder during debates in 1999 over whether to repeal the provision. He claimed that it 'is arguable whether the division that exists between the Director of Public Prosecutions and the Attorney General is a separation of powers, but that is a debate for later'.[92] He never returned to address the issue, nor did any other speaker acknowledge that because the Attorney General and the DPP were both part of the same branch of government, their relationship did not affect the separation of the powers, or check the exercise of powers between branches of government.

This confusion regarding the separation of powers was evident in other jurisdictions during the same period. As discussed further in chapter six, the Attorneys General of South Australia (SA) and Queensland exercised their independent prosecutorial powers, respectively, in the cases of *Nemer* in 2003 and *Hurley* in 2007. In both cases, members of the Opposition incorrectly criticised the Attorneys General for purported breaches of the separation of powers. The Queensland National Party Opposition Leader, Jeff Seeny, alleged that the intervention in *Hurley* was intended 'to override the independence of the DPP',[93] and destroy the 'separation of powers between the Government and DPP'.[94] In SA, Liberal Party MP Isabel Redmond alleged that in *Nemer*, the Attorney General contravened 'the fundamental concept of democratic government, known as the separation of powers'.[95] Some of these comments about the separation of powers may have been casual descriptions of the separation of the prosecutorial role from political interference and investigative functions, rather than intended to invoke its technical meaning. However, they demonstrate a lack of awareness of the fundamental relationship between the ODPP and the executive branch that has implications for the exercise of prosecutorial discretion.

V. Conclusions

The rationale for the establishment of the ODPPs was the recognition of a problem with the exercise of prosecutorial discretion by the executive branch, but the Australian parliaments demonstrated a myopic focus on the Attorney General. The ODPPs, axiomatically, achieved the parliaments' goal of separating the exercise of

[91] Victoria, *Parliamentary Debates*, Legislative Council, 27 May 1994, 993 (Donato Nardella).

[92] ibid 15 December 1999, 596 (Carlo Furletti).

[93] T Moore, 'Hurley Charge "Political": Seeney' *Brisbane Times* (21 June 2007) www.brisbanetimes.com.au/news/queensland/hurley-charge-political-seeney/2007/06/21/1182019252174.html.

[94] M McKenna and A Fraser, 'Beattie Backflip on Palm Case' *The Australian* (22 December 2006) www.theaustralian.com.au/news/nation/beattie-backflip-on-palm-case/news-story/9d8bed45d1dc8a309cd9ab96d7e396f4.

[95] South Australia, *Parliamentary Debates*, House of Assembly, 17 September 2003, 111 (Isabel Redmond).

prosecutorial discretion from direct political control. However, the parliaments' narrow approach meant they failed to give the actual prosecutorial discretion a level of attention that reflected its importance.

Parliamentary debates disclose the curious situation that parliamentarians were prepared to vigorously defend the separation of powers and yet repeatedly, wrongly, identified the Attorney General's occasional performance of their prosecutorial role as an incursion into the separation of powers. They also ignored the fact that the ODPPs are part of the executive branch of government, and are also overseen by an elected member of the executive branch. They are not an external check upon the executive branch. This misunderstanding overestimated the extent to which the ODPPs separated the decision to prosecute from the reach of political influence.

6

Nature of the Australian DPPs: A Political–Statutory Hybrid

Once the Australian parliaments agreed to adopt the English prosecutorial model, they each had to answer the central question posed by John Lenders in Victoria in 1999: 'What is the balance in the Westminster system between the chief legal officer, the Attorney-General – an honourable man – and the Director of Public Prosecutions, who carries out the executive acts?'[1]

The answer to that question was expressed across the Australian jurisdictions through varying legislative relationships between Directors of Public Prosecutions (DPPs) and Attorneys General. Despite the differences in legislation across the country, all jurisdictions adopted a DPP model that was a restricted form of reform that neither rejected the prosecutorial role of the Attorney General nor accepted its traditional form.

The Office of Director of Public Prosecutions (ODPP) system apportions responsibility for prosecutorial independence to the DPP and responsibility for prosecutorial accountability to the Attorney General. All the DPP models accepted two paradoxes: an Attorney General could be distanced from the decision to prosecute and yet be accountable to Parliament for prosecutorial decisions; and a DPP could be overseen by the Attorney General but keep the initiation and conduct of criminal prosecutions independent of political influence. This prosecutorial model creates hybrid statutory–political offices that sit at the intersection of criminal and administrative law, and contain an inherent tension that undermines prosecutorial independence. The Queensland case of *Hurley* demonstrates the tension created where the Attorney General can exercise concurrent prosecutorial powers with the DPP. The South Australian (SA) case of *Nemer* demonstrates the tension created where the Attorney General can direct the DPP to take action in particular cases. The prosecutorial model of Victoria demonstrates the tension created where the Attorney General can neither direct the DPP to take action in particular cases nor exercise concurrent prosecutorial powers.

[1] Victoria, *Parliamentary Debates*, Legislative Assembly, 9 December 1999, 1037 (John Lenders).

I. Independence and Accountability

The ODPPs were established to achieve prosecutorial independence, but reflected the English principle that accountability was as important as independence. In 1996, the Victorian DPP, Geoff Flatman QC, argued that 'Independence without accountability poses an obvious danger to the public interest'.[2] He also quoted one of his predecessor DPPs, John Coldrey, who maintained in 1990 that while 'prosecutorial independence is an essential element in the proper administration of criminal justice', without accountability, independence creates 'the potential for … arbitrary, capricious, and unjust decisions'.[3] Concerns about the ability of the ODPPs to uphold both independence and accountability pre-dated their establishment. Some parliamentarians focused on doubts about the likely independence of the proposed DPPs. In Victoria in 1982, Liberal MP Robert Maclellan stated that the proposed DPP was 'not a free and independent judicial or quasi-judicial appointment exercising independent and separate judgement from the Attorney-General', but, rather, 'the office boy' who would become 'a convenient whipping boy'.[4] In 1986, New South Wales (NSW) Liberal MP Max Willis agreed that the proposed DPP was 'really nothing more than a subordinate functionary of the Attorney General'.[5] There were, however, diametrically opposed concerns that the DPP would, in effect, suffer from 'over-independence'.[6] In Western Australia (WA), Peter Foss implicitly raised the 'classic problem of second-order accountability',[7] or 'guarding the guardians',[8] which has been identified by administrative lawyers and political scientists. He cautioned against isolating 'independent officers from the scrutiny of and accountability to Parliament … We occasionally go too far in trying to set up these independent people: The more independent they are, the less accountable they become'.[9]

Parliamentarians also questioned the likely effectiveness of the role of the Attorney General within the proposed ODPP system. Maclellan was as concerned about the Attorney General not being accountable as he was about the DPP not being independent. He argued that the Attorney General would avoid 'responsibility

[2] G Flatman, 'Independence of the Prosecutor', Conference Paper, Australian Institute of Criminology, Prosecuting Justice Conference, 18–19 April 1996, 4.

[3] J Coldrey, 'The Office of the Director of Public Prosecutions: Independence Professionalism and Accountability' (1990), cited in ibid 5.

[4] Victoria, *Parliamentary Debates*, Legislative Assembly, 9 December 1982, 2670 (Robert Maclellan).

[5] New South Wales, *Parliamentary Debates*, Legislative Council, 3 December 1986, 7851 (Max Willis).

[6] DC Langevoort, 'The Human Nature of Corporate Boards: Law, Norms, and the Unintended Consequences of Independence and Accountability' (2011) 89 *Georgetown Law Journal* 797, 814.

[7] JM Ackerman, 'Understanding Independent Accountability Agencies' in S Rose-Ackerman and PL Lindseth (eds), *Comparative Administrative Law* (Cheltenham, Edward Elgar Publishing, 2010) 265, 270.

[8] M Johnston, 'A Brief History of Anticorruption Agencies' in A Schedler et al (eds), *The Self-Restraining State: Power & Accountability in New Democracies* (London, Lynne Reinner Publishers, 1999) 217, 225.

[9] Western Australia, *Parliamentary Debates*, Legislative Council, 30 April 1991, 847–48 (Peter Foss).

in Parliament for decisions that are rightly his responsibility' and 'wash his hands of [any contentious] matter like Pontius Pilate' by claiming that 'he is only a sort of puppet in the House'.[10] Maclellan concluded that the Attorney General would have

> all the perks, powers and titles, without any responsibility. If anyone asks him a question, he will run down to the law offices. Perhaps honourable members should coin the phrase that we have an 'Ajax' Attorney-General. He has the fastest footwork in the south, but no responsibility.[11]

In WA, Joseph Berinson agreed that because an independent DPP needed 'full legal authority to make all decisions concerning the prosecution of criminal offences', the Attorney General could not 'be held accountable to Parliament and the community to the extent which many suggest is still appropriate in respect of prosecution decisions'.[12] In 1991, John Burdett summarised the concerns in the South Australian debates by stating that 'the Government cannot have its cake and eat it: it cannot appear to be setting up an independent Director of Public Prosecutions but still have him under the control of the Attorney General'.[13] In fact, the ODDPs are open to precisely that criticism. The hyperbole of parliamentarians actually revealed legitimate confusion about the proposed DPP–Attorney General relationship, and its limited potential to uphold independence and accountability. However, the concerns across the country were swamped by consensus that the Attorney General could be both distanced from the decision to prosecute and accountable for it, and the DPP could be both overseen by the Attorney General and independent from political influences.

II. The DPP's Independence

The debates about the DPP Acts recognised that the independence of the DPPs could, and should, be protected through conditions of employment that would address the internal tension inherent in the DPP being independent from, and yet subject to, the Attorney General. However, they also recognised that security of tenure could, as Peter Foss articulated in WA, undermine the 'obligation to continue as an actively involved, lifetime leader',[14] and remove the possibility of dismissal for 'not doing a good job – as opposed to acting improperly'.[15] Former South Australian Attorney General Trevor Griffin agreed that if a DDP could too easily be removed from office they could have, or be perceived to have,

[10] Victoria, *Parliamentary Debates*, Legislative Assembly, 9 December 1982, 2670, 2672–73 (Robert Maclellan).

[11] ibid.

[12] Western Australia, *Parliamentary Debates*, Legislative Council, 28 March 1991, 699 (Joseph Berinson, Attorney General).

[13] South Australia, *Parliamentary Debates*, Legislative Council, 9 October 1991, 982–83 (John Burdett).

[14] Western Australia, *Parliamentary Debates*, Legislative Council, 7 June 1990, 2015 (Peter Foss).

[15] ibid 30 April 1991, 844 (Peter Foss).

'a motivation to please the Government of the day, and then be insufficiently independent', but that without provisions for removal, the DPP would be 'virtually unaccountable'.[16] The conditions of DPP appointment, tenure and dismissal seek to achieve an appropriate balance.

A. Appointment

The appointment provisions of public officials are critical to their independence.[17] The Western Australian Opposition originally proposed that the DPP be appointed by an independent panel consisting of the Chief Justice, the Commissioner of Police, the Law Society and the Attorney General.[18] However, the government objected as a 'matter of principle. It believes that if it can be trusted to appoint judges and other high officers it should be trusted to appoint the DPP.'[19] The recommendation for appointment by panel was not adopted in WA or elsewhere in Australia, and the appointment processes adopted across the jurisdictions involve varying levels of protection against political influence. In the territories, the Administrator[20] and the executive[21] are responsible for the appointment of the DPP, so there is no apparent barrier to political influence in the appointment process. In NSW, there is some protection against political influence because the proposed appointment of a DPP must be referred to the Office of the Ombudsman.[22] In the remaining states and the Commonwealth, the DPP is formally appointed by the Governor,[23] but the government is instrumental in the selection of the candidate, so the process is susceptible to political influence. In all jurisdictions, the eligibility criteria for the position of DPP is extremely broad; being limited to between 5 and 10 years' experience as a legal practitioner,[24] and, in two cases, a maximum age at time of appointment.[25] The breadth of the criteria means there is a lack of legislative constraint exerted

[16] South Australia, *Parliamentary Debates*, Legislative Council, 8 October 1991, 870 (K Trevor Griffin).

[17] J Morgan, 'Securing the Administrative Appeals Tribunal's Independence: Tenure and Mechanisms of Appointment' (2018) 43 *Alternative Law Journal* 302, 307; MN Roy and SS Saha, *Statutory Auditors' Independence in Protecting Stakeholders' Interest: An Empirical Study* (Cham, Palgrave Macmillan, 2018) 64–98.

[18] Western Australia, *Parliamentary Debates*, Legislative Council, 30 April 1991, 844 (Peter Foss).

[19] Parliament of Western Australia, Legislative Council, *Report of Standing Committee on Legislation in Relation to the Director of Public Prosecutions Bill* (July 1990) 3.

[20] Director of Public Prosecutions Act 1990 (NT), s 4(1) (DPP Act (NT)).

[21] Director of Public Prosecutions Act 1990 (ACT), s 22(1) (DPP Act (ACT)).

[22] Director of Public Prosecutions Act 1986 (NSW), s 4A (DPP Act (NSW)).

[23] Director of Public Prosecutions Act 1991 (SA), s 4(2) (DPP Act (SA)); Director of Public Prosecutions Act 1973 (Tas) (DPP Act (Tas)) s 4; Director of Public Prosecutions Act 1991 (WA), s 5(1) (DPP Act (WA)); Director of Public Prosecutions Act 1984 (Qld), s 5(1) (DPP Act (Qld)); Director of Public Prosecutions Act 1983 (Cth), s 18(1) (DPP Act (Cth)).

[24] DPP Act (Cth) (n 23) s 18(2), DPP Act (ACT) (n 21) s 22(4): 5 years; Constitution Act 1975 (Vic), s 87AB 23, DPP Act (WA) (n 23) s 5(2): 8 years; DPP Act (NSW) (n 22) sch 1, s 2(2); DPP Act (SA) (n 23) s 4(3); DPP Act (Tas) (n 23) s 4(2): 7 years; DPP Act (NT) (n 20) s 4(1)(b), DPP Act (Qld) (n 23) s 5(1A): 10 years.

[25] DPP Act (ACT) (n 21) s 22(5): 70 years; DPP Act (NT) (n 20) s 4(1)(a): 72 years.

on the appointment process, which further enables the potential for political influence in the choice of candidate.

B. Dismissal

Western Australia also considered requiring a resolution of both Houses of Parliament to dismiss a DPP, in order to bring 'entirely apolitical integrity in matters of public prosecution'.[26] This suggestion, however, was not included in the original provisions in any jurisdiction. The suggestion was adopted in Victoria in the 1990s, in response to prosecutorial controversies discussed later in this chapter,[27] and in Tasmania after its DPP, Tim Ellis, was found guilty of negligent driving causing death in 2013.[28] Other state DPPs may be terminated by the Governor, and territory DPPs by the Attorney General[29] or the Administrator.[30] The independence of the DPP is protected by very narrow grounds for removal from office, such as physical or mental incapacity, bankruptcy, persistent absenteeism, unauthorised engagement in legal or other work outside of the ODPP, failure to comply with legal obligations, charge or conviction for a serious criminal offence, or engaging in conduct that brings the ODPP into disrepute.[31] Former NSW DPP Nicholas Cowdery was adamant that these restricted grounds for removal from office protected DPP independence. He reflected that other senior public servants were dismissed for 'giving advice their political masters didn't want to hear', 'refusing to appoint political hacks' and as 'scapegoats for mistakes made by politicians', but that 'What allowed me to do my job was how hard it was to get rid of a DPP'.[32] However, the relatively short duration of DPPs' tenure weighs against their independence, especially when compared to the provisions for judicial officers.

C. Tenure

Judicial independence is recognised as critical to the rule of law, and security of tenure is critical to judges' 'freedom from external control by the executive government'.[33] Australian judges are generally protected from retribution from

[26] Western Australia, *Parliamentary Debates*, Legislative Assembly, 15 June 1988, 1170 (Andrew Mensaros).

[27] Constitution Act 1975 (Vic), s 87AE(3) and (5).

[28] P Caruana, 'DPP Bill Stalls' The Examiner (17 June 2015) www.examiner.com.au/story/3154557/dpp-bill-stalls/; Law Officers (Miscellaneous Amendments) Act 2015 (Tas), s 6; DPP Act (Tas), s 9F.

[29] DPP Act (ACT) (n 21) s 28.

[30] DPP Act (NT) (n 20) s 8(2).

[31] DPP Act (Cth) (n 23) s 23; DPP Act (SA) (n 23) s 4 (8)–(9); DPP Act (Tas) (n 23) s 9A; DPP Act (NT) (n 20) s 8; DPP Act (WA) (n 23) sch 1, s 6(a); DPP Act (Qld) (n 23) s 6.

[32] N Cowdery, *Frank and Fearless* (Sydney, NewSouth Publishing, 2019) 86.

[33] K Mack and S Roach Anleu, 'The Security of Tenure of Australian Magistrates' (2006) 30 *Melbourne University Law Review* 370, 372.

an executive that disapproves of their decisions, because they are appointed for a period extending to the compulsory retirement age.[34] There was some initial support for DPPs having security of tenure similar to that of Australian judges and European prosecutors, who are subject to the 'principle of irremovability'.[35] Western Australia proposed life appointment,[36] to recognise that the first Commonwealth DPP was not reappointed because the government objected to his prosecutions of Lionel Murphy and Neville Wran.[37] Foss recognised that it 'is accepted in the community that if a person is appointed for life, he realises, because he is no longer beholden to any person for reappointment, that he is extremely independent'.[38]

In NSW, the DPP was originally 'appointed for life',[39] to remove 'any suggestion or appearance that he or she is open to political pressure' and to pre-empt accusations that DPPs may 'curry favour with the Government of the day, in order to secure reappointment or advancement'.[40] In 2007, life tenure was replaced by a 10-year fixed term.[41] The Attorney General, John Hatzistergos, asserted that life tenure was an 'anachronistic … remnant of a bygone age' that did not encourage improved performance, and that fixed terms would 'enhance the accountability' of the DPP.[42] However, the DPP, Nicholas Cowdery, revealed the continuing tension between independence and accountability. He observed that the purpose of life tenure was to 'take politics out of the prosecution', and he asked how a DPP could 'resist political pressure if politicians were the ones deciding whether to renew the DPP's contract'.[43] Tasmania also, originally, appointed the DPP for life, but reduced the term to 10 years as part of the legislative reform undertaken after the resolution of charges against Ellis.[44] Liberal MP Matthew Groom described the change as necessary for 'refreshment of skills' and 'reflective of contemporary recruitment and knowledge management practices'.[45] However, the political–legal commentator Patrick Billings observed that the changes demonstrated that 'whittling away the independence of rival institutions sometimes proves irresistible

[34] Australian Constitution, s 72.

[35] M Fabri, 'Clash of Visions: Regulating Judges and Prosecutors in Italy' in R Devlin and A Dodek (eds), *Regulating Judges: Beyond Independence and Accountability* (Cheltenham, Edward Elgar Publishing, 2016) 245, 249.

[36] Western Australia, *Parliamentary Debates*, Legislative Assembly, 15 June 1988, 1169 (Andrew Mensaros).

[37] Western Australia, *Parliamentary Debates*, Legislative Council, 28 November 1989, 5375 (Peter Foss). The controversies are documented at Commonwealth of Australia, *Parliamentary Debates*, House of Representatives, 17 February 1986, 663–68.

[38] Western Australia, *Parliamentary Debates*, Legislative Council, 30 April 1991, 843 (Peter Foss).

[39] New South Wales, *Parliamentary Debates*, Legislative Council, 3 December 1986, 7857 (Jack Hallam).

[40] New South Wales, *Parliamentary Debates*, Legislative Assembly, 1 December 1986, 7343 (Terence Sheahan, Attorney General).

[41] Crown Law Officers Legislation Amendment (Abolition of Life Tenure) Bill 2007 (NSW).

[42] New South Wales, *Parliamentary Debates*, Legislative Council, 17 October 2007, 2671 (John Hatzistergos, Attorney General).

[43] Cowdery (n 32) 89.

[44] Law Officers (Miscellaneous Amendments) Bill 2015 (Tas), s 5; DPP Act (Tas) (n 23) s 5.

[45] Tasmania, *Parliamentary Debates*, Legislative Assembly, 17 September 2015, 65 (Matthew Groom).

for politicians'.[46] Queensland does not specify a minimum duration for the tenure of the DPP,[47] and Victorian DPPs have tenure of up to 20 years.[48] The DPPs in the other jurisdictions are appointed for periods of between 5 and 10 years.[49] The limited tenure has created suspicions that reappointment depends on maintaining favour with the government of the day. Barrister and legal commentator Greg Barns alleged in 2007 that South Australian DPPs became 'targets' when they did not 'play ball with the Rann Government's hardline law and order agenda … The shamelessly populist Rann got rid of one DPP – Paul Rofe … And now, Rofe's successor, Stephen Pallaras, is in the gun.'[50] Pallaras was not reappointed, and he reflected later that he only reapplied so that 'If they wanted me to finish they would have to go through some discomfort by sacking me, by not reappointing me. I was not prepared to make it easy for a government that made it extremely difficult for me.'[51]

The personal independence of the DPP is not the only consideration in the assessment of the independence of prosecutorial decision-making. Foss argued in the lead-up to the establishment of the WA ODPP that 'There are two independences to be preserved; the first one is the independence of the person' and the 'second independence is that of the process'.[52] The conditions of the DPPs' employment do provide some protection for their own independence, but the prosecutorial powers of the Attorney General undermine the independence of the prosecutorial process.

III. Attorney General's Prosecutorial Powers

The Attorney General needed a prosecutorial role that reconciled the commitment to the independence of DPPs with the need for their accountability. Apart from the unique case of Victoria, the Attorneys General in every jurisdiction were given, in effect, a 'reserve' prosecutorial power. Australian Attorneys General may engage in prosecutions in one of three ways: they may direct the DPP to take action on specific cases, such as to appeal a sentence or initiate or terminate a particular prosecution; they may direct the DPP on matters of prosecutorial

[46] P Billings, 'Time Limits on Tenure of DPP Not the Answer' *The Examiner* (23 April 2015) www.examiner.com.au/story/3032571/time-limits-on-tenure-of-dpp-not-the-answer/.

[47] DPP Act (Qld) (n 23) s 5(2).

[48] Constitution Act 1975 (Vic), s 87AB(2).

[49] DPP Act (WA) (n 23) sch 1, s 1; DPP Act (Cth) (n 23) s 18(3); DPP Act (SA) (n 23) s 4(4)(a); DPP Act (NSW) (n 22) sch 1, s 2A(1). In the ACT, appointments are made for up to seven years: DPP Act (ACT) (n 21) s 22(2).

[50] G Barns, 'Pollies Who Don't Get the Independence of the DPP' *Crikey* (4 June 2007) www.crikey.com.au/2007/06/04/pollies-who-dont-get-the-independence-of-the-dpp/?wpmp_switcher=mobile.

[51] N Hunt, '"It was Revenge" – Stephen Pallaras Speaks About His Bitter Falling Out With the State Government' *The Advertiser* (24 April 2015) www.adelaidenow.com.au/news/south-australia/it-was-revenge-stephen-pallaras-speaks-about-his-bitter-falling-out-with-the-state-government/news-story/c3af321a70bedde792a7bbc842a261a9.

[52] Western Australia, *Parliamentary Debates*, Legislative Council, 19 October 1989, 3454 (Peter Foss).

policy; or they may have concurrent powers with the DPP that allow them to substitute their judgement for that of the DPP when they disagree on how to proceed in a particular case.

Irrespective of the type, or combination, of prosecutorial powers retained by, or conferred on, the Attorney General, parliamentarians agreed their use would be limited. Former Commonwealth Attorney General Peter Durack, then in Opposition, noted in 1983 that the DPP Bill would enable the Attorney General 'to conduct prosecutions in his own right, although, obviously, that would be done only in very rare cases'.[53] His successor, Gareth Evans, reflected the following year that his power to direct the DPP had 'not been exercised to date, nor do I anticipate that it will very often, if ever, be so exercised'.[54] Jack Hallam, further confirmed in the NSW Parliament in 1986 that directions by the Attorney General would be issued 'sparingly'.[55] However, the inescapable reality in relation to both concurrent powers and the power to direct the DPP was, as NSW National Party MP Adrian Solomons explained in 1986: 'when the Attorney General is given, and retains, exactly the same powers as the Director of Public Prosecutions is given, one must assume that it is the intention of the Attorney General to exercise those powers'.[56]

Table 6.1 summarises the statutory provisions that confer prosecutorial responsibilities on Attorneys General in each jurisdiction. It shows that only the Commonwealth Attorney General can exercise all three forms of power, and only the Victorian Attorney General cannot exercise any of them. Most jurisdictions allow the Attorney General either to exercise prosecutorial powers concurrently with the DPP or to direct the DPP to proceed in particular ways.

Table 6.1 Australian Attorneys General' prosecutorial powers by jurisdiction

Jurisdiction	Prosecutorial powers of Attorney General
Commonwealth	Direct the DPP on policy matters and in specific cases[a] Concurrent powers[b]
ACT	Direct the DPP on policy matters but not in specific cases[c] Concurrent powers[d]
Queensland	Retains all 'functions, powers, prerogatives and privileges of the Attorney-General for the State under the common law or equity or by tradition or usage',[e] but must provide a written report to Parliament on the independent exercise of prosecutorial power[f] May not direct or instruct the DPP to present an indictment or enter a *nolle prosequi*[g]

(continued)

[53] Commonwealth, *Parliamentary Debates*, Senate, 16 November 1983, 2672 (Peter Durack).

[54] G Evans, 'The Discretion to Prosecute' in IL Potas (ed), *Prosecutorial Discretion*, Seminar Proceedings No 6 (Australian Institute of Criminology, 7–9 November 1984) 7, 8.

[55] New South Wales, *Parliamentary Debates*, Legislative Council, 3 December 1986, 7857 (Jack Hallam).

[56] ibid 7848 (Adrian Solomons).

Table 6.1 ***(Continued)***

Jurisdiction	Prosecutorial powers of Attorney General
NSW	Issue guidelines on general policy but not specific cases, and only after consultation with the DPP[h] Concurrent powers which prevail over decisions of the DPP[i]
WA	Direct the DPP on policy matters but not in specific cases, except on request of DPP[j] DPP must not perform a function inconsistently with the action of the Attorney General[k]
Tasmania	Not explicit on directions by, or powers of, Attorney General, but DPP required to 'act as counsel for the Crown in right of the State or for any other person for whom the Attorney-General directs or requests the Director to act'[l] Concurrent powers[m]
SA	Direct the DPP on policy matters and in specific cases[n] No concurrent powers[o]
NT	Direct the DPP on policy matters but not in specific cases, except on request of DPP[p] DPP must not perform a function inconsistently with the action of the Attorney General,[q] so must have some concurrent powers
Victoria	DPP 'responsible' to Attorney General for the 'due performance of his or her functions and exercise of his or her powers'[r] Cannot give directions to DPP and has no concurrent powers except the ability to enter a *nolle prosequi*

[a] DPP Act (Cth) (n 23) s 8(1)–(2).
[b] ibid s 10(1)(a).
[c] DPP Act (ACT) (n 21) s 20(1), (2) and (3).
[d] ibid s 21.
[e] Attorney-General Act 1999 (Qld) s 8.
[f] ibid s 11(2).
[g] ibid s 7(2).
[h] DPP Act (NSW) (n 22) ss 26(1) and (3).
[i] ibid ss 27(1) 30.
[j] DPP Act (WA) (n 23) ss 27(1) and (2).
[k] ibid s 28.
[l] DPP Act (Tas) (n 23) s 12(1)(e).
[m] ibid s 12(2).
[n] DPP Act (SA) (n 23) s 9; *Nemer v Holloway and Others* (2003) 87 SASR 147, 153–57.
[o] *Nemer v Holloway and Others* (2003) 87 SASR 147, 157.
[p] DPP Act (NT) (n 20) ss 28(1), (2)–(3)(b).
[q] ibid s 29(1).
[r] Public Prosecutions Act 1994 (Vic) s 10.

The following analyses of the Queensland case of *Hurley* and the South Australian case of *Nemer* show how the Attorney General choosing to exercise prosecutorial powers can undermine prosecutorial independence.

A. Concurrent Powers

In the Commonwealth, the Australian Capital Territory (ACT), Queensland, NSW, WA, Tasmania and the Northern Territory (NT), the Attorney General has the same prosecutorial powers as the DPP. The Attorney General may 'exercise his statutory powers by himself initiating proceedings, by continuing proceedings or by discontinuing proceedings … of his own motion'.[57] This arrangement provides backup where the DPP has a personal conflict or for some other reason is unable to act impartially,[58] but it also allows the Attorney General to impose his or her judgement in the event of disagreement with the DPP.

Queensland's Parliamentary Committee for Electoral and Administrative Review explained in 1993 that while the Attorney General's exercise of concurrent power 'overrides the Director, in strict terms it is not a question of one overriding the other but rather two separate discretions being exercised'.[59] The DPP agreed that his independence was protected as long as an Attorney General openly took responsibility for any 'individual and independent course of action'.[60] This process would, indeed, protect the personal independence of the DPP, who would not be required to act contrary to their own judgement. However, the personal independence of the DPP may not protect the prosecutorial process where the Attorney General exercises concurrent powers to circumvent a decision of the DPP. The following study of the Queensland case of *Hurley* demonstrates a core tension in the ability of the Attorney General to exercise prosecutorial discretion: a DPP's decision to prosecute can undermine confidence in the criminal justice system and justify the exercise of the concurrent powers of the Attorney General. However, an Attorney General's use of concurrent powers can undermine prosecutorial independence where there is a motivation for using that power for short-term, partisan political interest.

(i) Hurley

In 2004 on Palm Island, Senior Sergeant Christopher Hurley arrested an intoxicated Aboriginal man, known by his traditional name, Mulrunji. Hurley transported Mulrunji to the local police station to charge him with creating a public nuisance.[61] Mulrunji unquestionably struck Hurley as he exited the police

[57] Parliamentary Committee for Electoral and Administrative Review, *The Independence of the Attorney-General, Review of an Electoral and Administrative Review Commission Report: Transcript of Proceedings* (Legislative Assembly of Queensland, 27 October 1993) 9–10 (Royce Miller, Director of Public Prosecutions).

[58] Western Australia, *Parliamentary Debates*, Legislative Council, 28 March 1991, 702 (Joseph Berinson, Attorney General).

[59] Parliamentary Committee for Electoral and Administrative Review, *Report on Review of Independence of the Attorney-General* (Legislative Assembly of Queensland, December 1993) 21.

[60] ibid 9–10.

[61] C Clements, Office of the State Coroner, *Finding of Inquest: Inquest into the Death of Mulrunji* (27 September 2006) 1–3.

van upon arrival, but Hurley and witnesses disagree on whether Hurley struck Mulrunji in return. The question of violence by Hurley is critical, because within an hour of their arrival at the station, Mulrunji died in the cells from internal blood loss resulting from internal and external injuries. Palm Islanders engaged in widespread rioting and public protest. They believed that Mulrunji's death resulted from racist police brutality, because Hurley had assaulted other Aboriginal people at the police station.[62] However, the events preceding Mulrunji's death were disputed. The uncontested medical finding was that Mulrunji's fatal injuries were caused by a massive compressive force to the front of his body while his back was immobilised on a hard surface, probably the floor. The autopsy identified that he sustained four broken ribs, a black eye and a rupture to the portal vein, and that his liver was almost cleaved in two.[63] The legal question was whether the injuries occurred accidentally through a fall or through Hurley administering deliberate force. The acting coroner concluded in 2006 that a retaliatory punch from Hurley caused Mulrunji's death. She referred the matter to the DPP.[64]

Several months later, the DPP, Leanne Clare, announced that no criminal charges would be laid against Hurley because the evidence could not prove that he 'was criminally responsible' for Mulrunji's death.[65] She addressed the inconsistency with the outcome of the coronial inquiry by explaining that her 'duties are different to those of the coroner. This may lead to different views being reached in the same case.'[66] A coronial inquest is 'a major inquiry into death with a constructive focus into how the avoidable can be avoided',[67] and the applicable rules of evidence are more permissive than in a criminal trial.[68] However, the different purposes and rules of evidence do not explain the DPP deciding that Mulrunji's 'death was a terrible accident' and a 'fall is the only satisfactory explanation' for his injuries[69] in the light of the coroner's finding that Hurley had delivered fatal blows. The DPP's decision was consistent with the findings of the Crime and Misconduct Commission (CMC) in 2006,[70] with Hurley's acquittal of charges of assault and manslaughter at trial in 2006,[71] with Hurley's 2008 application to the District

[62] J Corrin and H Douglas, 'Another Aboriginal Death in Custody: Uneasy Alliances and Tensions in the Mulrunji Case' (2008) 28 *Legal Studies* 531, 542, 547.

[63] B Hine, Office of the State Coroner, *Finding of Inquest: Inquest into the Death of Mulrunji* (14 May 2010) 49–52.

[64] Clements (n 61) 25.

[65] Office of the Director of Public Prosecutions, Queensland, 'Hurley Not to Face Criminal Charges', Media Release, 14 December 2006.

[66] ibid.

[67] I Freckelton, 'The Evolving Institution of Coroner' (1999) 24 *Alternative Law Journal* 156, 157.

[68] Corrin and Douglas (n 62) 542.

[69] Office of the Director of Public Prosecutions, Queensland, 'Hurley Not to Face Criminal Charges', Media Release, 14 December 2006.

[70] Crime and Misconduct Commission (Queensland), 'CMC Statement Regarding Palm Island Death in Custody', Media Release, 14 December 2006.

[71] 'Hurley Acquitted After Controversial Case' *ABC 7.30 Report* (20 June 2007) www.abc.net.au/7.30/content/2007/s1957282.htm.

Court to have the original coroner's findings set aside and the inquest reopened,[72] with the appeal of that decision in 2010[73] and with another coroner's finding in 2010.[74] However, it was highly controversial at the time. Part of the controversy relates to the legitimate role of the DPP. As Mackenzie et al argue, Clare's conclusion that Mulrunji's death was 'an accident is inappropriate and not within her jurisdiction. She may well form a personal view that an accident is the most likely explanation for the death, but it is the role of the Coroner to determine this.'[75]

The DPP's decision not to prosecute was of concern to the community and government because it was made under 'the long shadow cast by the Royal Commission into Aboriginal Deaths in Custody'.[76] The Palm Island community, and its supporters, interpreted it as continuing unequal and discriminatory treatment of Aboriginal people.[77] According to Keenan, Mulrunji's death and 'its legal and political aftermath were not isolated, local issues for Palm Island or for the state of Queensland, but were part of the ongoing, colonial process that is Australia'.[78] The long and well-documented history of colonialism, poor relations between Aboriginal people and police, incarceration of Aboriginal people and Aboriginal deaths in custody may or may not be relevant to the assessment of the reasonable prospects of conviction and the public interest test in an individual prosecution. However, that history certainly provides context for evaluating the following, specific features of the case, which would be highly problematic even without the historical and contemporary relations between Aboriginal people and Australian law enforcement.

The original coroner was not satisfied that Hurley had testified truthfully before the first inquest. She determined that the arrest was not an appropriate exercise of police discretion, and that Hurley had not checked on Mulrunji's welfare after his initial injuries. She was scathing of the police response because the investigation was conducted by friends and colleagues of Hurley, Mulrunji's cell was never classified as a crime scene, evidence was not properly collected, and Hurley socialised with the investigators and assisted them with their inquiries. These factors collectively undermined the actual and perceived independence of the investigation.[79]

[72] *Hurley v Clements & Ors* [2008] QDC 323.

[73] *Hurley v Clements* [2010] 1 Qd R 215 (Court of Appeal).

[74] B Hine, Office of the State Coroner, *Finding of Inquest: Inquest into the Death of Mulrunji* (14 May 2010).

[75] G Mackenzie et al, '"What Really Happened" Versus "What We Can Prove": Tension Between the Roles of Coroner and DPP in Queensland' (2006) 6 *Indigenous Law Bulletin* 6, 7.

[76] RS Bray, 'Death Scene Jurisprudence – The Social Life of Coronial Facts' (2010) 19 *Griffith Law Review* 567, 570.

[77] 'Beattie Stand Firm amid Hostile Palm Island Reception' *The 7.30 Report* (20 December 2006) www.abc.net.au/7.30/beattie-stand-firm-amid-hostile-palm-island/2680064.

[78] S Keenan, 'A Blue Wristband View of History: The Death of Mulrunji Doomadgee and the Illusion of Postcolonial Australia' (2009) 34 *Alternative Law Journal* 248, 249.

[79] Clements (n 61) 33.

At a 2006 public meeting on Palm Island, the Premier faced hostility and abuse over allegations of racial discrimination, inequality before the law and the breakdown of criminal justice in Queensland.[80] In this political climate, the Attorney General had to decide whether or not to intervene in the prosecution of Hurley. In keeping with the principles and purposes of the ODPP system, the Premier initially advised the public to accept the decision of the DPP. He argued: 'if we are going to have justice for the long term of Indigenous Australians, the only way you can do that is by ensuring that the DPP's independence is not corrupted by political processes'.[81] However, just a few weeks later, the Attorney General announced that the former Chief Justice of NSW, Sir Laurence Street, then QC, would independently review the DPP's decision.[82] Street determined that there were reasonable prospects of conviction, and the Attorney General used his statutory powers to present an ex officio indictment against Hurley.[83] The intervention of the Attorney General generated as much controversy as the DPP decision that prompted it.

(ii) Legitimate Involvement or Cynical Politics

The Attorney General faced allegations that his initiation of Hurley's prosecution constituted improper political interference that undermined prosecutorial independence.[84] National Party MP Ian Rickuss was outraged at how 'poor old Sergeant Hurley was handled', and concluded that 'when politics comes into it good common sense gets thrown out the window'.[85] After a jury acquitted Hurley, the Police Association launched a series of radio advertisements likening Queensland to Zimbabwe in having politicians override laws to suit their own purposes.[86] The allegations misstated the limits of the law and ignored the Attorney General's legal authority for involvement in prosecutorial decisions. However, the questioning of the appropriateness of the particular intervention raised a fundamental issue about the prosecutorial power of the Attorney General under the ODPP system that is not answerable by applicable law. On the view favourable to the Police Association, while the Attorney General's exercise of prosecutorial power was within its statutory power, it was not a legitimate use of that power. It was a cynical political response to threats by Palm Island residents never to vote for the Australian Labor

[80] 'Beattie Stand Firm' (n 77).

[81] ibid.

[82] 'Sir Laurence Street to Review Mulrunji Case' *ABC News* (4 January 2007) www.abc.net.au/news/2007-01-04/sir-laurence-street-to-review-mulrunji-case/2166016.

[83] K Shine, 'Attorney-General's Report on Palm Island Death-in-Custody Prosecution', Media Release, 18 July 2007.

[84] M McKenna and A Fraser, 'Beattie Backflip on Palm Case' *The Australian* (22 December 2006) www.theaustralian.com.au/news/nation/beattie-backflip-on-palm-case/news-story/9d8bed45d1dc8a309cd9ab96d7e396f4.

[85] Queensland, *Parliamentary Debates*, Legislative Assembly, 7 March 2007, 768 (Ian Rickuss).

[86] E Schwarten and R Desmond, 'Govt Meddled in Hurley Case: QPU' *Brisbane Times* (22 June 2007) www.brisbanetimes.com.au/news/queensland/govt-meddled-in-hurley-case-qpu/2007/06/21/1182019269454.html.

Party again, and to negative publicity resulting from the resignation of the state's highest ranking Aboriginal police officer in protest at the government's purported mismanagement of Aboriginal affairs.[87] The intervention circumvented the authority of the DPP, which was intended to uphold prosecutorial independence, and sought to avoid electoral backlash rather than uphold the public interest.

However, on the view favourable to the Attorney General and the government, Attorneys General retain prosecutorial power so that democratically elected officials can ensure that prosecutorial decisions reflect community standards. This case clearly enlivened the Attorney General's prosecutorial powers because it involved allegations that a police officer who had a reported history of racially motivated violence used lethal force against an Aboriginal man. The offender's actions were subject to an ineffective police investigation marred by blatant croneyism, and despite a coronial inquiry damning the conduct and its investigation, the DPP brought the criminal justice system into dispute by declining to prosecute the police officer.

Unfortunately, neither the Attorney General nor the Premier effectively explained the decision to intervene in the prosecution. Upon Hurley's acquittal, the Attorney General provided a media release that outlined the procedural history of the case. It stated: 'In light of Sir Laurence's opinion, and having given very careful consideration to the matter, I decided that it was in the public interest for the matter to be resolved in Court.'[88] He simply added: 'As Attorney-General, I exercised the independent legal power to present an indictment based on legal advice with respect for the separation of powers and the independence of the DPP.'[89] The Premier's response to the criticism of the intervention was brief yet controversial. He stated: 'I don't see it as any big deal.'[90] His statement was a cavalier shorthand that located the intervention within the legitimate prosecutorial power of the Attorney General. However, it ignored the fact that it was the first time an Attorney General had effectively overruled the decision of the independent ODPP. While the Police Association underestimated the legitimacy of the exercise of the Attorney General's powers, the Premier understated its significance. The intervention by the Attorney General was a 'big deal', and he left the accusations of the Police Association largely unchallenged by failing to explain the rationale for the Attorney General's prosecutorial role and the appropriateness of exercising that power in this case.

Hurley has implications beyond Queensland, and beyond jurisdictions where Attorneys General have concurrent prosecutorial powers. It illustrates just one problematic manifestation of the tension inherent in a DPP system that empowers Attorneys General to substitute their judgement for that of the DPP, even though ODPPs were established to distance the decision to prosecute from political

[87] 'Beattie Stand Firm' (n 77).
[88] Shine (n 83) [7].
[89] ibid.
[90] L Willis, 'Lawyer Accuses Government of Pushing for Palm Island Prosecution' *ABC The World Today* (29 January 2007) www.abc.net.au/worldtoday/content/2007/s1835505.htm.

influence. While the Attorney General's concurrent prosecutorial powers have the manifest potential to compromise the reality and perception of the independence of the prosecutorial process, they do at least minimally protect the formal independence of the DPP. The alternative prosecutorial model, which grants the Attorney General the legislative power to direct the DPP, can compromise prosecutorial independence in a more fundamental way.

B. Directions on Policy

The Attorney General is authorised to give directions to the DPP on policy matters in the Commonwealth, the ACT, WA, SA and the NT, and to issue guidelines on policy matters in NSW. Western Australian Attorney General Joseph Berinson explained the rationale for this power in parliamentary debates in 1991. He argued that the Attorney General should be able 'to stress to the director parliamentary or public disquiet about, say, sentencing trends or the effects of certain policies being followed by the director'.[91] Similarly, the NT debates noted that the Attorney General was in the best position to 'reflect the prevailing needs and views of the community' on prosecutorial policy matters.[92] Such directions are removed from the decisions on particular cases that are central to the independence of the DPP and the prosecutorial process. The absence of cases or commentary questioning the application or appropriateness of this power suggests that it fits, uncontroversially, within the Attorney General's legal and political responsibility for oversight of the criminal justice system.

C. Directions in Specific Cases

As with the English DPP, the Attorney General can give directions to the DPP in specific cases in the Commonwealth and SA, and likely in Tasmania, pursuant to the authority to direct the DPP to act as counsel for the Crown or any other person.[93] Unlike the power to direct the DPP on policy matters, this power was subject to controversy and judicial review in the South Australian case of *Nemer*. The case involved a successful Crown appeal against sentence, but the statutory interpretation used in its resolution also applies to the decision to prosecute.[94] The case raised issues of class, rather than race, but, like *Hurley*, caused public outrage,

[91] Western Australia, *Parliamentary Debates*, Legislative Council, 28 March 1991, 701 (Joseph Berinson, Attorney General).

[92] Northern Territory, *Parliamentary Debates*, Legislative Assembly, 28 February 1990, 8968 (Daryl Manzie, Attorney General).

[93] DPP Act (Tas) (n 23) s 12(1)(e).

[94] Other cases of Attorney General involvement in sentencing decisions are outside the scope of this book, but see *R v Watson; ex parte A-G (Qld)* [2009] QCA 279; R v CMB [2014] NSWCCA 5; *CMB v A-G (NSW)* (2015) 256 CLR 346.

mobilised the government and ventilated issues about political involvement in prosecutions that are relevant across the country.[95]

D. Nemer

In 2001, Paul Nemer shot Geoff Williams, a newsagent who was conducting early morning delivery rounds and was incorrectly accused of menacing two young women. The gun was fired at close range and caused serious injury to Williams, including the loss of one eye. Nemer was charged with attempted murder, but under an agreement negotiated between his defence counsel and the DPP, he pleaded guilty to a charge of endangering life and received a fully suspended sentence of imprisonment and a $100 bond.[96] The Attorney General directed the DPP to appeal the sentence, and the Court of Criminal Appeal (CCA) resentenced Nemer to serve 4 years 9 months' imprisonment, with a non-parole period of 1 year 9 months. The case was extensively reported by the local press according to two themes that resonated with the public: judicial sentences are too lenient; and wealthy people receive favourable treatment in the criminal justice system.[97]

Nemer was from a wealthy and high-profile business family. Michael Atkinson was the Attorney General during much of the time that *Nemer* was before the courts, although not when the direction to appeal was made. Atkinson later observed that the 'state was convulsed' by the prospect that 'postcode justice'[98] allowed Nemer to avoid the conviction and sentence that his conduct warranted.[99] The success of the Crown appeal supports the assertion that the original sentence was below the tariff appropriate to the offence. In sentencing Nemer at first instance, Soulio J told the defendant that he should consider himself 'very fortunate' because the DPP accepted a plea to a lesser charge. Nemer's own barrister, Lindy Powell, then QC, was quoted in the local press in 2010 as having told him at the time: 'you've had a very, very fortunate result and you are a very lucky young man'.[100] Nemer's representation by Queen's Counsel is the only factor that suggests a causal link between his financial situation and his legal outcome. However, like the possibility of race-based advantage in *Hurley*, the possibility of class-based advantage in *Nemer* needs to be considered in its broader context,

[95] See, eg 'Paul Nemer – and the Man Who Was Shot in the Head' *Today Tonight* (25 July 2003) www.youtube.com/watch?v=2WUqDzVYAdU&list=PLDCF344C3D68A2614&index=22&feature=plpp_video.

[96] *R v Nemer* [2003] SASC 375 [87].

[97] C Hockley, 'Power of the People' *The Advertiser* (31 July 2003) 1.

[98] J Williams, 'Law and Order' in J Spoehr (ed), *State of South Australia: Trends and Issues* (Adelaide, Wakefield Press, 2005) 260, 272.

[99] South Australia, *Parliamentary Debates*, House of Assembly, 29 November 2017, 12400 (Michael Atkinson, Speaker).

[100] P Debelle, 'A Law Unto Herself' *The Advertiser* (9 April 2010) www.adelaidenow.com.au/news/a-law-unto-herself/news-story/4a67395952a2c86290478f925ece0a1b?sv=3cd1c60166b60cd14b0d8d3fba4166c8.

and the risk of differential legal treatment based on economic circumstances is a legitimate political issue.

Limited access to justice for criminal defendants across Australia has been recognised for many years. Legal aid has historically been poorly funded by international standards, and growing social and economic inequality have increased both the demand for legal services and the pool of eligible applicants.[101] According to Rick Sarre, it 'is undeniable that in our prisons we find principally those who are economically marginalised'.[102] Morry Bailes, former president of the Law Society of SA, asked in 2016 whether the South Australian criminal justice system afforded 'Justice for all, or just the rich?' He grimly concluded that limited legal aid funding constitutes 'discrimination in favour of those who can afford legal services against those who cannot'.[103] Notwithstanding that systemic discrimination in the criminal justice system has been attributed to limited government funding, the allegation that a defendant facing an attempted murder charge received favourable treatment on account of his family's wealth is a justifiable concern for government. In *Nemer*, that possibility exerted a profound and demonstrable negative impact on public confidence in the criminal justice system, which was, in itself, another legitimate cause for the Attorney General to consider exercising his prosecutorial powers.

The Labor Premier at the time of *Nemer*, Mike Rann, maintained that the decision to direct the appeal against sentence was made by the 'attorney-general, strongly supported by me'.[104] However, multiple members of the state government engaged in relentless public criticism over the reduction in Nemer's original charge, the perceived leniency of the sentence and the DPP's decision not to appeal the sentence. Liberal MP Robert Lawson KC alleged that the Premier exceeded the role of 'supporter' of the Attorney General. He reminded the Parliament that two weeks before the Attorney General directed the DPP to appeal the sentence, the Premier issued a media release that stated: 'I want to see this case appealed.'[105] South Australian court reporter Sean Fewster reflected in later years that Rann expressed to the press his shock at the outcome of the *Nemer* case, and advised the media that he personally wanted to know the process that led to the plea agreement, the factual basis of the plea and the prosecution's attitude towards that factual basis.[106] The question of political involvement in *Nemer* was more complex than in *Hurley* because the concurrent prosecutorial powers of the

[101] MA Noone, 'Challenges Facing the Australian Legal Aid System' in A Flynn and J Hodgson (eds), *Access to Justice and Legal Aid* (Oxford, Hart Publishing, 2017) 23, 24–29.

[102] R Sarre, 'We Get the Crime We Deserve: Exploring the Disconnect in "Law and Order" Politics' (2011) 18 *James Cook University Law Review* 144, 156.

[103] M Bailes, 'Justice for All, or Just the Rich?' *InDaily* (19 May 2016) www.indaily.com.au/opinion/2016/05/19/justice-for-all-or-just-the-rich/.

[104] South Australia, *Parliamentary Debates*, House of Assembly, 16 February 2004, 1174 (Mike Rann, Premier).

[105] South Australia, *Parliamentary Debates*, Legislative Council, 6 May 2004, 1511 (Robert Lawson).

[106] M Rann address to reporters in South Australia, 2003, cited in Fewster (n 100) 133.

Attorney General were clear in Queensland and only the appropriateness of their use in the particular case was in issue. In SA, the limits of the Attorney General's statutory power to direct the DPP in SA were unclear, and had to be resolved before the appropriateness of the particular intervention could be assessed.

According to the reflections of former Attorney General Michael Atkinson upon his retirement, key South Australian legal figures initially disagreed on the limits of the Attorney General's power to direct the DPP. The Crown Solicitor 'doubted that an appeal could be directed under the DPP Act', and senior staff of the Attorney General's Department 'were appalled by the prospect of a directed appeal, which, they said, would undermine the independence of the DPP'.[107] However, the Solicitor General, Chris Kourakis, took a different view. On his advice, the Acting Attorney General, Paul Holloway, directed the DPP to appeal the sentence.[108] Nemer sought a declaration that the direction to appeal was invalid on the grounds that the DPP Act did not authorise the Attorney General to direct the DPP on a specific case. Three justices of the Supreme Court sat concurrently as the Full Court of the Supreme Court (the Full Court) to conduct the judicial review of the direction by the Attorney General and as the CCA to reconsider Nemer's sentence.[109]

The process of judicial review enabled the Full Court to interpret the relevant provisions, and the justices explicitly applied their reasoning to the decision to prosecute. The justices grappled with legislation that included seemingly contradictory provisions. Section 9(1) provides that the DPP is 'entirely independent of direction or control by the Crown or any Minister or officer of the Crown'.[110] However, the following sub-section provides that the Attorney General may 'give directions and furnish guidelines to the Director in relation to the carrying out of his or her functions'.[111] The Chief Justice, John Doyle, alluded to the essential tension under the ODPP system Australia-wide when he characterised this combination of provisions as 'odd'.[112] The Full Court resolved the apparent contradiction according to the principle of parliamentary accountability and its historical importance in prosecutions. The Chief Justice concluded that Parliament 'qualified the Director's independence … having regard to the long tradition that the Attorney General exercised powers in this area independently of control by other ministers', and because the 'public and the Parliament have an interest' in prosecutorial decisions.[113] Nonetheless, he concluded, in dissent, that the Attorney General did not have the power to direct the DPP. Prior J held that the ability of the Attorney

[107] South Australia, *Parliamentary Debates*, House of Assembly, 29 November 2017, 12400 (Michael Atkinson, Speaker).

[108] *Nemer v Holloway and Others* (2003) 87 SASR 147.

[109] After the majority determined in ibid that the Attorney General's direction was valid, the court considered the sentencing appeal in *R v Nemer* [2003] SASC 375.

[110] DPP Act (SA) (n 23) s 9(1).

[111] ibid s 9(2).

[112] *Nemer v Holloway and Others* (2003) (n 108) 153.

[113] ibid 152.

General to direct the DPP was not odd, but merely 'exceptional'.[114] Vanstone J agreed with Prior J that while

> the spectre of the Attorney-General regularly playing a decision-making role in the work of the Office of the Director of Public Prosecutions may be unpalatable today, until the passage of the DPP Act he had that very control and, indeed, responsibility with respect to criminal prosecutions.[115]

She concluded that 'the clear implication … is that while the Parliament expected that in future the Director would be responsible for the day-to-day operations of his office, it was not prepared to give absolute control to him'.[116]

The majority decision of the Full Court established the authority of the Attorney General to make directions to DPPs in particular cases. The CCA vindicated the Attorney General's decision to make the particular direction in the *Nemer* case by significantly increasing his sentence. The Premier argued that this combination of decisions confirmed that 'it is only right and proper' that the Attorney General has the power of direction[117] because the administration of criminal justice is 'a matter of public interest'.[118] He also argued that the judgments showed that the 'intervention was right in terms of morality, right in terms of justice and right in terms of law',[119] and 'should silence the critics' who questioned 'the Attorney-General's motives'.[120] However, the courts did not, and could not, actually make any determination regarding the appropriateness of the Attorney General's intervention, or quell concerns that the direction to the DPP was motivated by partisan political interests.

Unlike the Queensland government in *Hurley*, the SA government spoke repeatedly and publicly for over a decade about the reasons for the Attorney General's prosecutorial powers and their exercise in the *Nemer* case. However, far from legitimising the Attorney General's action, the government's commentary was consistently compatible with the Opposition's claim that the intervention was 'base political point scoring' undertaken by 'a knee-jerk, reactive government'.[121] In 2004, Premier Rann told the Parliament that the CCA's decision showed that the lawyers and politicians who opposed the intervention 'have been proved wrong and the talkback callers have been proved right'.[122] The following year, he confirmed that the government's stand on *Nemer* was part of a policy agenda that would leave a legacy of 'some big billboards – Labor, tough on crime; Liberals,

[114] ibid 160.
[115] ibid 165.
[116] ibid 165. An application by Nemer for special leave to appeal was refused by the High Court of Australia: Transcript of Proceedings, *Nemer v Holloway and Others* [2004] HCATrans 24.
[117] South Australia, *Parliamentary Debates*, House of Assembly, 16 February 2004, 1174 (Mike Rann, Premier).
[118] ibid 11 November 2003, 694 (Mike Rann, Premier).
[119] ibid 16 February 2004, 1174 (Mike Rann, Premier).
[120] ibid 11 November 2003, 694 (Mike Rann, Premier).
[121] ibid 20 September 2005, 3471 (Robert Brokenshire).
[122] ibid 16 February 2004, 1179 (Mike Rann, Premier).

soft on crime'.[123] In his valedictory speech in 2017, Atkinson explained that while *Nemer* was being prosecuted, justice was a 'combat portfolio' in which his office led 'the artillery barrage'.[124]

When Stephen Pallaras commenced as DPP in 2005, he denounced what he perceived as political interference in *Nemer*. He argued that SA 'made a conscious and deliberate choice to include in its legal system an independent DPP', but its independence was 'at risk and under siege' because it was being made 'a plaything of the political process'.[125] The Shadow Attorney General, Robert Lawson, agreed that by seeking to 'undermine and discredit' the DPP, the Attorney General and his government 'politicised and interfered in what is supposed to be an independent office'.[126] In 2007, Greg Barns described Rann as one of a number of 'Law and order politicians' who were 'bully boys and thugs' when dealing with the ODPP. He exhorted that the 'DPP is independent of government – yes, that's right, i-n-d-e-p-e-n-d-e-n-t', and bemoaned that Rann was not 'able to spell the word'.[127] In 2012, then SA DPP Adam Kimber observed that 'There can be no clearer indication than what happened in that case of the fact that the Director is not completely independent'.[128] The reflections of Chris Kourakis, the Solicitor General who advised the government on the Nemer appeal and later became the state's Chief Justice, provide some support for these concerns. He recounted in an interview with Appleby, published in 2016, that the '*Government* … took the view that the sentence didn't reflect the public conscience'.[129] His view that the government, rather than the Attorney General, made the decision to intervene is compatible with the claims of improper political influence.

However, the intervention in *Nemer* cannot justly be dismissed as mere political manoeuvring. Attorney General Atkinson pointed out in 2004 that rather than 'just willy-nilly' directing an appeal of Nemer's sentence, he commissioned a report from the Solicitor General that 'made an incontrovertible case for appealing the sentence'.[130] Similarly, the intervention does not indicate, as alleged by the President of the Law Society later that year, that 'the government will give directions to the DPP whenever it thinks it desirable'.[131] The Premier explained that the power to direct the DPP could not be abused because it was subject to the safeguards of prior consultation with the DPP, reporting in the gazette, tabling

[123] ibid 12 September 2005, 3256 (Mike Rann, Premier).

[124] ibid 29 November 2017, 12398 (Michael Atkinson, Speaker).

[125] S Pallaras, Speech, SA Press Club, 6 May 2005, 2–6.

[126] 'DPP Independence Queried' *Lawyers Weekly* (14 May 2004) www.lawyersweekly.com.au/news/8091-dpp-independence-queried.

[127] Barns (n 50).

[128] A Kimber, '20 Years of the DPP: How Far Have We Come?', Speech, Justice Oration, 18 October 2012, 4.

[129] Interview with Chris Kourakis (Gabrielle Appleby), cited in G Appleby, *The Role of the Solicitor-General: Politics and the Public Interest* (Oxford, Hart Publishing, 2016) 214 (emphasis added).

[130] South Australia, *Parliamentary Debates*, House of Assembly, 16 February 2004, 1179 (Michael Atkinson, Attorney General).

[131] ibid 3 May 2004, 1930 (Mike Rann, Premier), quoting comments made by the Law Society.

before Parliament for debate and censure, judicial review, and comment by the press and the public.[132] He promised that future directions would only be issued 'in extraordinary and exceptional circumstances and in the public interest',[133] and 20 years later, no further directions have been made by Attorneys General from either political party.

Despite the negative commentary from within the legal profession, both *Hurley* and *Nemer* were, ostensibly, appropriate vehicles for intervention by the Attorney General. In each case, the public and the Parliament were dissatisfied with the decision of an unelected statutory officer. A coronial inquest supported the view that *Hurley* involved fatal police brutality against an unarmed Aboriginal man accused of extremely minor offences, and yet the DPP declined to prosecute the police officer involved. *Nemer* involved a wealthy defendant who negotiated a favourable plea agreement that reduced his liability and penalty for using an illegal firearm to seriously injure an unarmed and blameless man. The cases raised the possibility of race- and class-based bias in prosecutions that was undermining the reputation of the criminal justice system for which the Attorney General is responsible. The Attorneys General used their prosecutorial powers to ensure that the courts assessed, in the case of *Hurley*, and reassessed, in the case of *Nemer*, relevant legal and factual issues. In both cases, the Attorney General took action that was unequivocally authorised by legislation. Much of the criticism of both interventions misrepresents the legal relationship between the Attorney General and the DPP, and exaggerates the level of independence the ODPPs were empowered to achieve. However, fundamentally, the establishment of the ODPPs was intended to remedy the loss of confidence in the independence of the prosecution system that resulted from impugned exercises of prosecutorial discretion by Attorneys General. Sossin and Smith argue that 'Public confidence is not an absolute; it shifts over time and in response to particular disputes or crises',[134] and the establishment of the ODPPs did not resolve concerns about prosecutorial independence. It perpetuated concerns about the Attorney General's prosecutorial decisions and added concerns about the DPP's prosecutorial decisions. It is still impossible to assess accurately the motives of an Attorney General in a particular case because, as Stoker argues, politics 'has the quality of being both the decent pursuit of the common good and a rather unedifying process that involves humans behaving badly'.[135] Stenning agrees that in the prosecutorial context, 'Differentiating the interests of the governing party from "the public interest" … is inherently, and inescapably, problematic, if not ultimately impossible'.[136] Wherever Attorneys

[132] ibid 11 November 2003, 693–94 (Mike Rann, Premier).

[133] ibid 3 May 2004, 1930 (Mike Rann, Premier).

[134] L Sossin and CW Smith, 'The Politics of Transparency and Independence Before Administrative Boards' (2012) 75 *Saskatchewan Law Review* 13, 40.

[135] G Stoker, 'Embracing the Mixed Nature of Politics' in P Fawcett et al (eds), *Anti-Politics, Depoliticization and Governance* (Oxford, Oxford Scholarship Online, 2017) 1, 2.

[136] P Stenning, 'Discretion, Politics, and the Public Interest in High-Profile Criminal Investigations and Prosecutions' (2009) 24 *Canadian Journal of Law and Society* 337, 341.

General exercise legitimate power over prosecutions, their conduct is open to the perception that it crosses the very fine line between representing community interests according to legal authority and improperly using legal authority to gain electoral advantage.

In the cases of *Nemer* and *Hurley*, the public and media responses to the original DPP decision were sustained enough, and virulent enough, to provide a motivation for the government to intervene to achieve electoral gain. The cases support Woodhouse's observation that 'where politically contentious decisions are concerned, the Attorney General is unlikely to escape criticism … a conflict of interest will always be suspected and the opposition will seek to make political capital out of any high-profile decision'.[137]

Unlike the other Australian jurisdictions, Victoria does not empower its Attorney General to give directions to the DPP, or to exercise concurrent prosecutorial powers. However, the absence of these powers does not result in Victoria's prosecutorial system more effectively upholding prosecutorial independence and public confidence in the criminal justice system.

E. Extreme Independence in Victoria

Victorian DPP legislation provides that the DPP is 'responsible' to the Attorney General.[138] The Opposition objected to the 'drafting curiosity'[139] that originally left the meaning and implications of that responsibility unresolved.[140] In 1982, the Parliament 'put beyond doubt' that the DPP would be 'totally independent and free of review in respect of decisions to prosecute or not to prosecute'.[141] A provision was added to clarify that nothing 'affects or takes away from the authority of the Director in respect of the institution, preparation and conduct of proceedings'.[142] The statutory language and commentary about independence is similar to that used in other Australian jurisdictions, but, unlike in the other jurisdictions, the rhetoric approximates reality in Victoria. After conducting an international comparison of independence and accountability in prosecutorial decision-making, the Canadian Department of Justice determined in 1990 that the Victorian prosecutorial model 'is at the extreme end of independence'.[143] Former SA Attorney General Trevor Griffin reached the same conclusion the following year, and opposed the adoption in SA of the 'virtually complete structural independence' of the Victorian model.[144]

[137] D Woodhouse, 'The Attorney General' (1997) 50 *Parliamentary Affairs* 97, 101–02.

[138] Public Prosecutions Act 1994 (Vic), s 10.

[139] Victoria, *Parliamentary Debates*, Legislative Assembly, 9 December 1982, 2681 (Robert Maclellan).

[140] ibid 2685–86 (Jeanette Patrick).

[141] ibid 15 December 1982, 2924, 2923 (John Cain, Premier and Attorney General).

[142] Public Prosecutions Act 1994 (Vic), s 10(2).

[143] Law Reform Commission of Canada, 'Controlling Criminal Prosecutions: The Attorney General and the Crown Prosecutor' (1990) Working Paper 62, 47.

[144] South Australia, *Parliamentary Debates*, Legislative Counsel, 8 October 1991, 868 (K Trevor Griffin).

When the Attorney General faced pressure in Parliament in 2023 to intervene in a dispute between a special investigator and the DPP, she accurately replied that

> as Attorney-General I have no decision-making role in either of these processes, and that is entirely appropriate. For you to suggest that I should consider legislation to support one person's view versus the other when we already have a role for the DPP is not actually a request I think you should be making if you understand the role of the DPP. It is certainly not a matter for me to make these decisions.[145]

However, the Victorian experience demonstrates that, irrespective of statutory provisions, prosecutorial independence can be undermined whenever the Attorney General retains oversight of the DPP.

Victoria in the 1990s provided a unique environment to test the limits of prosecutorial independence because the decade was beset with prosecutorial controversies.[146] John Elliott, a former state and federal president of the Liberal Party, was unsuccessfully prosecuted for offences involving foreign exchange transactions made during the 1980s. He caused antagonism between the government and the DPP when he responded by requesting the dismissal of the DPP and suing that DPP for conspiracy to damage his reputation. In 1993, that tension was heightened. The unsuccessful prosecution of 11 serving and former police officers over two fatal shootings in the late 1980s promoted sustained and influential public campaigning against the DPP by police and their advocates. Mutual antipathy peaked when the DPP openly considered charging the Premier, Jeff Kennett, with contempt of court over statements he made on television about a murder suspect.[147] The absence of concurrent powers or the power to direct the DPP that are held by the Attorney General in the other states did not prevent political involvement in prosecutions raising concerns about prosecutorial independence in Victoria. After the persistent tension over prosecutions, the government made legislative changes that significantly encroached on the power of the DPP. The 'Office of the Director of Public Prosecutions' was renamed the 'Office of Public Prosecutions', senior positions and committees were created to share decision-making with the DPP, and the Attorney General was given sole responsibility for the initiation of contempt of court proceedings. In addition, there was a particularly controversial proposal for a Deputy DPP to be responsible to the Attorney General, not the DPP, and whose views would prevail over those of the DPP in the

[145] Victoria, *Parliamentary Debates*, Legislative Council, 21 June 2023, 2010 (Jaclyn Symes, Attorney General and Minister for Emergency Services). The dispute related to investigations of the Office of the Special Investigator that was established on the recommendation of the Royal Commission into the Management of Police Informants and is discussed in chs 7 and 8.

[146] See, eg M Sexton, 'Uncertain Justice: Inside Australia's Legal System' (2001) 33 *Australian Journal of Forensic Sciences* 51, 55–56; Director of Public Prosecutions, Victoria, *The Pursuit of Justice: 25 Years of the DPP in Victoria* (Director of Public Prosecutions, 2008) 26–27.

[147] J McCulloch et al, 'Putting the Politics Back into Prosecution: The Kennett Government and the DPP' (1994) 19 *Alternative Law Journal* 78, 81; C Corns, 'The Politics of Prosecution' (1994) 68 *Law Institute Journal* 276, 279.

event of certain conflicts. While this deputy position was never actually created, it demonstrated the extent of the efforts to curtail the power of the DPP.[148]

In 1993, the Attorney General, Jan Wade, justified the prosecutorial reforms as necessary to replace the 'untrammelled power' of the DPP with 'time-honoured notions of checks, balances and accountability'.[149] However, the reforms were unprecedented in Australia, and were interpreted, in various quarters, as political revenge for the controversial prosecutions.[150] The Premier fuelled allegations of political motivation by publicly stating that the DPP was 'digging a crater for himself' by criticising the government.[151] Two years later, a former staff member of the Attorney General's office publicly confirmed that tension with the DPP drove the legislative changes.[152] Premier Kennett denied the allegations and claimed to have documents supporting his denial, but no such documents were ever proffered.[153] The allegations of political interference were enduring. More than two decades later, Labor member Anthony Carbines reminded the Parliament of the 'Kennett government's attempt to emasculate and undermine' the role of DPP, and to 'put in party apparatchiks as deputy directors of public prosecutions'.[154] Through the Public Prosecutions (Amendment) Bill 1999 (Vic), the Bracks Labor government restored the right of the DPP to institute contempt proceedings. The government also expressed an intention to 'depoliticise'[155] the ODPP, and strengthen its legal and symbolic status as one of the 'independent watchdogs'[156] that checked 'the exercise of executive power'.[157] The language was certainly rhetorical, but not merely so. The Constitution Act 1975 (Vic) was amended so that the DPP could only be removed from office by an absolute majority in each House of Parliament.[158]

Concerns about the Attorney General undermining prosecutorial independence have not been resolved by subsequent decades of policy, legislation and convention. In 2018, 15 Labor MPs faced criminal charges over a so-called 'red shirts rorts scandal'. They were accused of using public money to pay party campaign organisers as 'casual electorate officers'.[159] The Deputy Leader of the

[148] McCulloch et al (n 148) 81; C Corns, 'The Politics of Prosecution' (1994) 68 *Law Institute Journal* 276, 279.

[149] Article in *Sun-Herald* (23 December 1993), cited in McCulloch et al (n 148) 80.

[150] ibid.

[151] Comment of Premier J Kennett reported in *The Age* (16 December 1993), cited in McCulloch et al (n 148) 81.

[152] J McCulloch, 'The Bongiorno Affair' (1995) 20 *Alternative Law Journal* 140, 141.

[153] ibid.

[154] Victoria, *Parliamentary Debates*, Legislative Assembly, 13 December 2017, 4431–32 (Anthony Carbines).

[155] Victoria, *Parliamentary Debates*, Legislative Council, 15 December 1999, 600 (Dianne Hadden).

[156] ibid 10 November 1999, 304 (Ann Barker).

[157] ibid 9 December 1999, 1029 (Timothy Holding).

[158] Public Prosecutions (Amendment) Bill 1999 (Vic), s 11; Constitution Act 1975 (Vic), s 87AE.

[159] Parliament of Victoria, Legislative Council Privileges Committee, *Inquiry into Matters Relating to the Misuse of Electorate Office Staffing Entitlements* (Victorian Government Printer, August 2018) 9–19; Australian Communications and Media Authority, 'Seven News Broadcast on 21 March 2018'

Opposition argued that the allegations have 'ramifications for the law system of Victoria', because the DPP who has to decide whether or not to prosecute the parliamentarians reports to the Attorney General of the same political party.[160] The allegations did not result in criminal charges.[161] However, the case confirms that the mere involvement of the Attorney General in prosecutorial decisions can create a climate of suspicion that undermines the purpose of the ODPPs.

IV. Conclusions

The various prosecutorial models across Australia intended that the Attorney General's supervision of the DPP would achieve accountability without compromising independence. However, the retention of the prosecutorial role of the Attorney General embeds into the ODPP system the conflict between political allegiances and legal obligations that are inherent in the office of Attorney General. It creates a tension between independence and accountability that has never been resolved, and perpetuates the same possibilities for political interference that dogged its predecessor system and drove the establishment of the ODPPs. The controversies about independence under the ODPP system are strikingly similar to those that drove its establishment. However, the adoption of independent statutory offices added a new dimension to the controversies. The conflicting claims of the Attorney General and the DPP lead, apparently inexorably, to territorial disputes in which the public, the media and the legal profession aggressively take sides, and enliven political interests in prosecutorial decisions. These contrasting representations highlight that the ODPPs promise a level of prosecutorial independence that cannot be achieved because the DPP legislation also confers prosecutorial power on the Attorney General. The discrepancy between their promised and actual level of independence undermines the ODPP system's ability to satisfy community expectations and undermines the perception of prosecutorial independence.

(18 July 2018) Investigation Report No BI-405; Victorian Ombudsman, *Investigation of a Matter Referred From the Legislative Council on 25 November 2015* (March 2018) 32–91.

[160] Victoria, *Parliamentary Debates*, Legislative Assembly, 8 August 2018, 2632 (Peter Walsh).

[161] R Willingham and S Anderson, 'No Labor MPs Charged Over Red Shirts Victorian Election Rort, Police Announce' *ABC News* (14 February 2019) www.abc.net.au/news/2019-02-14/no-mps-charged-over-victorian-alp-red-shirts-scandal/10795058?pfmredir=sm.

7

The Reasonable Prospects of Conviction Test

When the Australian Office of Director of Public Prosecutions (ODPP) system was adapted from the English prosecutorial model, it inherited the problem that a broad discretion is resistant to, but in need of, some level of constraint. The requirement to prosecute in the public interest is meant to limit the discretion of the prosecutor, and the ODPP guidelines define the public interest through the reasonable prospects of conviction and public interest tests. As the tests jointly act as the main control over the decision to prosecute, they play a key role in determining whether prosecutorial discretion is constrained.

The reasonable prospects of conviction test is, ostensibly, an objective standard that constrains the prosecutorial discretion. However, its efficacy depends upon a precise definition that can be consistently and transparently applied across cases. The case of *Volkers* was investigated by the Royal Commission into Institutional Responses to Child Sexual Abuse (the Royal Commission). The case demonstrates that in assessing the reasonable prospects of conviction, prosecutors need to forecast how a jury will assess specialised topics, and apply a normative view of reasonableness to determine which cases should proceed to trial. This assessment requires a level of subjective judgement that is rarely acknowledged in discussions of the test.

I. Guiding the Decision to Prosecute

The decision to prosecute is guided by two tests, which are enumerated in enough detail to meet Hart's standard that discretion should be exercised by conscientiously weighing factors that are formulated and identifiable in advance.[1]

The Victorian prosecution policy most clearly articulates that a 'prosecution may only proceed if: there is a reasonable prospect of a conviction; and a prosecution is in the public interest'.[2] The reasonable prospects of conviction test involves a legal determination of whether a prosecution *can succeed* on the basis of the sufficiency of the available evidence. The New South Wales (NSW) guidelines characterise the test as requiring an evaluation of 'the likely strength of the admissible evidence the prosecution would present to the court, bearing in mind that the

[1] HLA Hart, 'Discretion' (2013) 127 *Harvard Law Review* 652, 661.
[2] *Policy of the Director of Public Prosecutions for Victoria* (2022) s 1.

prosecution has to prove each element of the offence beyond a reasonable doubt'.[3] The public interest test determines whether a prosecution *should proceed* as a matter of public policy, where there is evidence capable of proving the elements of the offence charged. It requires consideration of factors including the circumstances of the offender and the victim, the facts of the case overall, and the broader social and legal implications of the prosecution.

According to the Northern Territory (NT) guidelines, the 'assessment of prospects of conviction is … an exercise of discretion in the public interest'.[4] In keeping with this principle, the Western Australian, NT and Commonwealth guidelines include the reasonable prospects of conviction as part of the public interest test.[5] The adoption of a single test recognises that it is, generally, in the public interest to prosecute serious crimes where there is sufficient evidence. Conversely, as the Western Australian (WA) guidelines state, 'A prosecution is not in the public interest if it does not have reasonable prospects of conviction'.[6]

The Australian Capital Territory (ACT), South Australia (SA) and NSW consider the reasonable prospects of conviction and public interest tests separately. The ACT guidelines provide that the 'decision to prosecute can be understood as a two-stage process. First, does the evidence offer reasonable prospects of conviction? If so, is it in the public interest to proceed with a prosecution?'[7] The SA guidelines maintain a similar distinction, stating that once a prosecutor is satisfied with the sufficiency of the evidence, they must 'consider whether … the public interest requires a prosecution to be pursued'.[8]

Under either approach, the decision to prosecute considers both the sufficiency of evidence and the public interest in prosecuting, and involves some overlap between those tests. However, I discuss the tests separately, in consecutive chapters, because they contain discrete criteria that raise different issues.

II. Interpreting the Reasonable Prospects of Conviction Test

The SA prosecutorial guidelines describe the reasonable prospects of conviction test as 'the cornerstone' of Australian prosecution policy.[9] Despite its importance, the test presents a range of interpretative challenges. The preliminary difficulty is one of distinguishing the reasonable prospects of conviction test from the prima facie test.

[3] Office of the Director of Public Prosecutions, New South Wales, *Prosecution Guidelines* (2021) 8.

[4] *Guidelines of the Director of Public Prosecutions* (Northern Territory) (2016) s 2.4 (*DPP Policy* (NT)).

[5] Office of the Director of Public Prosecutions for Western Australia, *Statement of Prosecution Policy and Guidelines* (2022) s 25 (*DPP Policy* (WA)); *DPP Policy* (NT) (n 4) s 2.2.

[6] *DPP Policy* (WA) (n 5) s 25.

[7] Director of Public Prosecutions, *Prosecution Policy of the Australian Capital Territory* (2021) s 2.4 (*DPP Policy* (ACT)).

[8] Director of Public Prosecutions, South Australia, *Statement of Prosecution Policy & Guidelines* (2014) 6 (*DPP Policy* (SA)).

[9] ibid 5.

A. Distinction from Prima Facie Test

The WA guidelines provide that the prima facie test is met if the evidence 'appears on its face or initial assessment to prove the offence which has been charged'.[10] Most of the Australian prosecutorial guidelines specify that the prima facie test must be satisfied before a prosecution can be commenced.[11] However, its satisfaction does not justify the institution of a prosecution. As the ACT guidelines state, the consideration of whether or not to prosecute 'is not confined to a technical appraisal of whether the evidence is sufficient to constitute a prima facie case. The evidence must provide reasonable prospects of a conviction.'[12] The former Queensland Director of Public Prosecutions (DPP) Leanne Clare interpreted the equivalent guidelines for her state for the Royal Commission. She testified that 'Reasonable prospects involves a threshold test that goes further than simply saying: is there a prima facie case; is there evidence on which all elements could be proved?'[13] However, the written statement to the Royal Commission of her successor, Anthony Moynihan, conflates the tests. He contends that the 'prima facie case must have reasonable prospects of a conviction before a reasonable jury, which involves an assessment of the sufficiency of the evidence to satisfy the elements of the offence'.[14]

The case of *Hoy* further illustrates the difficulty of distinguishing these tests. In SA in 2015, Constable Hoy was prosecuted for seizing a driver by the shirt while issuing him with a vehicle defect notice in 2010. The conduct would have constituted an assault unless Hoy was honestly exercising his powers as a police officer to secure compliance with a valid direction.[15] The jury acquitted Hoy of assault in less than two hours. The presiding judge 'wholeheartedly' agreed with the jury's verdict, and called the trial a waste of the court's time because a 'proper assessment' of the evidence would have revealed no reasonable prospects of conviction.[16]

In response to the judge's criticism, the DPP issued a public statement explaining that 'it was open to a jury to find that the accused did not have the power to do what he did. This being so, I came to the view that there was a reasonable prospect of conviction.'[17] The Police Association commissioned former NSW DPP Nicholas

[10] *DPP Policy* (WA) (n 5) s 21.

[11] Director of Public Prosecutions (Tasmania), *Prosecution Policy and Guidelines* (2022) 5–6 (*DPP Policy* (Tas)); Department of Justice and Attorney-General (Queensland), *Director's Guidelines* (2016) 2 (*DPP Policy* (Qld)); *DPP Policy* (ACT) (n 7) 4; *DPP Policy* (NT) (n 4) s 2.3; *DPP Policy* (WA) (n 5) s 23.

[12] *DPP Policy* (ACT) (n 7) 4.

[13] Evidence to Royal Commission into Institutional Responses into Child Sexual Abuse, Sydney, 16 July 2014, 8926 (Leanne Clare) (Evidence to Royal Commission).

[14] Statement to Royal Commission into Institutional Responses into Child Sexual Abuse, 14 July 2014, 9 (Anthony Moynihan).

[15] Memorandum from Nicholas Cowdery to Police Association of South Australia, 27 April 2015, 1–2.

[16] S Fewster, 'SA Court Jury Finds Police Constable Norman Hoy Not Guilty of Assaulting Yasser Shahin' *The Advertiser* (23 January 2015) www.adelaidenow.com.au/news/south-australia/sa-court-jury-finds-police-constable-norman-hoy-not-guilty-of-assaulting-yasser-shahin/news-story/e778f1d1ff4b93c6556a55be6b368092.

[17] Director of Public Prosecutions, South Australia, '*R v Hoy*', Media Release, 4 February 2015, 1.

Cowdery to review the prosecution. Cowdery found that the DPP's interpretation of the reasonable prospect of conviction test was, incorrectly,

> a restatement of the prima facie case test. By saying that 'it was open' to a jury, the DPP is really saying that a jury 'could' so find and is making no evaluation, forecast or judgment about whether or not it should make such a finding.[18]

The implications of prosecutors 'forecasting' the judgement of the jury, and determining what decision the jury 'should' make, are considered later in this chapter. The relevant point here is that the disagreement between the two experienced DPPs was not on the application of the reasonable prospects of conviction test, but on its actual meaning. Hart observes that precisely because reasonable minds can differ on particular cases, it is necessary to establish 'the best conditions for decisions'.[19] The disagreement between Kimber and Cowdery occurred a quarter of a century after the publication of prosecutorial guidelines that adopted reasonable prospects of conviction as a major determinant of the decision to prosecute in Australia. It demonstrates fundamental uncertainty regarding one of the major tests expected to uphold the public interest. The criteria comprising the reasonable prospects of conviction test itself create additional interpretive difficulties, including regarding the meaning of reasonableness.

B. 'Reasonableness'

In the English common law tradition, reasonableness introduces an objective standard into 'the exercise of administrative discretion [by] mapping the legal space' that is not defined in the legislation empowering the decision-maker.[20] For centuries, it has guided the assessment of 'actions', 'decisions', 'persons', 'rules', 'institutions', 'arguments' and 'judgments',[21] in order to prevent arbitrary and unpredictable decisions. Criminal law has been described as 'the natural home of the idea of reasonableness',[22] and reasonableness as 'one of the cornerstones in criminal law'.[23] It defines the criminal standard: of proof beyond reasonable doubt,[24] and creates 'a species of objective liability … designed to eliminate the indeterminacy of subjective liability'[25] in offences including manslaughter[26] and

[18] Memorandum from Nicholas Cowdery to Police Association of South Australia, 27 April 2015, 2 (emphasis in original).

[19] Hart, 'Discretion' (n 1) 664.

[20] M Bobek, 'Reasonableness in Administrative Law: A Comparative Reflection on Functional Equivalence' in G Bongiovanni et al (eds), *Reasonableness and Law* (Dordrecht, Springer, 2009) 311, 316.

[21] R Alexy, 'The Reasonableness of Law' in Bongiovanni et al (n 20) 5, 7.

[22] A Ripstein, 'Reasonable Persons in Private Law' in Bongiovanni et al (n 20) 255, 258.

[23] H Ramadan, 'Reconstructing Reasonableness in Criminal Law: Moderate Jury Instructions Proposal' (2003) 29 *Journal of Legislation* 233, 233.

[24] *Briginshaw v Briginshaw* (1938) 60 CLR 336, 360.

[25] Ramadan (n 23) 236.

[26] *Nydam v R* [1977] VR 430; *R v Lavender* (2005) 222 CLR 67.

defences including self-defence.[27] It is also central to constraining the prosecutorial discretion, because the 'reasonable' prospects of conviction test introduces objectivity into the decision to prosecute.

The concept of 'objectivity' in the reasonable prospects of conviction test embraces two distinct, but interrelated, ideas that require prosecutors to subordinate their individual judgement to external standards. The first concept, made explicit in the guidelines, is the requirement that prosecutors make an impartial assessment of the evidence, not influenced by their personal feelings or opinions, biases or emotions. The NT guidelines state that the reasonable prospects of conviction test 'requires an exercise of dispassionate judgment … of the admissibility and weight of the available evidence and the persuasive strength of the Crown case'.[28] The WA guidelines agree that 'evaluation of prospects of conviction is a matter of dispassionate judgment'.[29] The Tasmanian guidelines confirm that the soundest basis for the decision to prosecute is the 'application of the reasonable prospect of conviction test dispassionately'.[30] This aspect of reasonableness provides a clear prohibition against, for example, factoring the ethnicity, socio-economic status, notoriety or celebrity of defendants or complainants into the decision to prosecute. It also prohibits emotional or populist decisions on allegations of particularly heinous or high-profile crimes. It provides a clear normative statement capable of guiding decisions. The concept of reasonableness, guided by these criteria, may achieve consistency in routine cases, where the determination of the reasonable prospects of conviction involves a relatively neutral assessment of the strength of evidence. For example, a robbery where security footage shows a person who looks like the defendant committing the offence and the defendant's DNA is found at the scene fits the taxonomy of a 'core' case, 'where rules readily settle decision[s]'.[31] In 2023, Walter Sofronoff KC, former Justice of the Supreme Court of Queensland, expressed satisfaction that

> experience has proved that idiosyncratic differences in opinion are rare. Consistency in decision making is achieved by dint of experience, by training, by mentoring, by open-minded consultation with others before making a decision and by honest and earnest striving for an application of that degree of objectivity that the word 'reasonable' demands.[32]

However, the varied opinions in *Hurley* and *Nemer* reflect Alexy's view that the concept of reasonableness is a 'coalescence' of objectivity and subjectivity,[33]

[27] See, eg Criminal Law Consolidation Act 1935 (SA), s 15.
[28] *DPP Policy* (NT) (n 4) s 2.4.
[29] *DPP Policy* (WA) (n 5) s 27.
[30] *DPP Policy* (Tas) (n 11) 6.
[31] N Lacey, 'The Path Not Taken: HLA Hart's Harvard Essay on Discretion' (2013) 127 *Harvard Law Review* 636, 645.
[32] W Sofronoff, *Australian Capital Territory, Board of Inquiry: Criminal Justice System, Final Report* (31 July 2023) 30–31.
[33] Alexy (n 21) 13.

because decision-makers 'import their own values – or their assessment of society's values – into the definition of what is or is not reasonable'.[34] Ripstein further suggests that reasonableness may serve as 'a smokescreen' for pre-existing views, interests or prejudices by erroneously suggesting it sets standards that are 'somehow eternal'.[35] Doubts about objectivity in decision-making are not novel, and have been expressed within the legal profession for centuries. Francis Bacon, the former Attorney General and Lord Chancellor of England and Wales, observed in 1620 that 'human understanding'

> draws all things else to support and agree with it. And though there be a greater number and weight of instances to be found on the other side, yet these it … neglects and despises [so that] the authority of its former conclusions may remain inviolate.[36]

In the USA, in particular, empirical studies in the twenty-first century have addressed racial disparities in prosecutions. Findings identified that prosecutors' belief that they were blind to the colour of suspects, defendants and witnesses was at odds with demonstrated differences in charging practices across races.[37] Similarly, variability in charging decisions has been found in factually similar prosecutions of women who kill abusive partners, and the variations have been explained by attitudes to domestic violence and traditional conceptions of self-defence.[38] As Schmittat et al observe, 'legal storytelling … is a widely accepted persuasion tool within the legal community', and the first exposure prosecutors have to all criminal cases is an incriminating, but possibly incomplete or biased, police file that can unfairly influence their perception of the evidence and the case.[39]

Beyond the legal environment, Nickerson confirms that decision-making is consistently characterised by 'unwitting selectivity in the acquisition and use of evidence [and] unwitting molding of facts to fit hypotheses or beliefs'.[40] Other studies agree that, despite the evidence of unconsciously one-sided decision-making, 'many biases work below the surface and leave no trace of their operation [so] an introspective search for evidence of bias often turns up empty'.[41] International

[34] JT Parry, 'Culpability, Mistake, and Official Interpretations of Law' (1997) 25 *American Journal of Criminal Law* 1, 27.

[35] Ripstein (n 22) 276.

[36] F Bacon, *The New Organon: Or True Directions Concerning the Interpretation of Nature* (1620) s XLVI, pages.uoregon.edu/kimball/Bacon.htm.

[37] RR Dunlea, '"No Idea Whether He's Black, White, or Purple": Colorblindness and Cultural Scripting in Prosecution' (2022) 60 *Criminology* 237, 239, 245; GL Brandon et al, 'Open Prosecution' (2023) 75 *Stanford Law Review* 1365, 1386.

[38] DR Follingstad et al, 'Decisions to Prosecute Battered Women's Homicide Cases: An Exploratory Study' (2015) 30 *Journal of Family Violence* 859.

[39] SM Schmittat et al, 'Alternative Stories and the Decision to Prosecute: An Applied Approach Against Confirmation Bias in Criminal Prosecution' (2022) 28 *Psychology, Crime & Law* 608, 610, 631.

[40] RS Nickerson, 'Confirmation Bias: A Ubiquitous Phenomenon in Many Guises' (1998) 2 *Review of General Psychology* 175, 175.

[41] J Ehrlinger et al, 'Peering into the Bias Blind Spot: People's Assessments of Bias in Themselves and Others' (2005) 31 *Personality and Social Psychology Bulletin* 680, 689.

studies have replicated these results across occupations, including government officials, scientists, judges and medical practitioners.[42] These findings suggest that prosecutors have limited ability to objectively assess evidence, and lack awareness of those limitations, which leads to individual and institutional underestimation of the amount of prosecutorial discretion involved in the decision to prosecute.

The second concept of objectivity within the test is that the assessment of the reasonable prospects of conviction is amenable to an incontrovertible standard not influenced or informed by judgement or analysis. However, reasonableness is 'an elastic'[43] and 'highly abstract'[44] concept. According to Ramadan, the expectation that it can objectively guide decision-making is 'misleading' and 'flawed'.[45] Nehushtan has been even more critical. In commentary on judicial review, he described the interpretation and application of reasonableness as 'a complete mess' that provided neither consistency nor clarity to the assessment of executive decisions.[46] This type of uncertainty has resulted in the reasonable prospects of conviction test historically resisting assessment to a common standard.

In 1980, the English DPP, Thomas Hetherington, provided a memorandum on the definition of the reasonable prospects of conviction test to a Parliamentary Select Committee on Deaths in Police Custody. He advised that the test considered whether the judge, jury or magistrate is 'more likely than not to be satisfied beyond reasonable doubt that the accused is guilty of the offence charged'.[47] He became pejoratively known as 'Mr Fifty-one Per Cent' for purportedly trying to impose mathematical standards on the assessment of the reasonable prospects of conviction.[48] Edwards objected to the 51 per cent measure because 'of the false conception implicit in such language that the prosecutor's decision-making bears the stamp of scientific objectivity. Nothing could be more misleading.'[49] Later commentators did not clarify a threshold for reasonable prospects of conviction. In 1984, Edwards himself concluded that it was a 'nebulous standard',[50] and Lezak and Leonard described it as providing 'a porous filtering process'.[51] However, there is general acceptance that, in the case of criminal prosecutions at least, further refinement of the term is neither necessary nor desirable. As then DPP, Shane Drumgold, submitted through counsel to an ACT Board of Inquiry into the

[42] Nickerson (n 40) 191–96.
[43] Ramadan (n 23) 240.
[44] Alexy (n 21) 7.
[45] Ramadan (n 23) 239.
[46] Y Nehushtan, 'The Non-Identical Twins in UK Public Law: Reasonableness and Proportionality' (2017) 50 *Israel Law Review* 69, 71.
[47] Memorandum of Thomas Hetherington to House of Commons Select Committee on Deaths in Police Custody, 1980, cited in J Edwards, *The Attorney General, Politics and the Public Interest* (London, Sweet & Maxwell, 1984) 414.
[48] ibid 415–16.
[49] ibid 416.
[50] ibid 415.
[51] SI Lezak and M Leonard, 'Prosecutor's Discretion: Out of the Closet – Not Out of Control' (1984) 63 *Oregon Law Review* 247, 253.

Criminal Justice System in 2023: 'any further definition of the term "a reasonable prospect of conviction" is counterproductive ... these words have stood the test of time and should remain unchanged'.[52] He elaborated that it 'is an irreducible test that cannot be further defined' and any attempt to substitute 'more complex tests for what are words that have their ordinary English meaning ... is likely to confuse and confound rather than assist those who are required to apply the test'.[53]

However, the lack of clarity in the reasonable prospects of conviction test weighs against it effectively providing a common standard compatible with the concept of the public interest. The Victorian Royal Commission into the Management of Police Informants (the Victorian Royal Commission) illustrated one example of how interpretations of the reasonable prospects of conviction can differ markedly between experienced legal practitioners.

C. The 'Lawyer X' Case – Nicola Gobbo and Victoria Police

In 2018, the Victorian government established a Royal Commission into the Management of Police Informants (the Victorian Royal Commission) to investigate Victoria Police's use of Nicola Gobbo as a 'human source', or police informant. The case gained public attention before Gobbo's identity was revealed, and she was referred to as 'Lawyer X' in the media and 'EF (a pseudonym)' in court proceedings.[54] The case continues to frequently be referred to as the 'Lawyer X scandal'.[55]

Gobbo was registered as an informant with Victoria Police for three separate periods between 1993 and 2010. Her informing activity started when she was a law student, and continued while she was a criminal defence barrister.[56] She represented and informed on leading figures in the so-called Melbourne 'gangland wars' between organised crime groups, which had proven difficult to investigate through traditional policing.[57]

Her informing activities included divulging details of clients' offending, defence strategy, advice on obtaining incriminating evidence, forensic issues arising and

[52] Sofronoff (n 32) 30.

[53] ibid Appendices 116–17.

[54] *AB & EF v CD* [2017] VSC 350; *AB v CD & EF* [2017] VSCA 338; *AB (a pseudonym) v CD (a pseudonym); EF (a pseudonym) v CD (a pseudonym)* (2018) 362 ALR 1.

[55] T Mills, 'The Nicola Gobbo, Lawyer X Scandal Explained' *The Age* (30 November 2020) www.theage.com.au/national/victoria/the-nicola-gobbo-lawyer-x-scandal-explained-20201124-p56hh9.html.

[56] Victorian Premier, Attorney-General, Minister for Police and Emergency Services, 'Royal Commission into Management of Informants', Media Release, 3 December 2018; M McMurdo, *Royal Commission into the Management of Police Informants: Final Report*, vol 1 (Victorian Government Printer, 2020) 6, 28.

[57] M McMurdo, *Royal Commission into the Management of Police Informants: Final Report*, vol 2 (Victorian Government Printer, 2020) 78–80; J Ayling and R Broadhurst, 'Organized Crime Control in Australia and New Zealand' in L Paoli (ed), *The Oxford Handbook of Organized Crime* (Oxford, Oxford University Press, 2013) 612.

strategies for investigating.[58] The relationship between Gobbo and Victoria Police compromised both parties. Gobbo created a conflict of interest by providing information about current clients that was, or at least may have been, protected by legal professional privilege and obligations of confidentiality where it was not necessary to prevent serious harm to any person. She purportedly had 'a mix of motivations for becoming an informer',[59] including disillusion with the ability of organised crime figures to manipulate the criminal justice system, serious health issues, feeling trapped in the criminal world[60] and fear of being charged as an accessory to certain of her clients' crimes.[61] The Victorian Royal Commission concluded that she had 'a propensity for deception and a fascination with criminals and police officers'.[62]

External investigations undertaken in 2012 and 2015 identified critical deficits in Victoria Police policy, supervision and legal understanding regarding police informants, and made recommendations that were largely ignored by the organisation.[63] A 2016 investigation by then DPP, John Champion, determined that miscarriages of justice may have occurred as a result of Gobbo's role as an informer because convictions were secured using evidence that was likely to have been excluded at trial as being obtained improperly or illegally. He concluded that he was obliged to disclose to seven people convicted of serious criminal offences, six of whom were sentenced to terms of imprisonment, that their barrister was a police informer.[64]

In 2016, Victoria Police and Gobbo took legal action in the Supreme Court to claim that public interest immunity and obligations of confidence to Gobbo prevented the DPP from making the disclosures. They emphasised the need to uphold the 'golden rule' of never revealing the identity of a police informer, especially since the criminal community had developed suspicions about Gobbo's informing conduct and she was receiving death threats as a result.[65] During 2017 and 2018, the Victorian Supreme Court, Victorian Court of Criminal Appeal and High Court of Australia (HCA) all determined that the DPP could make the disclosures that would identify Gobbo and reveal the conduct of Victoria Police.[66] As the HCA held in 2018, before Gobbo's identity was made public, acting as counsel and informing on her clients 'were fundamental and appalling breaches' of her

[58] McMurdo, vol 2 (n 57) 8, 34.
[59] *AB & EF* (n 54) [20].
[60] McMurdo, vol 2 (n 57) 81.
[61] *AB & EF* (n 54) [18]–[20].
[62] McMurdo, vol 2 (n 57)167.
[63] N Comrie, *Victoria Police Human Source 3838: A Case Review* (2012); M Kellam, *Report Concerning Victoria Police Handling of Human Source Code Name 3838* (2015), cited in McMurdo, vol 1 (n 56) 45–47.
[64] J Champion, *Report of the Director of Public Prosecutions in Relation to Recommendation 12 of the Kellam Report* (2016), cited in McMurdo, vol 1 (n 56) 47–48.
[65] *AB & EF* (n 54) [180]–[183]; D Plater and L de Vreeze, 'Is the "Golden Rule" of Full Prosecution Disclosure a Modern "Mission Impossible?"' (2012) 14 *Flinders Law Journal* 133.
[66] *AB & EF* (n 54); *AB* (n 54); *AB (a pseudonym)* (n 54).

professional obligations to them and to the courts.[67] It further found that Victoria Police was

> involved in sanctioning atrocious breaches of the sworn duty of every police officer to discharge all duties imposed on them faithfully and according to law without favour or affection, malice or ill-will. As a result, the prosecution of each Convicted Person was corrupted in a manner which debased fundamental premises of the criminal justice system. It follows, as Ginnane J and the Court of Appeal held, that the public interest favouring disclosure is compelling: the maintenance of the integrity of the criminal justice system demands that the information be disclosed and that the propriety of each Convicted Person's conviction be re-examined in light of the information.[68]

The Victorian Royal Commission agreed with the courts, and recommended the establishment of an Office of Special Prosecutor to investigate possible criminal conduct by Gobbo and Victoria Police, because Victoria Police could not effectively investigate itself and the independent, broad-based Anti-corruption Commission lacked appropriate investigative powers.[69]

Geoffrey Nettle was appointed as the Special Investigator in 2021, having served as a barrister for several decades, then as a judge of the Supreme Court of Victoria, the Victorian Court of Appeal and the HCA.[70] His commission was to investigate possible offences and 'compile briefs of evidence to give to the DPP for the purposes of determining whether charges should be filed'.[71] He was not authorised to institute or conduct prosecutions. By 2023, the Special Investigator had submitted to the DPP, Kerri Judd, three main briefs of evidence. On his assessment, one brief in particular implicated five suspects in the offence of perverting the course of justice. It included 'admissible real-time direct evidence of the acts and state of mind of some of the alleged offenders and powerful inferential evidence of the acts and states of mind of others', as well as more than 5000 pages of police records that 'attested powerfully to the deliberateness, planning and implementation of the alleged offences'.[72] Despite this confident assessment by the experienced and esteemed Special Investigator, the DPP disagreed on the strength of the evidence and the reasonable prospects of conviction of any person. She determined that no prosecutions would be commenced on the basis of the evidence provided to her. In her view, the Special Investigator had provided an 'inaccurate characterisation' of the 5000 page brief that contained material that was 'irrelevant to any likely facts in issue in the proposed proceeding or, if relevant, would have been inadmissible as

[67] *AB (a pseudonym)* (n 54) 3.
[68] ibid.
[69] McMurdo, vol 2 (n 57) 57; Independent Broad-Based Anti-corruption Commission, *What Is IBAC?* (2023) www.ibac.vic.gov.au/.
[70] High Court of Australia, *Former Justices: Geoffrey Nettle AC* (2020) www.hcourt.gov.au/justices/former-justices/page-4.
[71] Special Investigator Act 2021 (Vic), s 9(2)(b).
[72] G Nettle, *Special Report to Parliament* (20 June 2023) [38].

a matter of law'.[73] She identified the absence of statements from crucial witnesses, indications of witnesses who were uncooperative or potentially not compellable, evidence that would infringe the hearsay rule and evidence given at the Victorian Royal Commission that would not be admissible at criminal trial. Ultimately, she was not prepared to 'authorise a brief of evidence in circumstances where the prospects of conviction were contingent on the hypothetical prospect of obtaining further important evidence via a compulsory examination process after charge-sheets were filed'.[74] The perspectives of the DPP and the Special Investigator on the fundamental issue of the reasonableness of the prospect of conviction were so divergent, and their disagreement so intractable, that the Special Investigator advised Parliament that he would 'resign so that someone whose views more closely accord to the Director's position may be appointed'.[75]

D. The 'Reasonableness' Criteria

The Australian ODPP guidelines accord with the system that Green and Roiphe refer to as 'traditional' prosecution, based on 'decisions that are dictated by the law and facts without regard to political or policy preferences'.[76] There is no apparent trend in Australia towards the contrasting approach, commonly described, variously, in the USA as 'progressive prosecution',[77] or 'de-prosecution',[78] which does not uphold the 'pretense to be following well-trod paths to inevitable destinations'.[79] The progressive approach actively seeks to advance justice, emphasise public policy concerns and achieve criminal justice reform by declining to prosecute certain offences (commonly low-level drug offences or sex work) or seek certain penalties (particularly the death penalty) in order to achieve goals such as reducing incarceration and racial injustice, reducing police corruption and preventing poverty from thwarting bail applications.[80]

All the Australian guidelines seek to clarify the reasonable prospects of conviction test through a detailed, but non-exhaustive, list of factors to guide

[73] K Judd, *Response of Director of Public Prosecutions Kerri Judd KC to the Special Report of the Office of the Special Investigator* (1 December 2021) 3.

[74] ibid 4.

[75] Nettle (n 72) [43].

[76] BA Green and R Roiphe, 'A Fiduciary Theory of Progressive Prosecution' (2023) 60 *American Criminal Law Review* 1431, 1432.

[77] RC Meldrum et al, 'Progressive and Traditional Orientations to Prosecution: An Empirical Assessment in Four Prosecutorial Offices' (2021) 48 *Criminal Justice and Behavior* 354. There is critique that the term 'progressive prosecution' is a misnomer because it does not address the causes of crime. See, eg H Yamahiro and L Garzón-Montano, 'A Mirage Not a Movement: The Misguided Enterprise of Progressive Prosecution' (2022) *The Harbinger* 130.

[78] TP Hogan, 'De-prosecution and Death: A Synthetic Control Analysis of the Impact of De-prosecution on Homicides' (2022) 21 *Criminology & Public Policy* 489.

[79] Green and Roiphe (n 76) 1432, 1441, 1444, 1459.

[80] MD Wilson, 'The Common Prosecutor' (2022) 53 *Loyola University Chicago Law Journal* 325, 339.

its assessment. The criteria are relatively uniform across the country, and I have divided them into the three categories summarised in Table 7.1.

Table 7.1 Reasonable prospects of conviction test criteria

Category	**Issue for consideration**
Evidence	possibility of the exclusion of evidence[a]
Defendants	reliability of admissions by the accused;[b] available defences;[c] reasonable inferences consistent with innocence;[d] strength of evidence against multiple defendants[e]
Witnesses	veracity of identity evidence;[f] availability, competence and credibility of witnesses and their likely impression on the arbiter of fact;[g] relevant prior inconsistent statements; friendliness or hostility to the defence; physical or mental impairment[h]

[a] *DPP Policy* (ACT) (n 7) 5.
[b] ibid 4–5, *DPP Policy* (Tas) (n 11) 7; *DPP Policy* (SA) (n 8) 5.
[c] *DPP Policy* (Tas) (n 11) 6; *DPP Policy* (SA) (n 8) 5.
[d] *DPP Policy* (WA) (n 5) s 29(c)(iv).
[e] *DPP Policy* (ACT) (n 7) 5.
[f] ibid 5.
[g] *DPP Policy* (Tas) (n 11) 6; *DPP Policy* (SA) (n 8) 5–6.
[h] *DPP Policy* (WA) (n 5) s 95.

Despite the adoption of a test based on an objective concept, and the articulation of the criteria relevant to its assessment, subjective judgement is accepted as necessary in the assessment of the reasonable prospects of conviction test. The prosecutorial guidelines do not guarantee a consistent or predictable outcome in individual decisions to prosecute. According to the Tasmanian guidelines,

> there can never be an assurance that a prosecution will succeed. Indeed, it is inevitable that some will fail. It should be borne in mind that the test is not whether there is a reasonable prospect of an acquittal but whether there is a reasonable prospect of conviction. Both can exist simultaneously.[81]

The coexistence of a reasonable prospect of conviction with a reasonable prospect of acquittal indicates a high degree of subjective judgement in the assessment of the decision to prosecute, and the likelihood of disagreement between prosecutors on whether to proceed with a charge. The WA guidelines confirm that the reasonable prospects of conviction test 'does not mean that only cases perceived as "strong" should be prosecuted … A case considered "weak" by some may not seem so to others'.[82]

The acceptance of subjective judgement and variable outcomes reflects that the criteria comprising the reasonable prospects of conviction test are uncertain and evaluative. It requires a high level of subjective assessment, particularly in what

[81] *DPP Policy* (Tas) (n 11) 6.
[82] *DPP Policy* (WA) (n 5) s 26.

Hart refers to as 'penumbral cases'[83] and Dworkin refers to as 'hard' cases, where 'no settled rule dictates a decision either way'.[84] Assessing the criteria relating to evidence and defendants requires prosecutors to assess inherently unpredictable factors. In evidence before the Royal Commission into Institutional Responses to Child Sexual Abuse, Cowdery was explicit about the level of subjectivity involved in the decision to prosecute. He explained the need to consider factors 'both subjective from the accounts of … witnesses and objective from the circumstances that are objectively provable', but that, ultimately, there is no 'bright-line test. There are no objective and definite criteria to be met. It's a question of judgment.'[85] Similarly, the ACT DPP observed to the Board of Inquiry into the Criminal Justice System in 2023 that 'the test for a prosecution in every individual case requires an appraisal and judgement call by each individual prosecutor. Different prosecutors may well have different views.'[86]

Cowdery's written statement to the Royal Commission confirms that the test requires the prosecutor to 'forecast the future course of proceedings, legally and factually, on the basis of what is known at the time (bringing to bear the prosecutor's experience and perhaps in consultation with others)'. This process requires prosecutors 'to make a positive assessment of the case – to see and evaluate its strengths; but it is also necessary to notionally attack that case and assess the possible consequences for the verdict of any foreseeable attack'.[87]

In the category of 'evidence' I identified in Table 7.1, the exclusion of evidence by a trial judge is determined according to a complex set of discretions and rules relating to whether the evidence in question was unlawfully or improperly obtained and its admission would be contrary to the public interest;[88] whether the prejudicial effect of the evidence outweighs its probative value;[89] whether the admission of the evidence creates the risk of an unfair trial;[90] and whether confessions were made voluntarily.[91] The evaluation of these evidential matters requires prosecutors to anticipate the nature and persuasiveness of defence arguments, and the judge's attitude to those arguments.

Similarly, the matters in the category relating to 'defendants' involve complex and volatile matters. Prosecutors must: consider whether defendants will testify and, if so, how credible their evidence will be; anticipate a broad range of possible defences that are not, generally, revealed before trial; and predict the effectiveness of defence arguments undermining the prosecution case. On some occasions, prosecutors must consider these issues for multiple defendants giving conflicting evidence.

[83] HLA Hart, 'Positivism and the Separation of Law and Morals' (1958) 71 *Harvard Law Review* 593, 612.

[84] R Dworkin, 'Hard Cases' (1975) 88 *Harvard Law Review* 1057, 1060.

[85] Evidence to Royal Commission (n 13) 14 July 2014, 8825 (Nicholas Cowdery).

[86] Sofronoff (n 32) 30.

[87] Statement to Royal Commission into Institutional Responses into Child Sexual Abuse, 14 July 2014, 2 (Nicholas Cowdery).

[88] *Bunning v Cross* (1978) 141 CLR 54.

[89] *R v Christie* [1914] AC 545.

[90] *Cleland v The Queen* (1982) 151 CLR 1.

[91] *McDermott v The King* (1948) 76 CLR 501.

The need for the exercise of subjective judgement is greatest, however, in relation to the category of 'witnesses'. Prosecutors must anticipate whether expert witnesses will be persuasive in examination-in-chief and cross-examination compared to the alternative experts called by defence. They need to consider whether lay witnesses for prosecution and defence will attend, testify consistently with previous statements, perform under the stress of cross-examination and generally appear credible. As Margaret Cunneen, Senior Crown Prosecutor for NSW, explained in her written submission to the Royal Commission, credibility 'does not mean my personal view of a complainant's credibility but my assessment … of a complainant's credibility in the eyes of a properly instructed jury after the complainant has been cross-examined by competent defence counsel'.[92] Witness credibility is determinative where, for example, a defendant in a rape case argues that the complainant consented to sexual intercourse, or in a child sexual abuse case where the defendant argues that the complainant is lying. SA guidelines provide additional guidance on assessing the strength of witness testimony. They require that prosecutors take into account matters including the likelihood of witnesses appearing to exaggerate, to have faulty memory, to be either hostile or friendly to the accused, to have a motive for telling less than the whole truth or to be undermined by defence counsel.[93] The prosecutors' assessment of witness credibility will determine whether the reasonable prospects of conviction test is satisfied and the prosecution goes ahead, and all the criteria require the exercise of subjective judgement.

The reasonable prospects of conviction test has limited efficacy in guiding prosecutors to assess the objective strength of evidence available in particular cases. However, the more critical issue that extends the scope of the prosecutorial discretion is that prosecutors do not make a personal or professional assessment of whether the defendant is guilty as charged. As Cunneen explained above, they have the more difficult task of determining the likelihood of a jury finding a defendant guilty.

III. Applying the Reasonable Prospects of Conviction Test

A. Reasonable Prospects of Conviction and the Jury

The assessment of the reasonable prospects of conviction test crosses the legitimate spheres of the prosecutor and the jury. Cowdery testified before the Royal Commission that the prosecution has been granted 'by legislation, by practice, by

[92] Statement to Royal Commission into Institutional Responses into Child Sexual Abuse, 3 July 2014, 13 (Margaret Cunneen).

[93] See, eg *DPP Policy* (SA) (n 8) 5–6.

guidelines, the role of making an initial assessment of the case', and to 'just throw up every apparent case for some other body to adjudicate' would be an 'abrogation' of their responsibility.[94] Cunneen agreed that the reasonable prospects of conviction test was 'quintessentially a legal question and that's why lawyers decide it'.[95]

However, the prosecutorial discretion is exercised within a criminal justice system based on 'the abiding importance of the role of the jury'.[96] Unless a defendant elects to have their case heard by a judge alone, the jury is the finder of fact for serious criminal offences. Its representation of the community is intended to serve as an essential protection against the oppressive power of the state over the individual, and ensures that criminal defendants are judged according to community standards.[97] The decision to prosecute is intended to respect the respective roles of the prosecution and the court.

The WA guidelines state that 'Prosecutorial discretion will be exercised so as to recognise the central role of the courts in the criminal justice system in determining guilt and imposing appropriate sanctions for criminal conduct'.[98] The NT guidelines similarly provide that 'resolution of disputed questions of fact is for the court and not the prosecutor. The assessment of prospects of conviction is not to be understood as usurping the role of the court.'[99] In testifying before the Royal Commission, Clare confirmed that 'care has to be taken not to intrude into what is properly the province of the jury'.[100] The balance between the roles of the jury and the prosecutor is ostensibly achieved because the reasonable prospects of conviction test rests not on the prosecutor's own view of the evidence, but on their forecast of the jury's view of it. However, the forecasting of the jury decision requires a greater exercise of prosecutorial discretion than prosecutors and prosecutorial guidelines suggest.

B. Forecasting Jury Decisions

Queensland's Deputy DPP, Paul Rutledge, testified to the Queensland Crime and Misconduct Commission in 2003 that in assessing the reasonable prospects of conviction: 'I'm not making any judgments about whether something did or did not happen. I'm making judgments about the ability to persuade a jury at the end of the day that they should have no reasonable doubt.'[101] Cunneen agreed that the

[94] Evidence to Royal Commission (n 13) 14 July 2014, 8842 (Nicholas Cowdery).
[95] ibid 10 July 2014, 8625 (Margaret Cunneen).
[96] *R v Baden-Clay* (2016) 258 CLR 308, 329.
[97] J Walker Elrod, 'W(h)ither the Jury – The Diminishing Role of the Jury Trial in Our Legal System' (2011) 68 *Washington and Lee Law Review* 3, 7–8.
[98] *DPP Policy* (WA) (n 5) s 20.
[99] *DPP Policy* (NT) (n 4) s 2.4.
[100] Evidence to Royal Commission (n 13) 16 July 2014, 8926 (Leanne Clare).
[101] Crime and Misconduct Commission (Queensland), *The Volkers Case: Examining the Conduct of the Police and Prosecution* (March 2003) 56.

assessment requires a 'frank and fearless prediction of what would happen, given my experience in courts with juries, in a trial'.[102] Clare expressed the same principle in a letter to the lawyers of one of the complainants in the *Volkers* case. She explained that there 'is a significant distinction between the truth and the capacity to prove the truth', and she recognised the 'frustration and despair that this distinction can cause victims of crime'.[103] She confirmed in conference with one of the complainants that the process involves 'looking at what can be proved … it's not about saying yes I believe you therefore we can take it forward'.[104]

Prosecutors undoubtedly gain an understanding of jury decision-making from their experience and training. However, the evidence to the Royal Commission discloses a lack of precision in the actual process of determining how a jury will decide a particular matter. Clare testified that 'There is no precise formula or mathematical equation that can ever solve the question of reasonable prospects';[105] rather, it involves considering 'issues of credit and the way in which they might unfold in front of the jury'.[106] Rutledge, who had been Clare's Deputy DPP, further explained that: 'You take a look at whether there are any changes in stories over time … whether, having regard to the fact that we have to prove beyond reasonable doubt, you have sufficiently solid a story, account, to actually withstand a sustained attack.'[107] Lloyd Babb, the NSW DPP, simply stated: 'I try to, as best I can, clinically analyse how I expect the trial will proceed and foreshadow the result.'[108] This process means that disagreement between experienced and qualified decision-makers is inevitable. For example, Clare declined to prosecute Hurley for the death of Mulrunji because she was adamant that 'no law-abiding citizen – black or white, Christian or Muslim – would have found this man guilty … the evidence fell considerably short of that which would be required to put anyone on trial'.[109]

However, when Sir Laurence Street assessed the same evidence against the same legal standard a matter of weeks later, he identified a reasonable prospect of a conviction.[110] On Street's advice, the trial proceeded and a jury acquitted Hurley of assault and manslaughter.[111] The jury decision does not undermine the veracity of Street's assessment, however, because he only advised there was a reasonable prospect of a conviction, not a certainty of it.

[102] Evidence to Royal Commission (n 13) 10 July 2014, 8599 (Margaret Cunneen).

[103] Letter from Leanne Clare to Woodgate Hughes Solicitors, 9 April 2003, 1.

[104] Transcript of Interview between Leanne Clare, Darren Brazier, Julie Gilbert, Shane Gilbert, Hetty Johnston and Mr Tolhurst, 11 May 2004, 26.

[105] Evidence to Royal Commission (n 13) 16 July 2014, 8996–97 (Leanne Clare).

[106] ibid 8926.

[107] Evidence to Royal Commission (n 13) 11 July 2014, 8750 (Paul Rutledge).

[108] ibid 15 July 2014, 8909 (Lloyd Babb).

[109] 'DPP Stands Firm on Custody Death' *Sydney Morning Herald* (22 December 2006) www.smh.com.au/news/national/dpp-stands-firm-on-custody-death/2006/12/21/1166290684255.html.

[110] 'Palm Island Cop Suspended' *The Age* (26 January 2007) www.theage.com.au/news/national/palm-island-cop-suspended/2007/01/26/1169594473000.html.

[111] 'Hurley Acquitted after Controversial Case' *ABC 7.30 Report* (20 June 2007) www.abc.net.au/7.30/content/2007/s1957282.htm.

The prosecution of child sexual offences, in particular, reveal issues with the exercise of prosecutorial discretion because cases of this type have been found to be affected by multiple factors, including attitudes towards victims, perpetrators, caregivers and approaches to the assessment of evidence.[112]

The following case study of *Volkers* shows how much subjective judgement prosecutors exercise in assessing the reasonable prospects of conviction in a child sexual abuse case that involves professional fields where they have general but not expert knowledge. The case generated a memorandum of advice from NSW Crown Prosecutor Margaret Cunneen to NSW DPP Nicholas Cowdery to present to the Queensland DPP; testimony from Cowdery, Cunneen and Clare to the Royal Commission; media attention; two Crime and Misconduct Commission (CMC) inquiries;[113] and an unsuccessful application for a private prosecution.[114] The extensive commentary provides a unique insight into the assessment of the reasonable prospects of conviction test and the process for forecasting a jury decision.[115]

C. Case Study of *Volkers*

In 2002, Swimming Australia coach Scott Volkers was charged with multiple counts of indecent dealing with children under the age of 16. The charges were laid after three women complained to police about his conduct towards them during swimming coaching in the 1980s. Complainant 1 alleged that Volkers rubbed her bare buttocks during a massage at his home, and touched her vagina in his car; complainant 2 alleged that he massaged her bare breasts and put his tongue in her ear during a massage at his home; and complainant 3 alleged that he massaged her bare breasts during a training session at the pool, and touched her vagina until she experienced orgasm during a massage in his caravan at the swimming pool complex. Volkers faced a committal proceeding where the complainants were cross-examined and, on the basis of their testimony, he was committed to stand trial on seven of eight counts.[116] Clare explained in writing to the CMC that she

[112] SD Block et al, 'Predictors of Prosecutorial Decisions in Reports of Child Sexual Abuse' (2023) 28 *Child Maltreatment* 488, 489–90, 496–97.

[113] Crime and Misconduct Commission (n 101); Crime and Misconduct Commission (Queensland), *Seeking Justice: An Inquiry into How Sexual Offences Are Handled by the Queensland Criminal Justice System* (June 2003).

[114] *Gilbert v Volkers* [2004] QSC 436.

[115] The Royal Commission criticised the assessment that there were no reasonable prospects of conviction for allegations of sexual abuse of Aboriginal children in the NT's Retta Dixon home between 1946 and 1980. The issues were highly technical and related to latent ambiguity of charges and cross admissibility of evidence that are outside the scope of this book: Royal Commission into Institutional Responses into Child Sexual Abuse, *Report of Case Study No 17: The Response of the Australian Indigenous Ministries, the Australian and NT Governments and the NT Police Force and Prosecuting Authorities to Allegations of Child Sexual Abuse Which Occurred at the Retta Dixon Home* (July 2015).

[116] Royal Commission into Institutional Responses into Child Sexual Abuse, *Report of Case Study No 15: Response of Swimming Institutions, the Queensland and NSW Offices of the DPP and the*

originally intended to pursue the prosecution even though the complaints related to conduct that was alleged

> to have occurred more than 15 years prior to the disclosure to police, they were uncorroborated, and depended wholly on the word of the complainant. I was also aware that Mr Volkers had no criminal history and that evidence of good character was likely to come from some high-profile female swimmers.[117]

She concluded that while 'the case was not strong, I remained of the view that a jury could still reasonably accept the complainant's allegations'.[118] However, after submissions from defence counsel in 2002, the ODPP discontinued the prosecution.[119] The decision reflected that complainant 1's credibility was critically undermined because she had an extensive psychiatric history. She been committed to a psychiatric institution in 2001,[120] and medical records indicated that, at times, she could not 'distinguish between reality/not reality', and displayed 'almost psychotic behaviour'.[121] There were no issues with complainant 2's credibility, but Clare deemed that her allegation of an uncorroborated, single charge of low-level conduct, where any punishment would be nominal, was unsuitable to be prosecuted on its own.[122] Finally, the ODPP doubted a jury would believe complainant 3's allegations that Volkers absented himself from group training sessions for extended periods and committed sexual offences in an open area readily accessible by the public. These concerns were determined to have 'infected' her allegations about indecent dealings in the caravan.[123] These specific factors, combined with the general difficulties of prosecuting historical sexual offences, led to the decision that 'there was no realistic chance of satisfying twelve jurors of guilt beyond reasonable doubt'.[124]

The decision not to prosecute Volkers was controversial at the time. RV Hanson QC advised one of the complainant's solicitors about possible legal options after the DPP decided not to proceed. He described the ODPP's decision-making process as 'irregular'; the purported reasons for it 'inadequate'; and the complainant 'justified in feeling that there had been an injustice'.[125] In 2003, the CMC inquired into both the police investigation of Volkers and the DPP's decision not to prosecute him. It criticised both processes,[126] and police subsequently obtained new evidence that raised the possibility of reinstituting

Queensland Commission for Children and Young People and Child Guardian to Allegations of Sexual Abuse by Swimming Coaches (November 2015) 6–8.

[117] Crime and Misconduct Commission (n 101) 34.

[118] ibid 34.

[119] Letter from Leanne Clare to Nicholas Cowdery, 19 December 2003, 6–9.

[120] Memorandum from Margaret Cunneen to Nicholas Cowdery, 26 March 2004, 6.

[121] Letter from Michael J Byrne to Leanne Clare, 3 September 2002, 4.

[122] Crime and Misconduct Commission (n 101) 32.

[123] ibid 36.

[124] ibid 35.

[125] Letter from RV Hanson to Woodgate Hughes Solicitors, 20 February 2003, 1.

[126] Crime and Misconduct Commission (n 101) 58–73.

proceedings.[127] The Queensland DPP sought the opinion of the NSW ODPP on whether to reinstitute the prosecution, and accepted its advice that there were still no reasonable prospects of conviction.[128]

Clare and Cunneen testified to the Royal Commission that prosecuting similar cases had informed them of community attitudes towards child sexual offending, which indicated there were no reasonable prospects of Volkers's conviction. Clare explained that the attitude of juries 'evolves over time', and that, over her years in practice, she had discerned 'a real change in what juries are prepared to accept and their attitude to these kinds of cases'.[129] She reflected that, in 2003, limited knowledge of the extent of child sexual offending made it 'very difficult for juries to accept that, in normal-looking families, children were sexually abused'.[130] Cunneen agreed that there was 'much greater awareness of inappropriate touching and greater observation of the requisite standards today than there was 16–19 years ago'.[131]

In addition to the general difficulties of prosecuting child sexual abuse cases at the time, *Volkers* involved a broad range of complex and specialised scientific and social matters that I have divided into the following five categories:

1. Sexual biology and psychology: whether an offender could manage 'sufficient manual leverage' to manipulate the clitoris of a girl who had never before had an orgasm, while she was wearing tight bathers and a pair of shorts; and whether a sexually inexperienced 13-year-old girl could have the 'mental amenability' to experience orgasm while in a state of fear.[132]
2. Anatomy and child development: whether a 'flat chested' 13-and-a-half-year-old girl had sufficient breast tissue to be considered to 'have breasts'.[133]
3. Patterns of child sexual offending: whether Volkers would have offended in the 'high-risk situation' of the public area of the swimming complex;[134] indecently offended against girls without exposing himself or requesting they touch his genitals;[135] and would 'misconduct himself in the future'[136] given the publicity surrounding the allegations.[137]
4. The psychological effects of offending on victims: whether girls would return to be coached by a person who had abused them;[138] whether an incidence of sexual offending at the lower end of the scale of seriousness would lead to

[127] Memorandum from Margaret Cunneen to Nicholas Cowdery, 26 March 2004, 3.
[128] Letter from Nicholas Cowdery to Leanne Clare, 2 April 2004, 1.
[129] Evidence to Royal Commission (n 13) 16 July 2014, 9027 (Leanne Clare).
[130] ibid 9027.
[131] Memorandum from Margaret Cunneen to Nicholas Cowdery, 26 March 2004, 3.
[132] Evidence to Royal Commission (n 13) 10 July 2014, 8614–15 (Margaret Cunneen).
[133] ibid 8603.
[134] ibid 16 July 2014, 8961 (Leanne Clare).
[135] Memorandum from Margaret Cunneen to Nicholas Cowdery, 26 March 2004, 11.
[136] ibid 16.
[137] Evidence to Royal Commission (n 13)14 July 2014, 8818 (Nicholas Cowdery).
[138] Memorandum from Margaret Cunneen to Nicholas Cowdery, 26 March 2004, 3.

significant mental health problems for a victim;[139] whether a victim would deny being abused; and if 'the fondness' of the complainants for Volkers undermined their allegations.[140]

5. Memory patterns: whether one complainant's testimony that 'I couldn't explain what I felt, but now that I am an adult I experienced an orgasm' constitutes memory reconstruction, influenced by cognitive processes such as perception, imagination, life experience and belief systems.[141]

The prosecutors in *Volkers* had to forecast how these complex psychological, biological and criminological matters would be viewed by a hypothetical jury. Their assessment was that the combination of factors would prevent a jury from finding Volkers guilty. For example, complainant 3 alleged that Volkers offended in a public area, and Clare assessed that, at the time, 'juries had real difficulty with allegations that involved a substantial danger of discovery. The tendency – the climate really was to acquit unless there was the strongest of evidence, and this wasn't that kind of case.'[142] Similarly, Cunneen referred to the lack of community understanding of the damaging effects of child sexual abuse when she addressed complainant 1's claims of psychological damage. She surmised that 'a jury would not have regarded this single complaint, being so aged and being so relatively minor as being sufficient to cause … a massive mental health sequelae [*sic*]'.[143] A criminal jury would not, actually, have been required to determine whether or not the complainant developed a mental health issue as a result of offending by Volkers. Presumably, Cunneen assessed that a jury's scepticism about the purported effects of the offending would have adversely affected its assessment of its alleged cause, and/or that the existence of the mental health issue would have significantly undermined the complainant's credibility overall.

The prospects of conviction were affected not only by general community views on child sexual abuse. They also rested on specific issues that were beyond the knowledge of prosecutors and jurors, and highly contestable within the fields of evolutionary biology, evolutionary psychology, animal behaviour and neurology. For example, complainant 3's ability to experience orgasm in the circumstances she alleged weighed against prosecuting Volkers. Limited research has been undertaken on the neural pathways of female sexual arousal,[144] its physiology and evolutionary purpose,[145] and its reaction to 'threatening' situations.[146]

[139] Evidence to Royal Commission (n 13) 10 July 2014, 8599 (Margaret Cunneen).

[140] Memorandum from Margaret Cunneen to Nicholas Cowdery, 26 March 2004, 14.

[141] ibid 12.

[142] Evidence to Royal Commission (n 13) 16 July 2014, 8930 (Leanne Clare).

[143] ibid 10 July 2014, 8599 (Margaret Cunneen).

[144] CM Meston, 'Sympathetic Nervous System Activity and Female Sexual Arousal' (2000) 86 *American Journal of Cardiology* 30F, 30F.

[145] LLM Welling, 'Female Orgasm' in TK Shackelford and VA Weekes-Shackelford (eds), *Evolutionary Perspectives on Human Sexual Psychology and Behavior* (New York, Springer, 2014) 223.

[146] RJ Levin and W van Berlo, 'Sexual Arousal and Orgasm in Subjects Who Experience Forced or Non-consensual Sexual Stimulation – A Review' (2004) 11 *Journal of Clinical Forensic Medicine* 82, 84.

However, studies before the *Volkers* decision found that violence and sexual arousal may be 'an adaptive response to danger and threat of extinction',[147] which is possible during abuse of children.[148] In 2004, complainant 3 sought two medical evaluations of Cunneen's memorandum of advice. Psychiatrist Warwick Middleton determined that Cunneen's key conclusions on patterns of offending and on the physical and social effects of offending were 'uninformed by the scientific literature and widely documented contemporary clinical observations'.[149] Patricia Brennan, the Medical Director of a NSW Sexual Assault Service, agreed that Cunneen's determinations were 'misinformed medically', and showed 'ignorance about the nature of female anatomy and … sexual physiology'.[150] After an assessment of the totality of evidence in the *Volkers* case, counsel assisting the Royal Commission determined that Cunneen's reasoning for not prosecuting was 'flawed'.[151]

The lack of community understanding of child sexual abuse unquestionably presented a challenge for the prosecution. Any jury would have grappled with the range and complexity of matters raised, and their relevance to Volkers's criminal liability. However, Cunneen agreed in her testimony before the Royal Commission that the prosecutor's role included explaining to the jury the 'complex dynamics' involved in child sex cases.[152] Several years before allegations were made against Volkers, Flatman and Bagaric recognised that historical child sexual offences presented 'numerous' but not 'insurmountable' forensic difficulties.[153] Expert evidence on the nature and incidence of child sexual offending could have contextualised the complainants' testimony, as it had contextualised the testimony of women who killed abusive partners since the early 1990s.[154] In the USA, two decades before the charges against Volkers, Mason found that the admission of expert evidence about child sexual offending had proven useful to courts and not unduly prejudicial to criminal defendants.[155] According to Berliner, such expert evidence remediated limited 'knowledge about the nature of child abuse situations', 'prejudicial views about children who claimed to have been abused' and the

[147] ZR Kime, 'Aberrant Sexual Behavior, Violence, and Reproduction' (1992) 18 *Journal of Sex Education and Therapy* 231, 231–32.

[148] ibid 237.

[149] W Middleton, *Supreme Court of Queensland, Julie Therese Gilbert and Scott Alexander Volkers* (Expert Report, 15 October 2004) [6]–[7], [13]–[20].

[150] P Brennan, *Supreme Court of Queensland, Julie Therese Gilbert and Scott Alexander Volkers* (Expert Report, 31 October 2004) [4]–[11].

[151] Royal Commission into Institutional Responses to Child Sexual Abuse, Submissions of Counsel Assisting the Royal Commission (undated) 108.

[152] Evidence to Royal Commission (n 13) 10 July 2014, 8578 (Margaret Cunneen).

[153] G Flatman and M Bagaric, 'Problems in Prosecuting Cases Involving Historical Child Sexual Abuse: The Victorian Experience' (1997–98) 4 *Deakin Law Review* 1, 20.

[154] E Sheehy et al, 'Defending Battered Women on Trial: The Battered Woman Syndrome and Its Limitations' (1992) 16 *Criminal Law Journal* 369, 381–93.

[155] MA Mason, 'A Judicial Dilemma: Expert Witness Testimony in Child Sex Abuse Cases' (1991) 19 *Journal of Psychiatry and Law* 185, 212.

'long history of societal skepticism' about child sexual abuse.[156] Kovera et al found that in studies with mock jurors during the 1990s, 'participants who heard expert testimony … were more likely to convict the defendant' than in comparable cases where expert evidence was not adduced.[157]

Relevant expert evidence was obtained by one of the complainants in *Volkers*, but not by the prosecution. Cowdery's written statement to the Royal Commission admitted that in the contentious matters affecting the decision to prosecute, he 'did not rely upon any material, medical and scientific or otherwise'.[158] The admission of expert evidence would not necessarily have resulted in Volkers's conviction because a jury may not have been persuaded of his guilt beyond reasonable doubt. However, the decision not to prosecute eliminated the possibility of a conviction.

The assessment of the reasonable prospects of conviction requires prosecutors to exercise their gatekeeper role and anticipate the views of potential jurors on a range of specialised factors. It has the potential to extend the scope of the prosecutorial discretion beyond its intended role and to encroach on the legitimate province of the jury. The decision not to prosecute Volkers attracted precisely this criticism. At the time of the original decision, the Queensland Women's Legal Service[159] and a Queen's Counsel argued that the case should have been heard by a jury,[160] and the CMC found that the ODPP had erred because 'Too little attention was given to the possibility that Complainant 3 might simply be believed by a jury'.[161] The practical effect of the overreach of the prosecutorial discretion was the non-prosecution of an offence where evidence was capable of proving a course of child sexual offending by a person in a position of trust and authority over thousands of children. It also prevented prosecutors and the courts from gaining experience that would have assisted future prosecutions, even though international experience suggested that the use of expert evidence could have resulted in a conviction.

However, prosecutors do not merely engage in the fraught, but relatively passive, role of what Mansfield and Peay describe as 'socio-legal pundit, attempting to "second guess" the jury'.[162] The way that 'reasonableness' is formulated in the prosecutorial guidelines actually requires prosecutors to make normative decisions about what the jury should decide, which influences, rather than predicts,

[156] L Berliner, 'The Use of Expert Testimony in Child Sexual Abuse Cases' in SJ Ceci and H Hembrooke (eds), *Expert Witnesses in Child Abuse Cases: What Can and Should Be Said in Court* (American Psychological Association, 1998) 11, 12.

[157] MBl Kovera et al, 'Expert Testimony in Child Sexual Abuse Cases: Effects of Expert Evidence Type and Cross-Examination' (1994) 18 *Law and Human Behavior* 653, 667–68.

[158] Statement to Royal Commission into Institutional Responses into Child Sexual Abuse, 14 July 2014, 6 (Nicholas Cowdery).

[159] Australian Broadcasting Corporation, 'A Case to Answer: How the Justice System Failed Star Swim Coach Scott Volkers and the Women He Was Accused of Sexually Molesting' *Four Corners* (5 July 2004) www.thetvdb.com/series/four-corners-1961/episodes/4140107.

[160] Letter from RV Hanson to Woodgate Hughes Solicitors, 20 February 2003, 5.

[161] Crime and Misconduct Commission (n 101) 59.

[162] G Mansfield and J Peay, *The Director of Public Prosecutions: Principles and Practices for the Crown Prosecutor* (London, Tavistock Publications, 1987) 11.

the decision of the jury. This process supports Uviller's argument that the reasonable prospects of conviction test requires prosecutors to bend themselves 'into psychological pretzels',[163] which further extends the scope of their discretion.

D. Influencing Jury Decisions

The Queensland guidelines acknowledge that prosecutors employ a normative interpretation of 'reasonableness' by providing that a prosecution should not proceed if there is no '*reasonable* prospect of conviction before a *reasonable* jury'.[164] Other guidelines confirm the expectation that juries are rational, neutral and capable of making reasonable decisions. The WA guidelines specify that a 'preconception as to beliefs which may be held by a jury is not a material factor. Juries are presumed to act impartially.'[165] The Tasmanian guidelines similarly presume that 'the prosecution will be conducted before a reasonable jury not subject to any bias'.[166] The reasonable prospects of conviction test could, therefore, more appropriately be labelled the 'prospects of a reasonable conviction', or the 'reasonable prospects of a reasonable conviction' test.

However, jurors are not always, or not necessarily, rational and unbiased. They are influenced by prevailing social attitudes, which may involve stereotypes and prejudices that make their decisions unpredictable and/or undesirable. For example, studies have found that bias affects jury decisions related to consent in rape cases; homicide by police; women killing abusive partners; and protesting outside an abortion clinic.[167] Jurors may assume that their 'assessments reflect a logical, bottom-up progression from evidence and rational considerations to reasonable inferences and conclusions'.[168] In reality, according to Kahan, 'culturally motivated cognition' – the process by which 'individuals tend selectively to credit empirical information in patterns congenial to their cultural values'[169] – means that people tend to process factual information in a manner compatible with their personal values.[170]

The Royal Commission heard that both English and Australian ODPPs filter prosecutions based on expectations regarding juries' social attitudes. These expectations can result in discontinuation of prosecutions where prosecutors decide that

[163] HR Uviller, 'The Neutral Prosecutor: The Obligation of Dispassion in a Passionate Dispute' (2000) 68 *Fordham Law Review* 1695, 1697.

[164] *DPP Policy* (Qld) (n 11) 2 (emphasis added).

[165] *DPP Policy* (WA) (n 5) s 28.

[166] *DPP Policy* (Tas) (n 11) 5.

[167] DM Kahan et al, '"They Saw a Protest": Cognitive Illiberalism and the Speech–Conduct Distinction' (2012) 64 *Stanford Law Review* 851, 861–62, 884.

[168] E Pronin et al, 'Objectivity in the Eye of the Beholder: Divergent Perceptions of Bias in Self Versus Others' (2004) 111 *Psychological Review* 781, 789.

[169] Kahan (n 167) 859.

[170] E Balcetis and D Dunning, 'See What You Want to See Motivational Influences on Visual Perception' (2006) 91 *Journal of Personality and Social Psychology* 612, 613.

a jury could convict but should not, or would not convict though they should. For example, prosecutors might discontinue a rape case where evidence is weak but stereotypes applicable to the defendant or the complainant might influence the jury to convict. They may also choose not to proceed in cases like *Volkers*, where evidence is probative but might not persuade a sceptical or poorly informed jury. Alison Saunders, DPP for England and Wales, testified to the Royal Commission that in cases of men grooming disadvantaged young women for the purposes of sexual exploitation, prosecutors previously 'looked at those victims and said their credibility was not good enough [to] put them before a jury'.[171] She explained that even 10 years earlier they 'wouldn't have even entertained a prosecution' where complainants had addiction issues or prior convictions. However, by the time of her testimony, such cases were prosecuted and convictions did result.[172]

In addition to the complainants' testimony in *Volkers*, there were statements from other girls about 'various unsavoury incidents', and Volkers's stepbrother reported seeing Volkers massage girls under their T-shirts on the sides of their breasts.[173] Cunneen acknowledged that 'the inevitable conclusion from the brief as a whole, is that Scott Volkers was a thoroughly disreputable man given to inappropriate touching and comments towards young swimmers in his charge'.[174] However, the prosecutors did not proceed with the prosecution.

The introduction of a normative standard of reasonableness changes the task of prosecutors from anticipating what a jury is likely to decide to deciding if a jury should resolve a particular case. It creates a self-fulfilling problem. Prosecutions were not conducted where prosecutors did not expect a jury would understand or accept probative evidence, and then the decisions not to prosecute prevented the attainment of institutional knowledge within the ODPPs about how to inform and persuade juries. The knowledge of juries was not tested, and so forecasting by prosecutors may have reflected outdated and incorrect ideas about jury attitudes. As the decision to prosecute is not subject to judicial review, there is no independent adjudication of whether a prosecutor's assessment on a particular case is appropriate and no guidance on the application and interpretation of the test gained by case law. This assessment significantly enhances the scope of the discretion exercised by the prosecution and minimises the ability of the reasonable prospects of conviction test to constrain the prosecutorial discretion.

IV. Conclusions

The reasonable prospects of conviction test is applied without controversy in thousands of cases across Australia every year. However, it affords limited transparency

[171] Evidence to Royal Commission (n 13) 29 April 2016, 18 (Alison Saunders).
[172] ibid.
[173] Memorandum from Margaret Cunneen to Nicholas Cowdery, 26 March 2004, 13.
[174] ibid.

to the decision to prosecute in controversial and complex cases. The test is predicated on an objective assessment of evidence, but actually requires a high level of subjective judgement. Prosecutors are empowered to make the decision to prosecute according to their own judgement of evidence, circumstances, witness credibility and likely jury decisions. The legitimate roles of the prosecutor and jury are compatible, but the prosecutor alone decides the limits of its authority in relation to the role of the jury. Juries do not provide reasons for their decisions, and so even experienced prosecutors are not privy to why juries decided previous cases in particular ways. Prosecutors have to speculate on the attitudes of juries to legal and social issues, and to anticipate the impact of those views on jury decisions in particular cases, at particular times. The assessment of the jury's likely finding is filtered through the prosecutor's own biases and preconceptions, and limited by the prosecutors' own, necessarily partial, understanding of issues that might arise in any given case.

The reasonable prospects of conviction test purports to be about the sufficiency of evidence, but actually needs to encompass much broader considerations that expand the scope of the prosecutorial discretion in ways not fully recognised in guidelines or commentary. The range and number of the matters to be considered provides a significant amount of not only opportunity, but also necessity, for the exercise of prosecutors' subjective judgement. The Anglo-Australian system explicitly rejects mandatory prosecution and entrenches prosecutorial discretion, and so no legitimate issue can be taken with their exercise of discretion. However, the system also expects that the prosecutorial discretion is subject to legitimate and effective constraints, but the reasonable prospects of conviction test provides limited constraint.

8

The Public Interest Test

The establishment of the Offices of Director of Public Prosecutions (ODPPs) was a radical reform measure designed to ensure that the decision to prosecute is made independently in the public interest. The success of the ODPPs, therefore, rests significantly on the public interest test.

The concept of the public interest is resistant to precise definition, but the ODPP guidelines mitigate the risks associated with a broad discretion exercised in the public interest through the introduction of a detailed 'public interest test' that must be interpreted according to the principles of independence, fairness and justice. This test is comprised of two sets of criteria: those related to the characteristics of the individual case being prosecuted; and those related to the social implications of that type of offending and its prosecution. However, both sets of criteria have limitations, and the principles of independence, fairness and justice are as elusive as the public interest they are expected to uphold. Further discussion of the case of *Volkers* in particular demonstrates that the cumulative effect of these factors is that, like the reasonable prospects of conviction test, the public interest test requires too much subjective judgement to guide the public interest to any commonly accepted standard or protect the rule of law.

I. Prosecuting in the Public Interest

A number of Australian prosecutorial guidelines describe the public interest as the paramount'[1] or 'significant'[2] consideration in the decision to prosecute. While the ODPPs are creatures of modern Australian statute, prosecutorial guidelines across the country recognise that they have also inherited the English prosecutorial system's deeply rooted commitment to prosecuting in the public interest. The Queensland guidelines are explicit that prosecutions should proceed

> wherever it appears to be in the public interest. That is the prosecution policy of the prosecuting authorities in this country and in England and Wales. If it is not in the

[1] Office of the Director of Public Prosecutions, New South Wales, *Prosecution Guidelines* (2021) (*DPP Policy* (NSW)) 8.

[2] Director of Public Prosecutions, South Australia, *Statement of Prosecution Policy & Guidelines* (2014) (*DPP Policy* (SA)) 5; Director of Public Prosecutions (Tasmania), *Prosecution Policy and Guidelines* (2022) (*DPP Policy* (Tas)) 5.

> interests of the public that a prosecution should be initiated or continued then it should not be pursued.[3]

The provision makes clear that the decision to prosecute in the public interest is discretionary. The guidelines for Tasmania and South Australia (SA) confirm the existence and provenance of the discretion by directly quoting Shawcross's classic pronouncement on English prosecutions, cited in chapter two, that suspected criminal offences have never been automatically subject to prosecution.[4]

The commitment to upholding the public interest through a prosecutorial discretion reflects not only the Anglo-Australian prosecutorial tradition. It also reflects contemporary standards of individualised justice. As Bowers argues, 'legally identical cases should sometimes be handled differently for normative reasons'.[5] Murphy agrees that the 'tailoring of our retributive response to the individual natures of the persons with whom we are dealing – is a part of what we mean by taking persons seriously as persons and is thus a basic demand of justice'.[6]

Despite the commitment to discretionary decision-making, prosecuting in the public interest creates a dilemma. Airo-Farulla argues that the requirement to 'achieve the public policy purpose underlying the statute conferring the discretion' ensures that even 'the broadest, most open-textured discretions are subject to some limits'.[7] However, as Varuhas observes, the discretion still requires a decision-maker to determine 'What decision lies in the public interest'.[8] The authority of the ODPPs to impose their interpretation of the public interest at every stage of the prosecution process provides them with a very significant grant of discretion. As Wheeler argues, the public interest is 'one of the most used' but still 'least defined' terms in the discourse on democratic governance and public administration.[9] In 1989, the High Court of Australia (HCA) found that the concept of the public interest 'classically imports a discretionary value judgment to be made by reference to undefined factual matters'.[10] While the concept of the public interest is intentionally vague to accommodate multiple individual circumstances, it may be unsuited to constraining prosecutorial discretion in the way that Airo-Farulla suggests.

[3] Department of Justice and Attorney-General (Queensland), *Director's Guidelines* (2016) (*DPP Policy* (Qld)) 2.

[4] *DPP Policy* (SA) (n 2) 5; *DPP Policy* (Tas) (n 2) 5–6.

[5] J Bowers, 'Legal Guilt, Normative Innocence, and the Equitable Decision Not to Prosecute' (2010) 110 *Columbia Law Review* 1655, 1673.

[6] J Murphy, 'Mercy and Legal Justice' (1986) 4 *Social Philosophy & Policy* 1, 7.

[7] G Airo-Farulla, 'Reasonableness, Rationality and Proportionality' in M Groves and HP Lee (eds), *Australian Administrative Law: Fundamentals, Principles and Doctrines* (Cambridge, Cambridge University Press, 2007) 212, 225–26.

[8] J Varuhas, 'The Public Interest Conception of Public Law: Its Procedural Origins and Substantive Implications' in J Bell et al (ed), *Public Law Adjudication in Common Law Systems: Process and Substance* (Oxford, Hart Publishing, 2016) 45, 64.

[9] C Wheeler, 'The Public Interest Revisited – We Know It's Important but Do We Know What It Means?' (2013) 72 *Australian Institute of Administrative Law Forum* 34, 34.

[10] *O'Sullivan v Farrer* (1989) 168 CLR 210, 216.

The public interest has its origins in the concepts of the common interest, common good and public good developed over centuries by philosophers including Aristotle, Aquinas, Rousseau and Locke.[11] These origins are reflected in similarly general modern descriptions of the public interest, such as 'affecting the good order and functioning of the community and government affairs for the wellbeing of citizens' and for 'the benefit of society, the public or the community as a whole'.[12] In 1961, Miller warned that the 'built-in ambiguity' of the public interest permits 'a government of men and not of laws'.[13] He further warned that unless 'we are resigned to rule by unfettered discretion, without resort to principle or standard, an effort must soon be made to put content into the concept'.[14]

In addition to the disagreement about the reasonable prospects of conviction that was discussed in the previous chapter, the Special Investigator, Geoffrey Nettle, and the DPP, Kerri Judd, held opposing views on the public interest in prosecuting offences involving Victoria Police and Nicola Gobbo. Because the DPP deemed that the evidence available at the time provided no reasonable prospect of conviction, she did not need to consider the public interest.[15] However, in the two years before she reached that decision, such widely disparate views on the public interest emerged between her and the Office of the Special Investigator (OSI) that the Special Investigator cited it as one reason for deciding, in 2023, that it was 'pointless for OSI to continue' and recommending that it be 'wound up'.[16]

The disagreement was most pronounced over one particular charge of perjury, where the DPP identified a range of 'public interest considerations that would weigh against a decision' to prosecute.[17] She noted that the alleged offence was 'relatively old' and occurred in the course of a civil, not criminal, proceeding, and that the personal circumstances of the alleged offender suggested a non-custodial sentence was a possible outcome of any conviction.[18] However, in her assessment, the 'primary public interest consideration … was putting persons associated with the individual at risk'.[19] Overall, she questioned 'whether, having regard to those considerations, it was worth spending money' on prosecuting the offence.[20]

The Special Investigator was clear that he made no adverse finding or comment against or about the DPP, and merely identified apparently irreconcilable differences in their views regarding prosecuting the offences he had been commissioned to investigate.[21] The considerations the DPP identified are unquestionably relevant

[11] Wheeler (n 9) 35.
[12] ibid 34–35.
[13] AS Miller, 'The Public Interest Undefined' (1961) 10 *Journal of Public Law* 184, 187.
[14] ibid.
[15] K Judd, *Response of Director of Public Prosecutions Kerri Judd KC to the Special Report of the Office of the Special Investigator* (1 December 2021) 2.
[16] G Nettle, *Special Report to Parliament* (20 June 2023) [42].
[17] ibid [10].
[18] ibid.
[19] Judd (n 15) 2.
[20] Nettle (n 16) [10].
[21] ibid [41].

to the criteria of the public interest test, and the discretion to assess those criteria legitimately rests with the DPP.

However, the grounds for the opposing view of the Special Investigator, and his clear frustration with the decision of the DPP, are manifest. The offence deemed 'relatively old' was alleged to have occurred only four years before it was assessed for prosecution in 2021. Criticisms of the dealings of Victoria Police with Gobbo included the failure to seek legal advice, respond to the recommendations of reviews of its use of informants and to disclose to the DPP and the defendants its use of Gobbo as an informant.[22] These factors all delayed the identification and investigation of serious misconduct and possible corruption and, on the DPP's assessment, that delay could contribute to a decision not to prosecute a person involved in the impugned conduct. She further anticipated that the potential defendant would not receive a prison sentence, even though perjury attracts a maximum penalty of 15 years' imprisonment in Victoria.[23] Her 'primary consideration' of the risks to people associated with the suspected offender does not fit comfortably with the decisions of the three courts that considered the conduct of Gobbo and Victoria Police. As the High Court decided in 2018, albeit specifically in relation to police informers, where people 'corrupt the criminal justice system', public interest considerations can predominate over certain risks to them and those close to them.[24] Finally, Judd noted that the perjury offence was alleged to have been committed in civil, not criminal, proceedings. However, those civil proceedings related to the alleged commission of criminal offences in the course of unquestionably serious conduct. Over time, Gobbo's informing activities increased in scale and complexity, reaching 'industrial scale' following her third registration in 2005.[25] Gobbo herself estimated that information she provided resulted in 386 people being arrested and charged with serious criminal offences,[26] and the Royal Commission into the Management of Police Informants (Victorian Royal Commission) estimated that over 1000 people may have been affected by her conduct.[27] It captured the essence of Gobbo's wrongful conduct in the summary of the circumstances involving one particular client. Over a period of some months, she led him

> to believe that she was his lawyer, friend and confidant when, in truth, she was participating in a sophisticated, premeditated deception to assist Victoria Police. It is difficult to conceive of a more comprehensive abandonment of a lawyer's responsibilities than to inform on a client to police; to not discourage a client on bail for serious drug offences

[22] *AB & EF v CD* [2017] VSC 350 [29]–[40]; M McMurdo, *Royal Commission into the Management of Police Informants: Final Report*, vol 1 (Victorian Government Printer, 2020) 45–47.

[23] Crimes Act 1958 (Vic), s 314(1).

[24] *AB (a pseudonym) v CD (a pseudonym); EF (a pseudonym) v CD (a pseudonym)* (2018) 362 ALR 1, 4.

[25] M McMurdo, *Royal Commission into the Management of Police Informants: Final Report*, vol 2 (Victorian Government Printer, 2020) 15.

[26] *AB & EF v CD* [2017] VSC 350 [19].

[27] McMurdo, vol 2 (n 25) 5.

> from committing further like offences; to orchestrate the arrest of the client with police; to then act for the client after arrest, encouraging them to confess and implicate others and putting their safety and that of their family at risk; and to then ensure that this information was not disclosed, as it should have been, to the prosecution, the client, the courts and lawyers dealing with the scores of resulting charges against other individuals.[28]

The Victorian Royal Commission was also critical of the conduct of Victoria Police. It found that the organisation encouraged a defence lawyer to breach her obligations, and breached its own obligation of disclosure to defendants and to the DPP, which 'may have constituted misconduct and/or breaches of discipline at that time. That conduct was apt to bring Victoria Police into disrepute and diminish public confidence in it.'[29] The overall seriousness of the nature, context and effects of the alleged offending could be legitimately interpreted as outweighing the particular details that weigh against the public interest in prosecuting. The contrary decision of the DPP demonstrates the level of discretion involved in its assessment, and the potential for that assessment to create controversy.

Despite the demonstrated potential for alternative and even conflicting views of the public interest, Miller's call for clarity has received little support over subsequent decades. In 2013, Wheeler identified almost 190 Acts that include a public interest test in New South Wales (NSW) alone,[30] making it virtually impossible to agree on a singular definition. In its commentary on the Commonwealth Freedom of Information Bill in 1979, the Senate Committee on Constitutional and Legal Affairs accepted that the public interest 'does not need to be, indeed could not usefully, be defined'.[31] Similarly, in advocating reform of the public interest criteria in migration legislation in 2017, Appleby and Reilly opposed giving 'public interest discretions a singular "fixed and precise content" across all statutory contexts'.[32] When revisiting the issue of freedom of information in 2005, the Federal Court maintained that, irrespective of an agreed definition of the public interest, when applying the concept 'minds will differ as to what is, or what is not, in the public interest'.[33]

The limitations of the public interest as a guide to decision-making are exacerbated because, as Miller observed, the public interest is 'more than a legal or a

[28] ibid 41.

[29] M McMurdo, *Royal Commission into the Management of Police Informants: Final Report Summary and Recommendations* (Victorian Government Printer, 2020) 22.

[30] Wheeler (n 9) 46.

[31] The Parliament of the Commonwealth of Australia, Senate Standing Committee on Constitutional and Legal Affairs, *Report on the Freedom of Information Bill 1978, and Aspects of the Archives Bill 1978* (1979) Parliamentary Paper No 272/1979, 66.

[32] G Appleby and A Reilly, 'Unveiling the Public Interest: The Parameters of Executive Discretion in Australian Migration Legislation' (2017) 28 *Public Law Review* 293, 304. The term 'fixed and precise content' to the public interest was used in *Osland v Secretary to the Department of Justice* (No 2) (2010) 241 CLR 320, 329 and *Osland v Secretary, Department of Justice* (2008) 234 CLR 275, 300.

[33] *McKinnon v Secretary, Department of Treasury* [2005] 220 ALR 587, 655.

political principle. It has normative and ethical overtones as well.'[34] Appleby and Reilly agree that the concept of the public interest 'is used to import into the law a fundamentally affirming, positive and empowering force' that 'resonates positively with the public, the media and the Parliament'.[35] The combination of opacity of definition and normative force mean that the public interest as a benchmark for decision-making can 'cloak the exercise of an entirely subjective, unreviewable discretion'[36] and be a 'useless' tool that legitimises 'personal preference under the guise of pseudo-objectivity'.[37]

The public interest in prosecutions under the ODPPs is narrow enough to avoid some of the modern and historical ambiguity associated with the term. The Northern Territory (NT) and Queensland guidelines most concisely explain that the 'community's interest' is that those who are guilty of crimes be brought to justice and those who are innocent not be wrongly convicted.[38] However, the clarity of the purpose of the public interest does not necessarily reduce the level of discretion required in its assessment. As the senior prosecutor for NSW, Kara Shead, testified to the Royal Commission into Institutional Responses to Child Sexual Abuse (Royal Commission): 'Reasonable minds can differ upon whether or not, in the public interest, the prosecution should proceed.'[39]

II. Principles Guiding the Public Interest Test

The Director of Public Prosecutions (DPP) Acts do not define, or even refer to, the public interest, and so prosecuting in the public interest is a policy matter. The ability of prosecutors to prosecute in the public interest depends on prosecutorial guidelines translating the concept into criteria that guide the decision to prosecute. The guidelines seek to achieve consistent prosecutorial decisions through a public interest test interpreted according to the principles of independence, justice and fairness.

A. Independence

The clarification of the public interest in the prosecutorial guidelines includes elaboration of the concept of prosecutorial independence. The attention to

[34] Miller (n 13) 200.
[35] Appleby and Reilly (n 32) 295.
[36] ibid.
[37] DF Morgan, 'The Public Interest' in TL Cooper (ed), *Handbook of Administrative Ethics*, 2nd rev edn (New York, Marcel Dekker, 2001) 151, 166.
[38] *Guidelines of the Director of Public Prosecutions* (Northern Territory) (2016) (*DPP Policy* (NT)) s 1.2; *DPP Policy* (Qld) (n 3) 1.
[39] Evidence to Royal Commission into Institutional Responses into Child Sexual Abuse, Sydney, 29 April 2016, 97 (Kara Shead).

independence in the definition of the public interest is consistent with both the rationale for establishing the ODPPs and the historical link between those prosecutorial values that was discussed in chapter two. The Western Australian guidelines articulate the continuing importance of their connection by providing that a prosecutor 'acts independently in the public interest'.[40] The concept of prosecutorial independence in the prosecutorial guidelines has been expanded beyond the commitment to protection from political influence. It encompasses the principle expressed by Varuhas, that executive power should not be 'captured by private interests or extraneous concerns'.[41] The Tasmanian guidelines confirm that independent decisions are

> free from interference, political or otherwise. Prosecutors shall perform their duties without fear, favour or prejudice [and] remain unaffected by individual or sectional interests and public or media pressures and have regard only to the public interest.[42]

Other prosecutorial guidelines reflect the expanded concept of independence through statements such as: 'Prosecutors shall perform their duties without fear, favour or prejudice in particular they shall … remain unaffected by individual or sectional interests and public or media pressures and shall have regard only to the public interest',[43] and 'Prosecutors represent the DPP, not the government, the police, the victim, or any other person'.[44] Cunneen summarised to the Royal Commission that: 'The prosecutor is not there to serve any sectional interest. The prosecutor is there for the community at large.'[45]

The commitment to independence provides a clear statement on the factors that cannot influence the decision to prosecute, but does not provide positive guidance on the nature of prosecuting in the public interest. The concepts of fairness and justice are expected to provide positive guidance on making prosecutorial decisions in the public interest.

B. Fairness and Justice

The public interest in the decision to prosecute must be decided fairly and according to justice because, as the Australian Capital Territory (ACT) guidelines state, 'the criminal law reflects the community's pursuit of justice and the decision to prosecute must be taken in that context'.[46] Other guidelines confirm that the

[40] Director of Public Prosecutions for Western Australia, *Statement of Prosecution Policy and Guidelines* (2022) (*DPP Policy* (WA)) s 8.

[41] Varuhas (n 8) 64.

[42] *DPP Policy* (Tas) (n 2) 11.

[43] *DPP Policy* (WA) (n 40) s 3(b).

[44] Director of Public Prosecutions (Victoria), *Policy of the Director of Public Prosecutions for Victoria* (2022) (*DPP Policy* (Vic)) s 14.

[45] Evidence to Royal Commission (n 39) 11 July 2014, 8704 (Margaret Cunneen).

[46] Director of Public Prosecutions, *Prosecution Policy of the Australian Capital Territory* (2021) (*DPP Policy* (ACT)) ss 2.1.

'primary obligation on a prosecutor is one of fairness',[47] and that prosecutors must 'assist the court and do justice between the community and the offender according to law and the dictates of fairness'.[48]

The application of these principles is compatible with the traditions from which the ODPPs evolved and the administrative law principles with which they coexist. However, the principles are as ill-defined as the public interest they support. There is a vast literature on the subject of justice, which is beyond the scope of this book. It is sufficient to note that philosophers since Plato and Aristotle have debated the meaning of justice,[49] and yet D'Amato observed in 1993 that 'it's easier to spot an injustice than to say what justice is'.[50]

Fairness is, according to Lord Steyn, 'the guiding principle of our public law'.[51] The concept is, perhaps, less nebulous than justice, as it requires that where a statute 'confers an administrative power there is a presumption that it will be exercised in a manner that is fair in all the circumstances'.[52] However, as Lord Mustill acknowledges, fairness is 'essentially an intuitive judgment' to be exercised according to the circumstances and context of the case.[53] The ACT guidelines apply this observation to the decision to prosecute. They acknowledge that it 'is neither practicable nor desirable to fetter the prosecutor's discretion too much because the demands of justice and fairness will vary from case to case'.[54] The detailed enumeration of criteria comprising a public interest test seeks to balance defining the public interest and guiding prosecutors with allowing prosecutors to exercise an appropriate level of discretion.

III. The Public Interest Test

If the reasonable prospects of conviction test is met, the prosecutor needs to determine whether 'in the light of the provable facts and the whole of the surrounding circumstances, the public interest requires a prosecution to be pursued'.[55] It is presumptively in the public interest to prosecute where there is sufficient evidence, and so 'Most prosecutions will proceed if there is a reasonable prospect of a conviction'.[56] The presumption in favour of prosecution means the public interest

[47] *DPP Policy* (SA) (n 2) 3.
[48] *DPP Policy* (NT) (n 38) ss 1.2 and 3(f); *DPP Policy* (NSW) (n 1) 13.
[49] P Woodruff, 'Growing Toward Justice' in M LeBar (ed), *Justice* (Oxford, Oxford University Press, 2018) 13, 34–35.
[50] A D'Amato, 'On the Connection Between Law and Justice' (1993) 26 *UC Davis Law Review* 527, 562.
[51] *Anufrijeva v Secretary of State for the Home Department* [2004] 1 AC 604, 622.
[52] *Doody v Secretary of State for the Home Department* [1994] 1 AC 531, 560.
[53] ibid.
[54] *DPP Policy* (ACT) (n 46) 2.
[55] *DPP Policy* (Tas) (n 2) 7.
[56] *DPP Policy* (Vic) (n 44) s 5.

is likely to weigh against prosecution. However, the guidelines for Tasmania and SA acknowledge that 'While many public interest factors militate against a decision to proceed with a prosecution, there are public interest factors which operate in favour of proceeding with a prosecution (e.g. the seriousness of the offence and the need for deterrence)'.[57]

The exercise of discretion in the decision to prosecute must factor in the likely length and expense of a trial. As the SA guidelines explain, the resources of the ODPPs and the courts 'are finite and should not be wasted pursuing inappropriate cases, a corollary of which is that the available resources are employed to pursue those cases worthy of prosecution'.[58] However, the substance of the test is comprised of the two following sets of separate, but overlapping, criteria, which seek to provide a principled basis for assessing the public interest.

A. Particular Alleged Offending

The first set of criteria in the public interest test relates to the particular circumstances of the alleged offender and offending. It includes positive criteria that must be taken into account and negative criteria that must not be taken into account in making the decision to prosecute according to the principles of fairness and justice.

(i) Negative Criteria

The prosecutorial guidelines expressly exclude certain matters from factoring into the decision to prosecute. As the USA's National Committee on Law Observance and Law Enforcement reported in 1931, bias or discrimination by prosecutors represents 'a type of lawless enforcement of law' that creates the risk of wrongful convictions and resentment against the legal and political systems.[59] Accordingly, the ODPP guidelines uncontroversially specify that the decision to prosecute must not be influenced by the race, colour, ethnic origin, social position, marital status, sexual preference, sex, religion, political associations or beliefs of the alleged offender; the personal feelings of the prosecutor towards the alleged offender or victim; the political implications for the government or any political group or association; or the effects of the prosecution on the personal or professional circumstances of any prosecutor.[60] These criteria are unambiguous in their wording and purpose. They provide a strong normative standard for upholding

[57] *DPP Policy* (Tas) (n 2) 7; *DPP Policy* (SA) (n 2) 6.

[58] *DPP Policy* (SA) (n 2) 5. See also *DPP Policy* (Tas) (n 2) 5; *DPP Policy* (Qld) (n 3) 2; *DPP Policy* (NT) (n 38) s 2.8.

[59] National Committee on Law Observance and Law Enforcement, *Report on Prosecution* (1931), cited in S Hobbs, 'Prosecutor's Bias, an Occupational Disease' (1949) 2 *Alabama Law Review* 40, 56.

[60] *DPP Policy* (WA) (n 40) s 33; *DPP Policy* (Qld) (n 3) 4; *DPP Policy* (Vic) (n 44) s 6; *DPP Policy* (SA) (n 2) 7; *DPP Policy* (NT) (n 38) s 2.7; *DPP Policy* (NSW) (n 1) 10.

the public interest through the principles of fairness, justice and equality before the law, although, as discussed in chapter seven, they do not provide a guarantee against biases affecting individual decisions.

(ii) Positive Criteria

The criteria that must be taken into account in the decision to prosecute are open to competing considerations that do raise controversy at both a policy level and in individual cases. I have divided the positive criteria into the overlapping categories of 'the offending', 'the offender' and 'the victim' and summarised the key determinants for each category in Table 8.1.

Table 8.1 Public interest test criteria – particular alleged offending

Category	Positive criteria
The offending	seriousness or triviality of the alleged offence, and whether it is of a 'technical' nature only; whether there are mitigating or aggravating circumstances; the time since the alleged offence[a]
The offender	youth, age, intelligence, physical health, mental health or special infirmity of the alleged offender; whether the defendant knew or could reasonably be expected to know that the conduct was an offence; the criminal history of the alleged offender; whether the consequences of a conviction would be unduly harsh and oppressive; whether the alleged offender is willing to cooperate in the investigation or prosecution of others; likely sentence; availability and efficacy of alternatives to prosecution; relevance of compensation, reparation or forfeiture[b]
The victim	youth, age, intelligence, physical health, mental health or special infirmity of the alleged victim; attitude of the alleged victim to a prosecution[c]

[a] *DPP Policy* (Tas) (n 2) 8; *DPP Policy* (WA) (n 40) s 32; *DPP Policy* (SA) (n 2) 6; *DPP Policy* (NT) (n 38) s 2.5; Commonwealth Director of Public Prosecutions, *Prosecution Policy of the Commonwealth* (2021) (*DPP Policy* (Cth)) 5.

[b] *DPP Policy* (Tas) (n 2) 8; *DPP Policy* (Vic) (n 44) s 3; *DPP Policy* (WA) (n 40) s 32; *DPP Policy* (SA) (n 2) 6; *DPP Policy* (NT) (n 38) s 2.5; *DPP Policy* (Cth) (n 61) 6.

[c] *DPP Policy* (Tas) (n 2) 8; *DPP Policy* (Vic) (n 44) s 3; *DPP Policy* (WA) (n 40) s 32; *DPP Policy* (SA) (n 2) 6–7; *DPP Policy* (NT) (n 38) s 2.5; *DPP Policy* (Cth) (n 61) 6.

These criteria ostensibly restrict the public interest to the mitigating and aggravating circumstances of the offender and the offending, and to practical and compassionate decisions about individual cases. Some assessments on these grounds fit comfortably within the role of the ODPP. As Bowers argues, 'lawyers learn to think inside the proverbial legal box – a type of thinking that is critical when it comes to evaluating the legal merits of charges'.[61] For example,

[61] Bowers (n 5) 1690.

in the category of 'the offending', a prosecutor can distinguish the seriousness of a young woman selling an ecstasy tablet to a friend from an outlaw motorcycle club systematically trafficking large quantities of methamphetamine to young people in rural settings. Similarly, in the category of 'the offender', a prosecutor can distinguish a teenager with naked photos sent to him by his 15-year-old girlfriend from a 50-year-old man with 2000 pornographic videos of small children on his computer. Finally, a prosecutor can distinguish the seriousness of certain offences based on 'the victim' of offending. A small child being thrown against a wall by his mother constitutes a more serious offence than a single punch during a confrontation between adult males. In each of these examples, the prosecutor can situate offences on a spectrum of seriousness that generally accords with a community standard of the public interest.

The controversial 2022 prosecution of Bruce Lehrmann for the rape of Brittany Higgins was ultimately resolved through an uncontroversial application of the public interest test criteria in the category of 'the victim'. The prosecution related to an allegation that, late one night in 2019, after a social event, Lehrmann, a male Liberal Party advisor, raped Higgins, a female Liberal Party advisor, in the Parliament House office of the Minister for Defence. Higgins reported the alleged rape to police one week later, but the investigation was ceased because she did not want the matter pursued, partly because of the demands of an upcoming Federal election. In 2021, the investigation was reopened at the request of Higgins.

Investigating police had doubts about her motive, credibility and reliability. They found evidence contradicting aspects of her account of her level of intoxication, purported injuries and seeking of medical advice. They also noted her original unwillingness to provide her mobile telephone to investigators, and apparent deletion of data from it. The combination of these factors led the police to conclude that there was insufficient evidence to charge Lehrmann.[62] However, the ACT DPP, Shane Drumgold, determined that, due to independent corroboration of Higgins's demeanour after the alleged rape and of her inability to provide consent due to intoxication, 'there was a reasonable prospect that a properly instructed jury would reject [Mr Lehrmann's] denials of intercourse and the multiple reasons why he had gone to Parliament House'.[63] Walter Sofronoff KC, who led the inquiry, reviewed the prosecution brief and trial transcript, and agreed with the decision to prosecute on the basis that any 'inconsistencies and contradictions were certainly not incontrovertible proof that Ms Higgins was either dishonest or unreliable. There was evidence that a jury could accept that refuted these criticisms.'[64] Initially, the public interest test was also met, but the public interest considerations changed over time.

[62] W Sofronoff, *Australian Capital Territory, Board of Inquiry: Criminal Justice System, Final Report* (31 July 2023) 16–21, 26.

[63] ibid 21, 50.

[64] ibid 26, 52.

The only aspect of the public interest that the DPP described as being relevant to the decision to prosecute Lehrmann was Higgins's mental health. He observed that at the initiation of the prosecution, her

> mental health had clearly been precarious at times throughout the investigation process and had deteriorated [she] was mentally fatigued, but, in my experience, that is a relatively commonplace experience for most witnesses in prosecutions, particularly complainants in sexual assault prosecutions. At that point in time, I did not consider that her mental health issues were such that it was not in the public interest for a prosecution to be maintained.[65]

The trial proceeded and the jury retired to consider its verdict in October 2022. After five days, the jury was unable to reach a unanimous verdict and a 'hung jury' was a possibility. However, before the jury deliberations were resolved, a sheriff's officer provided the judge with evidence that one juror had accessed an academic research paper on sexual offending that had not been admitted into evidence or provided to the jury during trial. The jury was formally discharged and a new trial date was fixed for early in 2023.[66] However, before the date set for the new trial, Higgins advised the DPP that she 'did not want to proceed with a retrial because of mental health concerns'.[67] Drumgold decided that Higgins's mental health 'tipped the balance on the public interest considerations in favour of discontinuing the prosecution'.[68]

The DPP notified the court and the public that the prosecution was to be discontinued.[69] He explained that the 'non-exhaustive' public interest considerations include

> the actual or potential harm occasioned to any person as a result of the alleged offence … I have recently received compelling evidence from two independent medical experts, that the ongoing trauma associated with this prosecution presents a significant and unacceptable risk to the life of the complainant. The evidence makes clear that this is not limited to the harm of giving evidence in the witness box, rather applies whether or not the complainant is required to re-enter the witness box in the re-trial. Whilst the pursuit of justice is essential for my office and the community, the safety of a complainant in a sexual assault matter, must be paramount. In light of the compelling independent medical opinions, and balancing all factors, I have made the difficult decision, that it is no longer in the public interest to pursue a prosecution at the risk of the complainant's life.[70]

Sofronoff agreed with this assessment and decision of the DPP,[71] and there is no apparent commentary disputing the appropriateness of the decision not to continue to prosecute.

[65] ibid 50.
[66] *R v Lehrmann (No 5)* [2022] ACTSC 296 [2]–[5].
[67] Sofronoff (n 62) 155.
[68] ibid 155.
[69] *R v Lehrmann (No 6)* [2022] ACTSC 334 [2]–[3]; ACT Director of Public Prosecutions, 'RE: DPP v Lehrmann SCC 264 o021', Media Release, 2 December 2022, 1–2.
[70] ACT Director of Public Prosecutions (n 69) 1–2.
[71] Sofronoff (n 62) 157.

However, other prosecutorial decisions are less open to agreement because of strong but divergent views on what constitutes the public interest in criminal justice. For example, the category of 'the offending' requires prosecutors to consider concessions to the physical and mental condition of the offender and/or the availability of alternatives to their prosecution. This requirement is compatible with compassion in sentencing, avoiding crushing penalties[72] and the possibility of rehabilitation.[73] The criteria, therefore, uphold the public interest in two ways. They express the concept of individualised justice that benefits individual defendants by having their personal circumstances taken into account.[74] They also reflect research demonstrating that measures like diversion programmes are more effective at reducing crime than prison sentences, and so contribute to the safety of the community.[75]

However, recognising mitigating factors and compassion for offenders conflicts with a punitive approach to criminal justice that is also broadly accepted as being in the public interest. Brown's commentary on NSW politics in the 1990s, published in an article in the *Sydney Morning Herald* in 2009, is still relevant across Australia. He observes that with 'the law-and-order genie out of the bottle, it became standard political competition to posture over who was toughest on crime, setting up a dynamic that no-one, up to now, has had the courage to end'.[76] According to Weatherburn, this political rhetoric, and its support in the media, leads to 'public demands for tough law and order policies'[77] and creates a cycle of promotion, demand and delivery of ever harsher laws. Paradoxically, then, the measures that serve the public interest in having a safe and productive community also offend law and order politics and undermine the confidence in the criminal justice system that also constitutes the public interest.

Overlapping criteria and conflicting principles also affect decisions on individual prosecutions and prevent the public interest test from achieving a common standard. These issues are evident in the criteria related to 'the offending'. For example, 'time since the alleged offence' is highly controversial. As Leanne Clare informed one of the complainants in *Volkers* in 2002, the law required judges to warn juries that where there was delay between alleged offending and the report of that offending, it would be 'dangerous to convict' on a complainant's uncorroborated evidence unless they had carefully scrutinised that evidence and were

[72] D Chin, 'Sentencing: A Role for Empathy' (2012) 160 *University of Pennsylvania Law Review* 1561, 1576–84.

[73] P Raynor, 'Some Observations on Rehabilitation and Justice' 36 (1997) *Howard Journal of Crime and Justice* 248, 249–55.

[74] S Krasnostein, 'Too Much Individualisation, Not Enough Justice: Bugmy v The Queen' (2014) 39 *Alternative Law Journal* 12, 13–14.

[75] See, eg R Sarre, 'How I Would Spend $100 Million to Reduce Crime' (2017) 28 *Current Issues in Criminal Justice* 339.

[76] A West, 'Truce on Hardline Sentencing' *Sydney Morning Herald* (8 January 2009) www.smh.com.au/national/truce-on-hardline-sentencing-20090108-gdt8z8.html.

[77] D Weatherburn, 'Law and Order Blues' (2002) 35 *Australian & New Zealand Journal of Criminology* 127, 137.

satisfied of its truth and accuracy.[78] However, Newbury identifies that substantial delays in reporting crimes are 'almost unique' to child sexual offences.[79] Freiberg et al observe that such delay is particularly evident in 'institutional abuse cases'.[80] Child sexual offenders 'strategically manipulate the victim, their family, and the community to hide their deviant intentions',[81] so child victims may not report abuse until they reach adulthood. This is consistent with the findings of the Royal Commission that survivors delayed or declined to report abuse because 'they felt the abusing adult had greater credibility and power'.[82]

An examination of child sexual assault cases for the Judicial Commission of New South Wales found that 37.9 per cent of child sexual abuse offenders were sentenced more than 10 years after the offending and 18.2 per cent were sentenced more than 20 years after.[83] This trend creates a tension in the decision to prosecute. When evaluating 'time since the alleged offence', the prosecutor needs to recognise the principle articulated by the New Zealand Court of Appeal in 1999 that 'Avoidance of prosecution for a period does not diminish the criminal nature of the act alleged against an accused'.[84] Delay may justify non-prosecution where the alleged offender is aged, no longer working with children, has voluntarily ceased offending and/or undertaken rehabilitation, or where key witnesses are unavailable.[85] None of these factors applied to *Volkers*, yet delay in complaint was cited as a reason not to prosecute.[86]

On the other hand, as Mizzi observes, the importance of prosecuting child sexual offenders 'must be balanced with the requirement that the trial of an accused person be fair', and lengthy delay between alleged offending and prosecution can forensically disadvantage a defendant.[87] A defendant's right to a fair trial and the need to have child sexual offences prosecuted are both fundamental to the public interest, and the concept of fairness cannot resolve conflict between them.

[78] Transcript of interview between Leanne Clare, Darren Brazier, Julie Gilbert, Shane Gilbert, Hetty Johnston and Mr Tolhurst, 11 May 2004, 7; *Longman v The Queen* (1989) 168 CLR 79. The 'Longman warning' was heavily criticised and has been largely abolished by statute: Australian Law Reform Commission and NSW Law Reform Commission, *Family Violence – A National Legal Response* (Final Report, October 2010) 1317–21.

[79] M Newbury, 'Historical Child Sexual Abuse Investigations: A Case for Law Reform' (2014) 26 *Current Issues in Criminal Justice* 43, 43.

[80] A Freiberg et al, *Sentencing for Child Sexual Abuse in Institutional Contexts* (Royal Commission into Institutional Responses to Child Sexual Abuse, 2015) 89.

[81] GM Winters and EL Jeglic, 'Stages of Sexual Grooming: Recognizing Potentially Predatory Behaviors of Child Molesters' (2017) 38 *Deviant Behavior* 724, 724.

[82] Royal Commission into Institutional Responses into Child Sexual Abuse, *Final Report: Sport, Recreation, Arts, Culture, Community and Hobby Groups*, vol 14 (2017) 131.

[83] G Hazlitt et al, *Sentencing Offenders Convicted of Child Sexual Assault: Judicial Commission of New South Wales*, Monograph Series 25 (September 2004) viii.

[84] *R v O* [1999] 1 NZLR 347, 350–51.

[85] Freiberg et al (n 83) 45.

[86] Letter from Woodgate Hughes Solicitors to Leanne Clare, 26 March 2003, 1.

[87] P Mizzi, 'Balancing Prosecution with the Right to a Fair Trial: The Child Sexual Abuse Reforms in NSW' (2019) 31 *Judicial Officers Bulletin* 11, 18.

The category of 'the offender' also raises controversy. For example, a prosecutor might have to decide whether to prosecute a 19-year-old woman for having consensual sexual intercourse with a 16-year-old boy when the boy had reached 18 years of age, was in a committed relationship with the woman and did not want the matter prosecuted. A prosecution could be interpreted as enforcing a law based on arbitrary age designations and dated attitudes to sexual relationships, and to unfairly expose a young woman to conviction for a serious offence, a prison sentence and registration as a sexual offender. In 2014, Muscat J, of the District Court of SA, called for reform of laws that legitimately target 'sexual predators' but could be 'draconian and out of touch' with modern values when applied to young people.[88] Muscat J also observed that in cases involving consenting teenagers, 'only the boy is charged'.[89] The decision not to prosecute could create a real or perceived gender bias in the application of the law that saw young women avoid liability for the same conduct that has serious implications for young men. It could also undermine the public interest through the perception that prosecutors were thwarting the intention of Parliament by selectively not prosecuting certain offences and making decisions about sexual offences that are properly addressed by Parliament in consultation with the electorate.

Finally, *Volkers* demonstrates that the assessment of the category of 'the victim', particularly the criteria of 'attitude of the alleged victim to a prosecution', is difficult to reconcile with other public interest criteria. The complainants in *Volkers* maintained that 'justice would have been served' if their complaints were tested at trial before a jury.[90] Their view reflects the fact that victims generally 'see the law as more fair and legitimate when they have some control over the process … whether or not they control ultimate outcomes'.[91] The rights of victims to access judicial mechanisms to obtain redress is recognised in the United Nations Declaration of Basic Principles of Justice for Victims of Crime and Abuse of Power,[92] and is indisputably in the public interest. However, the concept of justice within Australian criminal law does not fully incorporate the perspective of the victim.

[88] J Schriever, 'SA District Court Judge Paul Muscat Says "Draconian" Child Sex Laws Need Reviewing' *The Advertiser* (11 June 2014) www.adelaidenow.com.au/news/south-australia/sa-district-court-judge-paul-muscat-says-draconian-child-sex-laws-need-reviewing/news-story/5135f1dda7fca6f6a93e6113e5412f5b.

[89] T Akerman, 'South Australian District Court Judge Paul Muscat Questions Why "Only Boys" Are Charged With Underage Sex' *The Advertiser* (28 May 2014) www.adelaidenow.com.au/news/south-australia/south-australian-district-court-judge-paul-muscat-questions-why-only-boys-are-charged-with-underage-sex/news-story/b8c77c652f26fc6100411710cb73cee2.

[90] Australian Broadcasting Corporation, 'A Case to Answer: How the Justice System Failed Star Swim Coach Scott Volkers and the Women He Was Accused of Sexually Molesting' *Four Corners* (5 July 2004) www.thetvdb.com/series/four-corners-1961/episodes/4140107.

[91] S Bibas, 'Transparency and Participation in Criminal Procedure' (2006) 81 *New York University Law Review* 911, 954.

[92] United Nations Declaration of Basic Principles of Justice for Victims of Crime and Abuse of Power, GA Res 40/34 (29 November 1985), Art 5.

In 2014, Marilyn Warren, Chief Justice of Victoria, characterised justice in criminal law as covering 'a fair hearing, a fair sentence that punishes not too harshly and offers hope', and 'the application of the rule of law'.[93] She did not refer to the experiences of victims of crime at all. The DPP for WA acknowledged in 2018 that the 'important role of victims of crime in the criminal justice process has not always been properly recognised', but contended that the adoption of a Policy and Guidelines for Victims of Crime addressed that oversight.[94] However, the current policy makes clear that the 'views of the victim … are important but not determinative' of if and how a matter proceeds.[95]

The views of victims must be factored into the process of making the decision to prosecute across Australia. The ODPP guidelines oblige prosecutors to consult with victims before terminating proceedings, substituting charges or entering plea agreements. However, as *Volkers* demonstrates, this obligation does not guarantee that victim perspectives influence the decision to prosecute. Tasmania mandates the lowest level of victim involvement, requiring only that 'great care must be taken in the interests of the victim … to ensure that the right decision is made'.[96] Other jurisdictions require victims to be informed about the progress of prosecutions. In Queensland, information will be provided to victims 'If requested',[97] and victims in the ACT are 'told about any decision not to proceed with a charge', without having to request information.[98] In the Commonwealth, prosecutors are required to consider the views of victims 'where it is appropriate' and to inform victims about prosecutorial decisions 'on request'. However, the guidelines provide that 'it may not be appropriate or practical' to seek individual views in cases where there are multiple victims.[99] In WA, a victim can 'request to be kept informed about' the progress of investigations and charges.[100] SA and NSW require victims to be consulted on prosecutorial decisions. South Australian victims have to be informed about the progress of investigations and prosecutions in all cases, not just where it is deemed practicable.[101] Prosecutors in NSW are required to 'have a talk' with victims before changing or dropping charges.[102] The NT marks the highest level of involvement of victims because its guidelines specify that the views

[93] M Warren, 'What Is Justice?', Speech, Newman Lecture Mannix College, 20 August 2014, 3.

[94] Director of Public Prosecutions (Western Australia), *Statement of Prosecution Policy and Guidelines* (2018) 3. The statement was not included in the Director of Public Prosecutions for Western Australia, *Statement of Prosecution Policy and Guidelines* (2022).

[95] *DPP Policy* (WA) (n 40) s 71.

[96] *DPP Policy* (Tas) (n 2) 5.

[97] *DPP Policy* (Qld) (n 3) 33.

[98] *DPP Policy* (ACT) (n 46) 27.

[99] Commonwealth Director of Public Prosecutions, *Victims of Crime Policy* (Cth) ss 4 and 7.

[100] Government of Western Australia, *Victim Treatment Guidelines and How to Make a Complaint* (19 June 2023) www.wa.gov.au/organisation/department-of-justice/commissioner-victims-of-crime/victim-treatment-guidelines-and-how-make-complaint.

[101] *DPP Policy* (SA) (n 2) 25.

[102] *DPP Policy* (NSW) (n 1) 24–25; New South Wales Government, *Charter of Victims Rights* (2022) s 5.

of victims *will* be taken into account when determining how relevant charges will proceed.[103]

Prosecutorial guidelines undoubtedly encourage, and sometimes require, prosecutors to incorporate victim preferences into the decision to prosecute. However, that decision involves balancing a variety of competing factors, and the views of victims are never determinative. Even reasonable and adamant views of victims cannot override the judgement of the prosecutor on whether the overall circumstances of the case justify prosecution. However, even with this proviso in mind, the way the 'attitude of the alleged victims' was assessed in *Volkers* failed to uphold the public interest. The DPP acknowledged that while complainant 3's allegations involved a 'breach of trust', it 'was an isolated act [and] on sentencing patterns it was unlikely to attract a sentence of any particular significance'.[104] This assessment critically understates the significance of the breach of trust involved in the offending. As Freiberg et al recognised, the established principle that sexual offences 'committed by those known to, or loved or respected by, the victim will be regarded even more seriously because of the abuse of power, or betrayal of trust' involved.[105] This oversight was made worse because the sentencing criteria and the lack of relevant prior convictions that were weighted more significantly than the breach of trust were themselves inadequately understood.

In 1993, the Queensland Court of Appeal reviewed child sexual abuse sentence appeals from the previous decade. It found that in cases not involving sexual penetration or physical injury, but where the offender was in a position of authority, 'very special circumstances' were required for 'a non-custodial sentence to be imposed'.[106] Counsel for the complainants in *Volkers* also analysed contemporary sentencing practices and confirmed that 'in 2004, custodial sentences were more likely than non-custodial sentences for indecent assault offences against children'.[107]

In a report for the Royal Commission in 2016, Cashmore et al analysed appeal decisions involving child sexual offences from 2005 to determine the effect of delayed reporting on prosecutions. They identified the 'counterintuitive' result that sentences were higher where there was a delay between alleged offending and its report, as well as the more predictable result that offences were treated more seriously where there was a significant age difference between offender and victim.[108]

[103] *DPP Policy* (NT) (n 38) ss 6.5 and 12.3.

[104] Evidence to Royal Commission (n 39) 16 July 2014, 8956 (Leanne Clare).

[105] Freiberg et al (n 83) 15.

[106] *R v H* (1993) 66 A Crim R 505, 510.

[107] Royal Commission into Institutional Responses to Child Sexual Abuse, Submissions on Behalf of Julie Gilbert, Simone Boyce, Kylie Rogers, Sharyn Rogers and John Rogers as to the Effect of R v Wruck [2014] QCA 3, 14 July 2014, 3. See, eg *R v Goulding* [1994] QCA 276; *R v Solway* [1995] QCA 374; *R v Jackson; ex parte AG* [2001] QCA 445.

[108] J Cashmore et al, *The Impact of Delayed Reporting on the Prosecution and Outcomes of Child Sexual Abuse Cases* (Royal Commission into Institutional Responses to Child Sexual Abuse, August 2016) 46, 95, 206–07.

All of these criteria suggest that if convicted, Volkers could have faced a significant penalty. Other international and Australian research suggests, however, that a sentence imposed on Volkers could have been at the lower end of the spectrum, because the alleged offending involved older children and there was no allegation of aggression or sexual penetration.[109] In any event, as Lamer CJ held in Canada seven years before the decision in *Volkers*, the length of the sentence is not its primary characteristic. It 'represents a symbolic, collective statement that the offender's conduct should be punished for encroaching on our society's basic code of values'.[110] In the same year that *Volkers* was discontinued, Vincent J in Victoria similarly found that a sentence 'signifies the recognition by society of the nature and significance of the wrong that has been done to affected members … and the public attribution of responsibility for that wrongdoing to the perpetrator'.[111] The prosecutors in *Volkers* ignored the deterrent and symbolic value that a sentence could have delivered if the allegations were proven.

Additionally, Volkers's lack of prior convictions was cited as a reason not to prosecute him.[112] The suggestion that a first-time child sexual offender should avoid prosecution is improper, particularly given the difficulty of identifying child sexual abuse. According to Mathews and Collin-Vézina, international studies demonstrate that 'Child sexual abuse is endemic worldwide',[113] and levels of victimisation could be as high as 20 per cent for girls and 10 per cent for boys.[114] However, according to Winters and Jeglic, extensive research indicates 'that many cases of child sexual abuse are never disclosed', and as few as 5 per cent of offenders are ever apprehended.[115] Offenders avoid detection because abuse rarely leaves physical evidence, children do not disclose abuse due to 'fear, embarrassment, and guilt', and most observers cannot identify signs that abuse has occurred.[116] A Victorian study found that while the numbers of adults reporting suspected child abuse increased between 1993 and 2012, the only 'statistically significant' increase occurred between 2007 and 2012.[117] A similar Victorian study in 2014 found that only 15 per cent of offenders convicted of child sexual offences had prior convictions for similar offending.[118]

Similar evidence on child sexual abuse and its prosecution was available before the *Volkers* case. Hawkins and Briggs identified in 1997 that in Australia, 'about

[109] T Lewis et al, 'Sentencing in Child Sexual Assault Cases: Factors Influencing Judicial Decision-making' (2014) 20 *Journal of Sexual Aggression* 281, 285, 292.

[110] *R v M (CA)* [1996] 1 SCR 500 [81].

[111] *DPP v DJK* [2003] VSCA 109 [18].

[112] Crime and Misconduct Commission (Queensland), *The Volkers Case: Examining the Conduct of the Police and Prosecution* (March 2003) 34.

[113] B Mathews and D Collin-Vézina, 'Child Sexual Abuse: Raising Awareness and Empathy Is Essential to Promote New Public Health Responses' (2016) 37 *Journal of Public Health Policy* 304, 305.

[114] B Mathews et al, 'Reports of Child Sexual Abuse of Boys and Girls: Longitudinal Trends Over a 20-Year Period in Victoria, Australia' (2017) 66 *Child Abuse & Neglect* 9, 9.

[115] Winters and Jeglic (n 84) 724.

[116] Mathews et al (n 117) 18.

[117] ibid 13.

[118] Lewis et al (n 112) 288.

2% of reports of child sexual abuse result in prosecution and only about half of those result in a conviction'.[119] In 2004, the psychiatrist engaged by complainant 3 in *Volkers* described child sexual offenders as 'elusive predators', and estimated that only 1–2 per cent of them would ever be imprisoned.[120] This evidence demonstrates the possibility that prior offending by Volkers was not identified before 2003, and he could have appeared in 'court with a clean legal record but an extensive history of criminal conduct'.[121] However, the Deputy DPP of Queensland informed complainant 2 that one of the reasons for not prosecuting Volkers was that he had trained over 1000 young female swimmers over many years without facing any previous complaints.[122] The decision not to prosecute suspects who lack relevant prior convictions perpetuates repeat offending and undermines the public interest by enabling suspects to escape prosecution where incriminating evidence finally emerges. This outcome clearly offends the concepts of 'fairness' and 'justice'.

B. Effects of the Offending and its Prosecution

The second set of criteria for the public interest test relates to the social impact of the type of alleged offending and its prosecution. I have divided these criteria into three categories, and summarised them and their key determinants in Table 8.2.

Table 8.2 Public interest test criteria – effects of the offending and its prosecution

Category	**Key determinants**
The social effects of the offence	effect on public order and morale; whether the alleged offence is of public concern[a]
The criminological effects of the offence and its prosecution	prevalence of the alleged offence and need for prosecutions to encourage personal and general deterrence[b]
The effect of the prosecution on the reputation of the law	whether prosecution would bring the law into disrepute; obsolescence or obscurity of the law; necessity to maintain public confidence in Parliament and the courts[c]

[a] *DPP Policy* (Tas) (n 2) 8; *DPP Policy* (WA) (n 40) s 32; *DPP Policy* (NSW) (n 1) 9; *DPP Policy* (Qld) (n 3) 3; *DPP Policy* (SA) (n 2) 6; *DPP Policy* (NT) (n 38) s 2.5.
[b] *DPP Policy* (Tas) (n 2) 8; *DPP Policy* (WA) (n 40) s 32; *DPP Policy* (NSW) (n 1) 9; *DPP Policy* (Qld) (n 3) 3; *DPP Policy* (Vic) (n 44) s 3; *DPP Policy* (SA) (n 2) 7; *DPP Policy* (NT) (n 38) s 2.5.
[c] *DPP Policy* (Tas) (n 2) 8; *DPP Policy* (WA) (n 40) s 32; *DPP Policy* (NSW) (n 1) 10; *DPP Policy* (Qld) (n 3) 4; *DPP Policy* (Vic) (n 44) s 3; *DPP Policy* (NT) (n 38) s 2.5.

[119] R Hawkins and F Briggs, 'The Institutionalised Abuse of Children in Australia: Past and Present' (1997) 133 *Early Child Development and Care* 41, 47.
[120] W Middleton, 'Julie Therese Gilbert and Scott Alexander Volkers' Expert Report (15 October 2004) [14].
[121] Freiberg et al (n 83) 76.
[122] Letter from Paul Rutledge to Simone Boyce, 27 September 2002, 1.

Some of these social factors are amenable to relatively objective measurement and so are within the expertise of the DPP. For example, on the 'criminological effects of the offence and its prosecution', the ODPPs annually report on matters related to the occurrence of offences, so can identify trends in offending over time. Similarly, they record penalties imposed and alternatives to prosecution pursued for various offences.[123] These records provide a basis to determine how recidivism rates for various offences are affected by different case resolutions.

However, as Bowers argues, these criteria also cover politico-legal matters that do not rest on 'legal or factual guilt or innocence, but on evaluations of relative blameworthiness'.[124] These matters involve what Bibas describes as 'deeply moral issues … that busy, legal-minded prosecutors are ill-suited to decide'.[125] *Volkers* demonstrates, for example, the difficulty involved in assessing the 'social effects' of child sexual offences, including 'whether the alleged offence is of public concern'. In her memorandum and testimony before the Royal Commission, Cunneen explained that the type of offending alleged against Volkers did not concern the public in 2003. She testified that people would frequently ask '"Are you still doing those kiddy sex cases?", in the most pejorative fashion as though it was some sort of adjunct to the criminal law and not really crime'.[126] She did acknowledge that if the complainants had alleged 'sexual penetration … it may well have been in the public interest to proceed'.[127]

Research does indicate that sexual penetration can increase the trauma of child sexual abuse.[128] However, most of the harm of abuse arises because 'immature psychosexual development is disrupted by the intrusion of the adult's mature sexual contact' and creates confusion, betrayal of trust, powerlessness, fear and isolation.[129] Complainant 1 in *Volkers* specifically addressed the assertion that the abuse against her was 'minor' compared to cases involving penetration. In her written statement to the Royal Commission, she reflected that 'the abuse was not at all minor to me and its effect has been, and still is, devastating'.[130] In this sense, the decision not to prosecute Volkers was affected by misinformed views on child sexual abuse. As discussed in chapter seven, the forecasting of jury decisions is an integral part of assessing the reasonable prospects of conviction, and prosecutors could not ignore ill-informed or outdated public opinion. However, the decision

[123] See, eg New South Wales, Office of the Director of Public Prosecutions, *Annual Report 2021–2022* (14 October 2022) Appendix A, 63.

[124] Bowers (n 5) 1658.

[125] S Bibas, 'The Pitfalls of Professionalized Prosecution: A Response to Josh Bower's Legal Guilt, Normative Innocence, and the Equitable Decision Not to Prosecute (2011) 111 *Columbia Law Review* 14, 15.

[126] Evidence to Royal Commission (n 39) 10 July 2014, 8644 (Margaret Cunneen).

[127] Memorandum from Margaret Cunneen to Nicholas Cowdery, 26 March 2004, 16.

[128] E Rowan, *Understanding Child Sexual Abuse* (Jackson, University of Mississippi Press, 2006) 30.

[129] D Glaser, 'Treatment Issues in Child Sexual Abuse' (1991) 159 *British Journal of Psychiatry* 769, 770–71.

[130] Statement to Royal Commission into Institutional Responses into Child Sexual Abuse, 6 July 2014, 11 (Kylie Rogers).

to reflect, rather than challenge, those opinions at trial could significantly undermine the public interest because, as St George and Spohn argue, it institutionalises stereotypes and prevents 'instrumental change in sexual assault case processing'.[131]

The decision not to prosecute *Volkers* also reflected the public interest criteria of the 'effect of the prosecution on the reputation of the law'. This category includes 'maintaining public confidence in the Parliament and the Courts' and not 'bringing the law into disrepute'. Cunneen's memo proposed that prosecuting 'relatively trivial allegations, occurring so long ago, would tend to bring all sexual assault prosecutions into disrepute' and 'erode public confidence in the Courts and the criminal justice system'.[132] She maintained to the Royal Commission, over a decade later, that extensive publicity and the 'inevitable result of not guilty' resulting from a prosecution would have worked 'against the progress' of similar prosecutions.[133] Her priority was to avoid creating a public impression of 'zealous prosecutors putting up very old, relatively minor cases' that would result in acquittals and conclusions that the complainants were lying.[134]

The experience of Attorneys General, discussed in previous chapters, illustrated the difficulty of an elected public official obtaining a representative view of complex questions of public interest. These difficulties are magnified for statutory officers. Keating's question of what 'legitimises a senior bureaucrat's perception of the common good'[135] recognises that statutory officers lack established channels of communication with the public. Despite this deficit, prosecutors can decline to prosecute conduct deemed by Parliament to be criminal and for which police have gathered sufficient evidence. *Volkers* indicates that such decisions can constitute an explicit policy against prosecuting historical child sexual offences that do not involve sexual penetration. US Circuit Judge Stephanos Bibas highlights that this discretion raises tension between accountability and independence because prosecutors 'imperfectly represent the community',[136] and their 'low-visibility exercises of discretion' are a 'chronic source of friction in a democracy'.[137] Brandon et al agree on the existence of a 'longstanding democratic deficit in prosecution, which is a global problem'.[138]

The concerns about the authority of prosecutors to assess the public interest do not recognise the many decisions of prosecutors that withstand scrutiny against

[131] S St George and C Spohn, 'Liberating Discretion: The Effect of Rape Myth Factors on Prosecutors' Decisions to Charge Suspects in Penetrative and Non-Penetrative Sex Offenses' (2018) 35 *Justice Quarterly* 1280, 1302.

[132] Memorandum from Margaret Cunneen to Nicholas Cowdery, 26 March 2004, 15–16.

[133] Evidence to Royal Commission (n 39) 10 July 2014, 8642 (Margaret Cunneen).

[134] ibid 8645.

[135] M Keating, 'Managing for Results in the Public Interest' (1990) 49 *Australian Journal of Public Administration* 387, 394.

[136] Bibas, 'Pitfalls' (n 128) 17. See, eg K Toole, 'The Making of Prosecutorial Decisions in Australia' (2014) 39 *Alternative Law Journal* 268; WJ Stuntz, 'Self-Defeating Crimes' (2000) 86 *Virginia Law Review* 1871 on systematic non-prosecution of certain offences undermining the will of the legislature.

[137] Bibas, 'Transparency' (n 94) 915.

[138] GL Brandon et al, 'Open Prosecution' (2023) 75 *Stanford Law Review* 1365, 1414.

the standard of the public interest, or the decisions of elected officials that do not. Nevertheless, the decision not to prosecute Volkers reveals the significant level of subjective judgement exercised by prosecutors determining the public interest. They have to assess complex social, legal, political and moral issues according to a vague concept of the public interest defined by criteria open to opposing interpretations and weightings. Without formal avenues for public consultation, the prosecutors in *Volkers* responded to limited snapshots of public opinion that did not represent the public's legitimate interest in the prosecution of all types of child sexual abuse. Their attempts to preserve the reputation of the criminal justice system actually exposed it to continuing criticism.

Complainant 1 testified to the Royal Commission that the stress of the committal proceedings caused her to experience a psychotic episode: 'I was injured, psychologically, by the abuse and have never recovered. I do not understand why the effects of what Scott did to me can be treated as a reason not to hold him to account for it.'[139] Similarly, complainant 2 described the legal process as 'extremely stressful, humiliating and compounded the harm that I had suffered at Scott's hands'.[140] Complainant 3 agreed that the prosecution was a 'process of re-victimisation' that left her feeling isolated, unsupported and not believed.[141] As discussed in previous chapters, the Crime and Misconduct Commission, the Royal Commission, members of the profession and the media all supported the complainants' opposition to the decision not to prosecute.

IV. Conclusions

The ODPPs introduced a detailed public interest test to challenge the idea, evident in both contemporary administrative law and the English prosecutorial tradition, that the concept of the public interest is not receptive to a clear benchmark for assessment. The detailed criteria for the public interest test, however, confirm the inherent ambiguity of the concept of the public interest, rather than providing any meaningful explanation of it.

The public interest test has the potential to produce more controversy than the ostensibly objective reasonable prospects of conviction test, yet it has actually generated little debate in Australia. It is possible that in order to neutralise public and political concerns, prosecutors justify public interest decisions according to the less controversial concept of reasonable prospects of conviction.

However, the need for a flexible approach to the public interest is widely accepted. The public interest test has functioned adequately enough to ensure that

[139] Evidence to Royal Commission (n 39) 7 July 2014, 8273–74 (Kylie Rogers).

[140] Statement to Royal Commission into Institutional Responses into Child Sexual Abuse, 4 July 2014, 16 (Simone Boyce).

[141] ibid 23 May 2014, 7–8 (Julie Gilbert).

thousands of cases per year, all over the country, for several decades have been resolved without controversy. Nonetheless, conflicting criteria inherent in the test have as much potential to divide as to achieve the public interest.

Like the reasonable prospects of conviction test, the criteria of the public interest test require a high level of subjective judgement over the exercise of prosecutorial discretion. This prevents its assessment according to a common standard accepted as upholding the public interest. The difficulty of assessing the inherently vague concept is aggravated because the decision to prosecute is made in a statutory environment, where critical aspects of the public interest are beyond the expertise of the decision-makers. Like the value of independence, the value of the public interest is only partially upheld by the ODPPs.

9

Accountability of the Attorney General

The introduction of independent, statutory Offices of Director of Public Prosecutions (ODPPs) transformed Australian prosecutions, but commitment to the tradition of parliamentary accountability within the Westminster system limited the extent of the reform. Maintaining the prosecutorial role of the Attorney General does not actually protect the accountability of the prosecutorial process, because the reporting requirements introduced with the ODPP system do not call and hold the Attorney General to account to Parliament or constrain prosecutorial decisions. Rather, the focus on the ODPPs' independence undermines accountability and promotes the view that Attorneys General cannot, and should not, be involved in prosecutorial decisions. The examples of Italy and South Africa show how a particular commitment to either independence or accountability, rather than to finding a balance between values, can undermine the integrity of a prosecutorial system. Despite the lessons from international jurisdictions, the ODPP system privileges prosecutorial independence over prosecutorial accountability. The prosecutions of Witness K and Bernard Collaery show that the attempt to balance independence and accountability within the prosecution system enables Attorneys General to engage covertly in politically motivated prosecutions and so avoid accountability.

I. The Attorney General and Accountability

Accountability is another concept that is critical to prosecutions but not amenable to precise definition. The concept of prosecutorial accountability, unlike the concept of prosecutorial independence, was not refined by centuries of debate in England. According to Mulgan, the term 'accountability' was, historically, 'used only rarely and with relatively restricted meaning'.[1] He elaborates that even in the twenty-first century, when the term 'crops up everywhere performing all manner of analytical and rhetorical tasks', its meaning remains 'complex and chameleon-like'.[2]

[1] R Mulgan, '"Accountability": An Ever-Expanding Concept?' (2000) 78 *Public Administration* 555, 555.
[2] ibid.

In 2007, Bovens noted that contemporary discourse on accountability referenced similarly diverse concepts, including 'transparency, equity, democracy, efficiency, responsiveness, responsibility and integrity'.[3] The concept has not achieved clarity in subsequent years. Manes-Rossi argued in 2019 that while accountability was 'universally accepted as a pillar of democracy', differing interpretations left the concept 'in crisis'.[4]

In the absence of a coherent political or scholarly discourse on accountability, the traditional English response to prosecutorial controversies focused on the integrity of the Attorney General. It involved a narrow conception of accountability that was satisfied by a process of 'questioning the transgressor and the transgression and debating the consequences' of any contentious decisions.[5] The concept of accountability was still under-developed when prosecutorial controversies arose in late-twentieth-century Australia. However, the Australian parliaments took a more sophisticated approach to accountability and engaged in 'deeper questioning of … procedures and how these can be abused through the exercise of power'.[6] This deeper analysis accepted that tension existed between the political and legal roles of the Attorney General, irrespective of the character of the office holder. It resulted in the establishment of independent, statutory offices that, implicitly, reflect Suchman's view that a prosecution system needed to generate 'a generalized perception' that decisions are 'proper, or appropriate within some socially constructed system of norms'.[7]

The retention of the Attorney General's prosecutorial role purported to reconcile the prosecutorial values of independence and accountability. Their political oversight intentionally restricted the independence of the Director of Public Prosecutions (DPP), to reflect Larkin's view that 'from a legitimacy perspective, parliament is the only accountability institution directly elected by the citizenry and directly accountable to it through the ballot box'.[8] Bricker's more strongly worded view was that 'the accountability function served by elections provides the defining feature of a democratic (as opposed to autocratic) regime'.[9] The accountability of the prosecutorial system, therefore, depends on parliamentary processes that both *call* the Attorney General to account to explain prosecutorial decisions and *hold* the Attorney General to account through rectification and sanction for those decisions.[10]

[3] M Bovens, 'Analysing and Assessing Accountability: A Conceptual Framework' (2007) 13 *European Law Journal* 447, 449.

[4] F Manes-Rossi, 'New Development: Alternative Reporting Formats: A Panacea for Accountability Dilemmas?' (2019) 39 *Public Money & Management* 528, 528.

[5] S Brenton, 'Ministers and Scandals' in K Dowding and C Lewis (eds), *Ministerial Careers and Accountability in the Australian Commonwealth Government* (Canberra, ANU Press, 2012) 135, 139.

[6] ibid.

[7] MC Suchman, 'Managing Legitimacy: Strategic and Institutional Approaches' (1995) 20 *Academy of Management Review* 571, 577.

[8] P Larkin, 'Ministerial Accountability to Parliament' in Dowding and Lewis (n 5) 95, 97.

[9] B Bricker, 'Citizens United and Political Accountability' in NS Lind and CE Rabe-Hemp (eds), *Corruption, Accountability and Discretion* (Bingley, Emerald Publishing, 2017) 185, 187.

[10] Larkin (n 8) 110–11.

In 1982, Victorian Premier and Attorney General, John Cain, expressed exasperation at a Parliament that could not comprehend how the Attorney General would achieve prosecutorial accountability under the ODPP system. He stated: 'there is a final accountability and responsibility to Parliament through the Attorney General. I cannot say it any louder. If honourable members opposite do not understand that, I cannot help them.'[11]

Cain's frustration did not recognise the challenges involved in securing the Attorney General's parliamentary accountability over the ODPPs. The first challenge was Parliament's limited ability to call and hold Attorneys General to account for prosecutorial decisions.

A. Calling the Attorney General to Account

Attorneys General are called to account to the Parliament, the people and the media by the requirement to provide public statements explaining controversial prosecutorial decisions made by themselves or the DPP.[12] This process provides transparency and generates public discussion that are hallmarks of prosecutorial accountability.[13] For example, in June 2018, the Commonwealth Attorney General, Christian Porter, issued a media release advising that a former staff member of the Australian Secret Intelligence Service (ASIS) and his lawyer, Bernard Collaery, were facing charges under the Criminal Code (Cth) and the Intelligence Services Act 2001 (Cth). The charges related to allegations of a conspiracy to communicate information acquired or prepared by ASIS in connection with the performance of its functions. The media release explained the legal basis of the charges, the identity of one defendant, the reasons for the suppression of the name of the other defendant and the legal requirement of the Attorney General's consent for the prosecutions. It also stated that the DPP made the decision to prosecute and that the Attorney General consented to it proceeding.[14] This public explanation was important because, as discussed later in this chapter, the case generated widespread accusations that the Attorney General instigated the prosecution for improper, political reasons.

Public explanations of prosecutions are not only provided by elected officials. For example, in 2019, the then Australian Capital Territory (ACT) DPP, Neville Drumgold, released a public statement in order to provide 'transparency and accountability'[15] regarding the decision not to prosecute a man for assisting the

[11] Victoria, *Parliamentary Debates*, Legislative Assembly, 9 December 1982, 2683 (John Cain, Premier and Attorney General).

[12] R Mulgan, 'Ministerial Responsibility in Australia' in Dowding and Lewis (n 5) 177, 178.

[13] R Mulgan, 'The Extended Scope of Accountability in Public Administration' in *Oxford Research Encyclopedia, Politics* (Oxford, Oxford University Press, 2020) 1, 2.

[14] Attorney-General for Australia and Minister for Industrial Relations, 'Prosecution Matter', Media Release, 28 June 2018.

[15] ACT Director of Public Prosecutions, 'Police v O – CC2019/3260 Charge of Aiding Suicide under Section 17(1) Crimes Act 1900', Statement of Reasons, 28 June 2019, 1.

suicide of his terminally ill partner. The statement was necessary because laws related to assisted dying are controversial and, as the statement acknowledged, the decision could have been misinterpreted as DPP policy that would undermine 'Parliament's intention that aiding suicide should be an offence'.[16]

However, parliamentary accountability privileges explanations from elected officers on the basis that unelected public officers 'can drift policies away from the[ir] original intent'.[17] In 2018, Atkinson disputed this distinction. He claimed that the limitations on parliamentary accountability enable ministers to 'increasingly stray from their functional mandates'[18] in the same way as the unelected officers they oversee. The evidence of the Queensland DPP to the Parliamentary Committee for Electoral and Administrative Review in 1993 confirms that calling Attorneys General to account does not ensure accountability of prosecutorial decisions. The DPP testified that the Attorney General was 'accountable' in the literal sense of being 'required to give an account to the Parliament' for prosecutorial decisions, but did 'not bear any political responsibility for any decisions' of the DPP.[19]

B. Holding the Attorney General to Account

Despite the perceived deficiencies in the processes for calling ministers to account, the principle of parliamentary accountability still involves the expectation that elected officials are held to account through criticisms in Parliament and in the media, public protests, elections, litigation in the courts and calls for their resignation.[20] The threat of these sanctions is supposed to motivate Attorneys General to 'advocate' for and 'remain attuned' to 'the aspirations of their voters. Their democratic mandate justifies their watchdog relationship vis-à-vis the bureaucracy'.[21] Under the ODPP system, Attorneys General fulfil their supervisory, prosecutorial role through the exercise of their own prosecutorial powers in particular cases.

C. Exercise of Attorney General's Prosecutorial Powers

Attorneys General involve themselves in prosecutions by making their own prosecutorial decisions or directing the DPP to take particular action, which may run

[16] ibid 3.

[17] UW Chohan, 'Legislative Oversight of Bureaucracy' in A Farazmand (ed), *Global Encyclopedia of Public Administration, Public Policy, and Governance* (Cham, Springer Nature, 2018) 3762, 3763.

[18] CL Atkinson, 'Legitimacy in Public Administration' in Farazmand (n 17) 3781, 3785.

[19] Parliamentary Committee for Electoral and Administrative Review, *The Independence of the Attorney-General, Review of an Electoral and Administrative Review Commission Report: Transcript of Proceedings* (Legislative Assembly of Queensland, 27 October 1993) 9–10, 13 (Royce Miller, Director of Public Prosecutions).

[20] P Stenning, 'Discretion, Politics, and the Public Interest in High-Profile Criminal Investigations and Prosecutions (2009) 24 *Canadian Journal of Law and Society* 337, 340.

[21] Chohan (n 17) 3763.

counter to the judgement of the DPP. The earlier discussions of *Nemer* and *Hurley* demonstrate how the media and the public can induce the Attorney General to intervene in prosecutions where DPPs have made decisions they resolutely defend. These cases could be interpreted as illustrating that Attorneys General are effectively held to account under the ODPP system. The extent and nature of the commentary on the cases demonstrated profound community concerns about possible prosecutorial injustice, and an expectation that the government, through the Attorney General, would reverse the controversial decisions.

The sustained pressure exerted in the media provided a powerful incentive for the Attorney General to ensure that prosecutorial decisions reflected community values and concerns. It also provided a more cynical motivation to prevent dissatisfaction with the original decision being converted into electoral backlash. In each case, the Attorney General intervened with actions that accorded with community sentiment, and calmed criticism of the prosecutorial system. However, for the Attorney General to be meaningfully accountable for prosecutorial decisions, media pressure and parliamentary processes would have to apply consistently and routinely. While most prosecutorial decisions may be acceptable to the public, sporadic response to particular cases will not reliably identify the outlier cases that do not accord with community standards.

The impracticality of Attorneys General consistently reviewing executive decisions has been evident since the time the ODPPs were established. In 1986, Galligan argued that the growth of executive decision-making precluded 'accountability in any direct or populist sense'.[22] Three years later, Sir Anthony Mason observed that Dicey's nineteenth-century doctrine of ministerial responsibility 'provided an adequate legal and political framework' for its time, but that Parliament cannot 'maintain a comprehensive overview of … the vast field' of modern administrative action.[23] The ability of parliamentary processes to constrain executive decision-makers did not improve over subsequent decades. In 2000, McMillan reiterated that 'the functions of government are too numerous and specialised for the parliamentary or electoral process to provide effective accountability for the myriad decisions that are made'.[24] The limitations of parliamentary accountability apply to the complex field of prosecutorial decision-making. They limit the likelihood that Attorneys General will become aware of controversial decisions, or will take action where they are aware of controversial decisions.

It would be neither possible nor desirable for the Attorney General to have oversight of all routine matters undertaken by the ODPP. For example, in the reporting period 2021–22, Australia's largest ODPP, New South Wales (NSW), resolved 5656 committal matters in the local court; dealt with 1970 sentences, 1100 trial matters

[22] DJ Galligan, *Discretionary Powers: A Legal Study of Official Discretion* (Oxford, Oxford University Press, 1986) 4.

[23] A Mason, 'Administrative Review: The Experience of the First Twelve Years' (1989) 18 *Federal Law Review* 122, 128.

[24] J McMillan, 'Parliament and Administrative Law' (Department of the Parliamentary Library, 7 November 2000) Research Paper No 13, 31.

and 4523 severity appeals in the District Court; received 52 homicide prosecutions in the Supreme Court; and completed 316 Court of Criminal Appeal matters.[25] Attorneys General cannot even be aware of all potentially controversial decisions, as neither the media nor the public consistently draw attention to them. The public is largely dependent on the media for its knowledge of prosecutorial issues, as few members of the public attend court and decisions not to prosecute are not decided in court. As Mulgan observes, the mainstream media largely report on the small number of cases that are 'particularly newsworthy'.[26] The significant racial and class issues evident in *Nemer* and *Hurley* generated an unusual amount of attention. The cases do not indicate that the media will routinely inform the public of prosecutorial decisions that might activate community members to lobby the Attorney General to take action. Rather, the cases that gain public attention are not necessarily the ones where the prosecutorial decision has miscarried, but those with particular factual characteristics that capture the public imagination.

Similarly, parliamentary processes do not ensure that Attorneys General will take action where they are aware of prosecutorial decisions that do or will offend community views. Ministerial responsibility 'remains a key constitutional convention',[27] but, as the discussion below demonstrates, neither processes for questioning the Attorney General nor those for removing them from office effectively hold them to account.

(i) Questions

According to the Federal Parliament website, the 'accountability of the Government is demonstrated most clearly and publicly at Question Time', when 'questions without notice are put to Ministers … to seek information or press for action'.[28]

However, several factors undermine the effectiveness of Question Time in any parliament. Stuart observes that, fundamentally, Question Time cannot ensure that ministers answer any questions directly or honestly.[29] This limitation has particular application to the Attorney General, and raises what Schuh identifies as an inherent 'tension between leadership discretion and accountability to the will of the people'.[30] According to Booth, discretionary decision-makers can avoid accountability where their 'professional judgement is accorded high status'.[31] The

[25] New South Wales, Office of the Director of Public Prosecutions, *Annual Report 2021–2022* (14 October 2022) 22, 24–26, 28 and 74.

[26] Mulgan, 'Ministerial Responsibility' (n 12) 190.

[27] ibid 177.

[28] Parliament of Australia, 'Question Time', www.aph.gov.au/About_Parliament/House_of_Representatives/Powers_practice_and_procedure/Practice7/HTML/Chapter15/Question_Time.

[29] D Stuart, 'Prosecutorial Accountability in Canada' in P Stenning (ed), *Accountability for Criminal Justice: Selected Essays*' (Toronto, University of Toronto Press, 1995) 330, 335.

[30] AM Schuh, 'Leadership in Organizations' in Farazmand (n 17) 3677, 3681.

[31] P Booth, *Controlling Development: Certainty and Discretion in Europe, the USA and Hong Kong* (London, Routledge, 1996) 111.

Attorney General occupies the most privileged position within the legal and political systems, which can prevent scrutiny of their decisions. Woodhouse claims that the Attorney General has been able, historically, to 'retreat behind the cloak of quasi-judicialdom and assert that in his opinion (all that really matters), given all the facts, it was the correct decision at the time'.[32] Prosecutorial decisions made by the Attorney General are particularly open to these types of responses because of the breadth of the prosecutorial discretion and the broad range of legal and factual matters that inform the decision to prosecute.

The Attorney General can even more effectively deflect questions about DPP decisions. They can assert that the independence of the DPP demands that they, as Attorney General, keep a distance from those decisions. They can also explain why prosecutors need a broad discretion, and how that discretion is informed by policies and budgets that are well-established, publicly available and largely uniform across the country.

(ii) Resignations and Voting

The Attorney General is ostensibly held to account by the possibility of removal from office through forced resignations and elections. Dowding et al note that ministerial resignations are rare,[33] so their effectiveness as an accountability measure is limited. These limitations apply to responses to prosecutorial controversies. The discussion above, and in previous chapters, shows that Attorneys General formulate their infrequent involvement in prosecutions to meet public expectations, and would not make prosecutorial decisions that would alienate the public and provoke calls for their resignation.

Prosecutorial decisions made by the DPP provide a tenuous basis for the resignation of Attorneys General. Marshall argues that in England, ministers cannot 'in the full executive sense be responsible' for tasks allotted to their agencies, and suggesting otherwise creates 'a muddle … of quasi-responsibility'.[34] Mulgan agrees that ministers are not 'vicariously liable' for actions of decision-makers within their portfolio, and claims that they have never been obliged to resign over decisions for which they bear no personal responsibility.[35] As Goldring explains, the development of the 'new' administrative law recognised that 'administrative structures are now way beyond a size where a minister can possibly be expected to know the details of every decision made under his authority'.[36] Attorneys General cannot

[32] D Woodhouse, 'The Attorney General' (1997) 50 *Parliamentary Affairs* 97, 103.

[33] K Dowding et al, 'The Pattern of Forced Exits from the Ministry' in Dowding and Lewis (n 5) 115, 119–26.

[34] G Marshall, 'The Evolving Practice of Parliamentary Accountability: Writing Down the Rules' (1991) 44 *Parliamentary Affairs* 460, 468–69.

[35] Mulgan, 'Ministerial Responsibility' (n 12) 180–81.

[36] J Goldring, 'The Foundations of the "New Administrative Law" in Australia' (1981) 40 *Australian Journal of Public Administration* 79, 80.

be aware of all prosecutorial decisions, as independent statutory offices expressly distance the decision to prosecute from the Attorney General. It is unlikely that Attorneys General could be held responsible for decisions made within the ODPP at all, and especially not to the standard that would result in any legitimate call for their resignation.

The factors that weigh against Attorneys General resigning from office over prosecutorial decisions, similarly, weigh against them being voted from office on account of such decisions. Booth's observations on electoral pressure and parliamentary accountability over planning decisions are relevant to prosecutorial decisions. He argues that while elections can hold 'politicians to account for the cumulative effect' of their decisions, they are so infrequently voted out of office for individual decisions that 'the link between electorate, politicians and administrators may be so attenuated that there is no effective accountability at all'.[37]

The processes meant to call and hold ministers to account are so ineffective over the Attorney General in prosecutorial matters that, in 1995, Edwards identified international 'scorn on the principle of ministerial accountability' for prosecutors.[38] However, as the following sub-section demonstrates, the ODPP system addresses the limits of parliamentary accountability through reporting requirements.

(iii) Reporting Requirements

The ODPP system enhances traditional parliamentary accountability processes through two, overlapping, requirements for reporting the Attorney General's involvement in prosecutions. The first requirement is that exercises of prosecutorial discretion be reported directly to Parliament; the second is that they be reported in the ODPP annual reports.

Attorneys General have few obligations to directly report to Parliament the exercise of their independent prosecutorial powers. In Queensland, the Attorney General must report to the Legislative Assembly within three sitting days whenever they present an indictment or enters a *nolle prosequi*.[39] In most jurisdictions where the Attorney General can direct the DPP to take particular action, they must 'as soon as practicable', and within a maximum of 15 sitting days, ensure that notice of the direction is published in the Gazette and tabled before Parliament.[40] These measures provide direct and timely notification of prosecutorial action by

[37] Booth (n 31) 134.

[38] J Edwards, 'The Office of Attorney General – New Levels of Public Expectations and Accountability' in Stenning, *Accountability for Criminal Justice* (n 29) 294, 310.

[39] Attorney-General Act 1999 (Qld), s 11(2).

[40] Director of Public Prosecutions Act 1983 (Cth), s 8(3) (DPP Act (Cth)). They must be reported within five days in the ACT: Director of Public Prosecutions Act 1990 (ACT), s 20(6); six days in SA: Director of Public Prosecutions Act 1991 (SA), s 9(3); and 14 days in Qld and NSW: Director of Public Prosecutions Act 1984 (Qld), s 10A(3) and (4); Director of Public Prosecutions Act 1986 (NSW), s 26(4) (DPP Act (NSW)).

the Attorney General, but both types of prosecutorial power are infrequently exercised. Additionally, the DPP's annual reporting process is intended to ensure the Attorney General's 'parliamentary and public accountability',[41] 'not only in the general sense of a Minister responsible for what occurs within his administration, but also in a more direct sense'.[42] The annual reports record cases where, for example, the Attorney General periodically requests information about the supervision and detention of offenders who pose an unacceptable risk of committing serious terrorism offences,[43] as well as when they institute or terminate a prosecution or appeal a sentence.[44] In Western Australia (WA) and the Northern Territory (NT), the direction of the Attorney General to the DPP is included in the annual report, rather than made directly to Parliament.[45]

Edwards was so impressed with this combination of reporting mechanisms that he recommended every jurisdiction 'take a good hard look at the Australian initiatives and then ask themselves, can we justify not accepting a similar degree of total prosecutorial accountability?'[46] No combination of parliamentary processes and reporting requirements is likely to achieve 'total prosecutorial accountability' in any system. The ODPP system presents a significant further barrier to its achievement, because it emphasises independence over accountability. The contrasting experiences of Italy and South Africa starkly demonstrate the dire consequences to a prosecutorial system where independence and accountability are in disequilibrium because one of the values is privileged over the other.

II. Balancing Independence and Accountability

Cain's frustration with the Victorian Parliament also overlooked the fact that the inherent problem of balancing prosecutorial independence and accountability that was evident in England was exacerbated in Australia because the ODPP system was designed to be independent from political influence.

A. International Experience

During a review of the New Zealand (NZ) prosecution service in 2011, Spencer argued that in the prosecutorial context, independence and accountability 'are

[41] Northern Territory, *Parliamentary Debates*, Legislative Assembly, 28 February 1990, 8969 (Daryl Manzie, Attorney General).

[42] New South Wales, *Parliamentary Debates*, Legislative Assembly, 1 December 1986, 7340 (Terence Sheahan).

[43] New South Wales, Office of the Director of Public Prosecutions, *Annual Report 2019–2020* (12 October 2020) 44.

[44] See, eg DPP Act (NSW) (n 40) s 27.

[45] Director of Public Prosecutions Act 1990 (NT), s 28(5); Director of Public Prosecutions Act 1991 (WA), s 27(6).

[46] Edwards (n 38) 309.

not mutually exclusive'.[47] This conclusion is not specific to NZ or to prosecutions. Burbank argued that in the USA, judicial independence and accountability are 'not at war with each other but rather are complements'.[48] However, experiences in Italy and South Africa demonstrate the difficulty of achieving a balance between the two prosecutorial values.

In Italy during World War II, the Fascist Code granted prosecutors extraordinary powers over arrest, detention, interrogation, and search and seizure, but did not impose corresponding procedural or ethical constraints, or judicial or other oversight.[49] These prosecutorial powers were used 'in a politically discriminating fashion'[50] that strengthened executive power. At the end of the war, prosecutorial powers were reduced and new conditions were introduced to achieve prosecutorial independence from the executive. Di Federico argues that prosecutors are now entitled to automatic promotion based on seniority, to high salaries and to pursue additional paid work, including in political roles. They are subject to limited professional evaluation or supervision, and there are few mechanisms for their removal or transfer between offices.[51] According to Di Federico, this 'extreme version of prosecutorial independence' shows 'utter disregard for "the democratic requirement of accountability"'.[52] Caianiello warns that, on a practical level, it carries 'a genuine threat of arbitrary or inconsistent decisions',[53] which, Di Federico further argues, risks 'defeat of one of the ultimate goals it is intended to guarantee, i.e. the equality of all citizens before the criminal law'.[54]

South Africa took the opposite approach to Italy, and privileged prosecutorial accountability over prosecutorial independence. South Africa's Attorney General was historically responsible for prosecutions in the same way as their Australian counterpart. Following the end of Apartheid during the early 1990s, the National Prosecuting Authority (NPA) was established to achieve independence in prosecutorial decision-making.[55] However, the President retains authority to appoint and dismiss DPPs in order to uphold prosecutorial accountability.[56] The protracted

[47] J Spencer, *Review of Public Prosecution Services (NZ)* (September 2011) 64.

[48] SB Burbank, 'Judicial Independence, Judicial Accountability and Interbranch Relations' (2007) 95 *Georgetown Law Journal* 909, 912.

[49] M Ploscowe, 'Purging Italian Criminal Justice of Fascism' (1945) 45 *Columbia Law Review* 240, 247–51.

[50] G Di Federico, 'Prosecutorial Independence and the Democratic Requirement of Accountability in Italy: Analysis of a Deviant Case in a Comparative Perspective' (1998) 38 *British Journal of Criminology* 371, 375.

[51] ibid 376–82.

[52] ibid 385, 378.

[53] M Caianiello, 'The Italian Public Prosecutor: An Inquisitorial Figure in Adversarial Proceedings?' in E Luna and M Wade (eds), *Transnational Perspectives on Prosecutorial Power* (Oxford, Oxford University Press, 2011) 250, 261.

[54] Di Federico (n 50) 385.

[55] Constitution of the Republic of South Africa (1996), s 179(4).

[56] P De Vos, 'When Political and Prosecutorial Prerogatives Clash in a "Neo-Patrimonial" State: The Case of South Africa's National Prosecuting Authority', Conference Paper, The Evolving Role of the Prosecutor Domestically and Internationally, 28–29 July 2016, 3.

prosecution of former President Jacob Zuma evidences how this authority can be misused.

In 2007, Zuma was charged with having received payments in exchange for political influence while in the position of Deputy President. However, the National Director of Public Prosecutions (NDPP) cited insufficient prospects of conviction for the decision not to prosecute him.[57] In 2008, the High Court of South Africa described the NDPP's decision as a 'bizarre' 'negation of the Constitutional imperatives … to prosecute without fear and favour, independently'.[58] The NDPP resigned, and his replacement announced that Zuma would be indicted. However, the replacement NDPP was suspended by President Mbeki,[59] and then permanently removed from office.[60] The subsequent Acting NDPP issued an 87-page indictment against Zuma alleging racketeering, corruption, money laundering, tax evasion and fraud offences.

In 2008, Mbeki resigned the presidency after the High Court of South Africa ruled he had improperly interfered with the operations of the NPA, including in Zuma's prosecution. In 2009, just before Zuma's election as President, the NDPP again discontinued his prosecution. In 2016, the High Court of South Africa found that the decision was 'irrational', and that the NDPP had 'ignored the importance of the oath of office which demanded of him to act independently and without fear or favour'.[61] The focus on prosecutorial accountability enabled profound political interference in a prosecution relating to allegations of corruption by the most senior political official in the country. It undermined prosecutorial independence to a catastrophic degree.

Italy and South Africa are extreme examples arising from unique political histories. However, they demonstrate the difficulty of balancing the ostensibly compatible values of independence and accountability, and how imbalance can undermine the integrity of any prosecution system seeking to uphold both values.

As discussed in chapter six, minority voices in the early parliamentary debates anticipated problems with the dual commitment to independence and accountability under the ODPP system. They doubted that an Attorney General's prosecutorial role could be limited enough to ensure independence but extensive enough to ensure accountability. Despite local concerns and international warnings about

[57] *National Director of Public Prosecutions v Zuma* [2009] ZASCA 1 [40].

[58] *Zuma v National Director of Public Prosecutions* 1 All SA 54 [150].

[59] F Ginwala, *Report of the Enquiry into the Fitness of Advocate VP Pikoli to Hold the Office of National Director of Public Prosecutions* (4 November 2008) 15.

[60] *National Director of Public Prosecutions v Zuma* [2009] ZASCA 1 [4]–[15].

[61] *Democratic Alliance v Acting National Director of Public Prosecutions and Others* (19577/2009 [2016] ZAGPPHC 255 [92]. The Democratic Alliance is the official opposition party in the Republic of South Africa. Both the NDPP and Zuma unsuccessfully appealed the decision to the Supreme Court: *Acting National Director of Public Prosecutions and Others v Democratic Alliance Re: Democratic Alliance v Acting National Director of Public Prosecutions and Others* [2016] ZAGPPHC 489. Zuma initiated various legal challenges and, in October 2023, the Supreme Court of Appeal of South Africa dismissed his appeal, claiming bias on the part of the members of the High Court of South Africa: *Zuma v Downer and Another* [2023] ZASCA 132.

imbalance between these values, the commitment to independence that drove the establishment of the ODPPs is still promoted above accountability. This emphasis exacerbates the tension inherent in seeking to achieve both independence and accountability.

B. Australian Focus on Independence

On the twenty-fifth anniversary of the Commonwealth ODPP in 2009, Attorney General Robert McClelland described himself as 'accountable to the Parliament for decisions made in the prosecution process'.[62] However, he also stressed that 'operational decisions are, and must continue to be, made by the CDPP – independently from the political process. Independence is the key'.[63] In 2018, the Victorian Shadow Attorney General, John Pesutto, did not even mention prosecutorial accountability when he addressed the appointment of the new DPP:

> I cannot emphasise enough how important independence is for the DPP … I encourage the DPP and the chief Crown prosecutor to assert their independence and not be guided by any influences that seek in any way to qualify or fetter that very important independence.[64]

While the focus on independence reflects the origins of the ODPPs, it ignores the fact that accountability was also a core value of the ODPP system. It creates the erroneous, but influential, view that Attorneys General either cannot or should not be involved in prosecutorial decisions. This situation discourages the Attorney General from openly undertaking their prosecutorial role, which undermines their ability to achieve accountability.

(i) Belief that Attorney General Cannot be Involved in Prosecutions

The infrequent, modern parliamentary debates on prosecutorial issues demonstrate uncertainty about the limits of the Attorney General's prosecutorial role. They create an overall misapprehension that Attorneys General do not have the power to be involved in prosecutorial decisions. The extended attention to the decision in *Nemer* did not clarify the extent and nature of the South Australian Attorney General's prosecutorial role. In 2016, six years into his term of office and more than a decade after *Nemer* was decided, the Attorney General, John Rau, tentatively stated: 'If I am not mistaken (and I am sure somebody will correct me), the Attorney already has the power, if they choose to exercise it, to direct the

[62] R McClelland, 'Remarks at the Commonwealth Director of Public Prosecutions' 25th Anniversary Dinner', Speech, Old Parliament House, 5 March 2009, 5.

[63] ibid 5.

[64] Victoria, *Parliamentary Debates*, Legislative Assembly, 9 December 1982, 7 June 2018, 1909 (John Pesutto).

Director of Public Prosecutions.'[65] This statement about the scope of his prosecutorial role was cautious, but correct.

Other Australian parliamentarians have proffered confident, but incorrect, characterisations of the Attorney General's prosecutorial role. In 2015, Independent Tasmanian MP Teunis Mulder asked:

> Would we entertain the Director of Public Prosecutions being told which cases to prosecute and which cases not to prosecute? Not in a fit. Prosecutions must be independent of political control or else who will be deciding who goes to the salt mines?[66]

His comments recognise that the Attorney General does not have power to direct the Tasmanian DPP in particular cases. However, they ignore the fact that the DPP is required to act as counsel for the Crown upon the direction or request of the Attorney General,[67] and that the Attorney General can initiate or terminate prosecutions upon their own initiative.[68] In the following year, the South Australian Shadow Attorney General, Vickie Chapman, claimed that prosecutors 'have autonomous responsibility and they are protected by law from interference. Any of the ministers … cannot ring up the DPP and say, "I want this person's backside. I want this person charged."'[69] While this is an accurate statement on the prohibition on Attorneys General demanding a prosecution for personal or political reasons, it ignores their statutory power to direct the DPP in particular cases.

The focus on independence, and the fear of improper political involvement in prosecutions that underpins it, does not just obscure the existence and importance of the Attorney General's prosecutorial powers. Even more significantly, it results in the normative view that Attorneys General should not exercise any prosecutorial power they do have, because any involvement in prosecutions inappropriately infringes the independence of the DPP and, therefore, the prosecutorial process.

(ii) Belief that Attorney General should not be Involved in Prosecutions

In 2015, Senator Matthew Canavan claimed that Attorneys General should not oversee prosecutorial decisions made by the ODPPs. During debate referencing the Australian Wheat Board and the 'oil-for-food scandal',[70] he objected to the suggestion that any politician 'should be double-guessing and questioning the judgement of the various directors of public prosecutions in our state and federal

[65] South Australia, *Parliamentary Debates*, House of Assembly, 17 May 2016, 5308 (John Rau, Attorney General).

[66] Tasmania, *Parliamentary Debates*, Legislative Council, 15 March 2016, 46 (Teunis Mulder).

[67] Director of Public Prosecutions Act 1973 (Tas), s 12(1)(e).

[68] ibid s 12(2).

[69] South Australia, *Parliamentary Debates*, House of Assembly, 23 March 2016, 4828 (Vickie Chapman).

[70] A Royal Commission found in 2006 that the Australian Wheat Board contravened Australian law and the United Nations Oil-for-Food Humanitarian Programme by supplying wheat to the regime of

jurisdictions'.[71] His assertion ignores the obligation of oversight of the DPP by the Attorney General that is critical to prosecutorial accountability.

The requirement of consent to prosecutions by an Attorney General is outside the scope of this book, because it is mandated in a small number of statutes, rather than forming part of the overall legislative and policy framework for prosecutions.[72] However, parliamentary debates on consent provisions have revealed opposition to the exercise of the Attorney General's prosecutorial powers that are part of the overall framework.

In South Australia (SA) in 2016, the Attorney General, John Rau, argued that it would not be 'good public policy' to require the Attorney General to consent to prosecutions of minors for sexual offences.[73] He explained that the prosecutorial system was based on 'trust in the prosecutorial discretion being exercised by … independent people', and that 'politicising the prosecutorial determination … as a matter of principle, is a bad idea'.[74] These statements fail to acknowledge that the Attorney General's consent to certain prosecutions would be compatible with their role of overseeing the prosecutorial system to ensure its accountability.

The appropriateness of the exercise of the Attorney General's statutory power to give directions to the DPP has also been disputed. NSW Minister Brad Hazzard was questioned in 2015 about an Independent Commission against Corruption investigation.[75] He responded: 'if you expect as Attorney General … that it is appropriate for you to give directions to the independent Director of Public Prosecutions, then, sir, you also should never be a leader in this place'.[76] This comment ignored the fact that the political leadership of the Attorney General was a critical component of prosecutorial accountability, and that the NSW Attorney General can issue guidelines to the DPP on general policy, although not in specific cases.[77]

Saddam Hussein: T Cole, *Report of the Inquiry into Certain Australian Companies in Relation to the UN Oil-for-Food Programme* (27 November 2006).

[71] Commonwealth of Australia, *Parliamentary Debates*, Senate, 13 August 2015, 5219 (Matthew Canavan).

[72] See, eg Criminal Code Act 1995 (Cth), s 83.5: 'Consent of Attorney-General required for prosecutions.' The possibility of political bias affecting consent to prosecutions has been identified in the United Kingdom: Law Commission, *Consents to Prosecution: Item 11 of the Sixth Programme of Law Reform Criminal Law* (19 October 1998) 29–30.

[73] South Australia, *Parliamentary Debates*, House of Assembly, 17 May 2016, 5308 (John Rau, Attorney General).

[74] ibid 5309.

[75] New South Wales, Office of the Inspector of the Independent Commission Against Corruption, *Report* Pursuant to Section 77A Independent Commission Against Corruption Act 1988 Operation 'Hale': ICAC re Margaret Cunneen SC & Ors (4 December 2015). Operation Hale investigated allegations that Margaret Cunneen and her son attempted to pervert the course of justice by advising the driver of a motor vehicle involved in an accident to feign chest pains to avoid a blood-alcohol level test. The investigation has been criticised: I Dobinson and L Houston, 'ICAC's Operation "Hale": A Low Point in the History of the Agency' (2017) 29 *Current Issues in Criminal Justice* 57.

[76] New South Wales, *Parliamentary Debates*, Legislative Assembly, 18 February 2016 (no page reference) (Brad Hazzard).

[77] DPP Act (NSW) (n 40) ss 26(1), (3).

The inherent conflict involved in upholding both independence and accountability generates confusion about the extent of the Attorney General's prosecutorial powers and the appropriateness of their exercise. The conflict inadvertently undermines the ability of the Attorney General to fulfil the role that was considered fundamental to upholding community standards in the criminal justice system. However, more dangerously, accountability mechanisms depend on Attorneys General exercising their prosecutorial role openly. The confusion about the Attorney General's prosecutorial role enables them to exploit the independence of the DPPs. They can covertly engage in prosecutions, obscure the exercise of their own prosecutorial powers and influence prosecutions but avoid accountability.

C. Deliberately Avoiding Accountability

According to Ackerman, independent agencies can be established to 'cover up problems instead of actually to address the issues they were created to solve'.[78] A number of commentators warned that ODPPs would have just this character, and that Attorneys General could use them for 'political cover' to consciously avoid accountability for prosecutions. In 1989, WA parliamentarian Phillip Pendal suggested that an ODPP would enable the Attorney General to 'escape accountability' to Parliament.[79] This view was shared by Bradley Selway, Crown Solicitor of SA during the establishment of the ODPPs.[80] He agreed that 'conferring the function of a statutory officer may protect the Attorney General and the government as a whole from accountability for tough decisions'.[81] This view was substantiated, at least in part, by the experience of the first DPP for WA. John McKechnie reflected in 1996 that he was never subject to political influence because 'each of the three Attorneys General has recognised the considerable political advantage of remaining distant from the prosecution process'.[82] Commonwealth parliamentary debates about the related issues of consent provisions in national security legislation and prosecutions of former ASIS agent Witness K and his lawyer, Bernard Collaery, also vindicated the concerns about Attorneys General deliberately avoiding accountability for prosecutorial decisions.

The Australian Security Intelligence Organisation Act 1979 (Cth) establishes Australia's national security service to gather information and produce security

[78] J Ackerman, 'Understanding Independent Accountability Agencies' in S Rose-Ackerman and P Lindseth (eds), *Comparative Administrative Law* (Cheltenham, Edward Elgar Publishing, 2010) 264, 267.

[79] Western Australia, *Parliamentary Debates*, Legislative Council, 24 October 1989, 3461–62 (Phillip Pendal).

[80] J Williams, 'Bradley Maxwell Selway: A Personal Tribute' (2005) 33 *Federal Law Review* 181, 182.

[81] B Selway, 'Nemer: Ethics and the DPP', Lecture, Selected Issues in Criminal Law & Procedure, University of Adelaide, 7 July 2004, 4.

[82] J McKechnie, 'Directors of Public Prosecutions: Independent and Accountable' (1996) 26 *University of Western Australia Law Review* 266, 275.

intelligence on activities such as espionage and politically motivated violence.[83] In 2014, section 35P was inserted into the Act to address unauthorised disclosure of information about special intelligence operations. In 2015, Parliament debated its amendment. Attorney General George Brandis argued that requiring the Attorney General to consent to certain prosecutions provided a 'safeguard' for accountability, because a 'political officer would accept personal and public responsibility. So it would not merely be a matter of prosecutorial discretion exercised by the Commonwealth DPP.'[84] Brandis expressed the same sentiments in debates later that year on the Australian Citizenship Amendment (Allegiance to Australia) Bill (Citizenship Amendment Bill). The Bill sought to amend the Australian Citizenship Act 2007 (Cth) so that dual citizens would lose Australian citizenship if they engaged in conduct including involvement in terrorist activities or wars against Australia. He confirmed that the 'commencement of a prosecution is ordinarily entirely a matter for the exercise of a discretion' by the DPP, but qualified that in national security cases, the Attorney General must take responsibility 'as the politically answerable minister'.[85]

Brandis's comments express the orthodoxy that the ODPP system is independent but requires political oversight, especially on national security matters, to ensure prosecutorial accountability. The comments would have been uncontroversial if not for contemporaneous commentary on the prosecutions of Witness K and Collaery. That commentary supported not only the general warnings about Attorneys Generals avoiding accountability for prosecutions, but also Stenning's specific warning that 'national security' can be used as 'a fig-leaf to cover more prosaic, partisan interests' in prosecuting.[86]

D. Prosecutions of Witness K and Bernard Collaery

Witness K and Bernard Collaery faced charges related to an alleged conspiracy to disclose details of a 2004 espionage operation. During the operation, the Australian government placed illegal recording devices in Timor-Leste's cabinet rooms and office of the Prime Minister to fraudulently gain advantage in negotiations for an oil and gas treaty.[87] In 2021, Witness K pleaded guilty to one charge of conspiring with his lawyer, Bernard Collaery, to disclose intelligence information to the government of Timor-Leste. He was convicted of the offence and placed under a three-month suspended sentence.[88] Collaery contested four charges of

[83] Australian Security Intelligence Organisation Act 1979 (Cth), ss 4, 17.

[84] Commonwealth of Australia, *Parliamentary Debates*, Senate, 26 March 2015, 2649 (George Brandis, Attorney General).

[85] ibid 1 December 2015, 9513 (George Brandis, Attorney General).

[86] Stenning, 'Discretion, Politics' (n 20) 361.

[87] *Seizure and Detention of Certain Documents and Data (Timor-Leste v Australia) (Provisional Measures Order)* [2014] ICJ; Porter (n 14).

[88] R Payne, 'Witness K and Bernard Collaery: Civil Liberty and Rule of Law Concerns' (New South Wales Council for Civil Liberties, 14 October 2021) www.nswccl.org.au/witness_k_and_bernard_collaery.

breaching section 39 of the Intelligence Services Act 2001 (Cth) and one charge of conspiracy to breach section 39, contained in a 2019 indictment based upon events alleged to have occurred during 2012 and 2014.[89] In 2022, after a change in Federal government, the charges against Collaery were withdrawn.[90]

After investigations were commenced but before charges were laid, Attorney General Brandis was questioned in Parliament about possible prosecutions. The questioning occurred in December 2015, just two days after debate on the Citizenship Amendment Bill, where Brandis stressed the importance of the Attorney General's involvement in prosecutions involving national security. However, he refused to answer questions on the prosecutions and explained that it 'would be absolutely wrong of me to respond … as it would involve, among other things, interfering with the discretion of the Commonwealth DPP. It would be absolutely wrong of me, and I will not be drawn.'[91] This was an orthodox statement of prosecutorial independence, just as his previous comments were an orthodox statement of prosecutorial accountability. However, together, they disclosed more than the tension inherent in upholding prosecutorial independence and accountability. The diametrically opposed comments were made within two days of each other. The conflict between them suggested that, as various commentators had foreshadowed, the Attorney General could take or avoid political responsibility for prosecutorial decisions according to political expedience. Brandis did not consent to the prosecutions of Witness K and Collaery before he left office,[92] but his successor Attorney General, Christian Porter, consented to them in 2018.

As in the cases of *Nemer* and *Hurley*, the Attorney General's motivation for involvement in the prosecutions of Witness K and Collaery is opaque. It can plausibly be interpreted as either the appropriate exercise of prosecutorial power to uphold accountability or the inappropriate exercise of prosecutorial powers for partisan, political gain.

On one hand, the Attorney General's consent to the prosecutions of Witness K and Collaery was appropriate and necessary. ASIS gathers and analyses foreign intelligence and conducts counter-intelligence activities with international intelligence and security services.[93] A high level of secrecy is clearly required over secret foreign intelligence related to the protection of Australia and its interests.[94] Any unauthorised disclosure of intelligence could undermine ASIS's ability to disrupt investigations into crimes like terrorism and people smuggling, and

[89] *Collaery v The Queen* [2021] ACTCA 1.

[90] S Zifcak, 'The Unconscionable Prosecution of Bernard Collaery Was an Assault on the Values Australia Holds Dear' *The Conversation* (12 July 2022) theconversation.com/the-unconscionable-prosecution-of-bernard-collaery-was-an-assault-on-the-values-australia-holds-dear-186560.

[91] Commonwealth of Australia, *Parliamentary Debates*, Senate, 3 December 2015, 9922 (George Brandis, Attorney General).

[92] S Cannane and P Cronau, 'Former Attorney-General George Brandis Had "Misgivings" About Prosecuting Witness K and Collaery' *ABC News* (26 August 2019) www.abc.net.au/news/2019-08-26/brandis-had-misgivings-about-prosecuting-witness-k-and-collaery/11449758.

[93] Intelligence Services Act 2001 (Cth), s 6.

[94] Australian Secret Intelligence Service, 'Our Mission' (2021) www.asis.gov.au/About-Us/ASIS-Overview/.

jeopardise Australia's international diplomatic relationships. Attorney General Porter explained in 2018 that he consented to the prosecution after the Commonwealth DPP 'considered the brief of evidence and subsequently made an independent decision that a prosecution was the appropriate course of action'.[95] According to this explanation, the Attorney General's consent was appropriate for this *type* of prosecution because it involved national security issues that were within the portfolio of the Attorney General and beyond the expertise of the DPP. It was also appropriate in the *particular* prosecution because the available evidence was independently assessed by the Commonwealth DPP as meeting the reasonable prospects of conviction and public interest tests.

However, prosecution of the cases generated a strong counter-narrative. The cases originated in allegations of unlawful conduct by the Australian government, including criminal trespass committed by planting surveillance devices in Timor-Leste's cabinet room, and breaches of domestic and international law by taking documents from Witness K and Collaery's offices that belonged to the Timor-Leste government and were subject to legal professional privilege.[96] The applications to have the case heard in a closed trial, and repeated applications for orders to restrict the public disclosure of evidence,[97] heightened suspicions that the prosecution was intended to punish the defendants for revealing government espionage, rather than to address a national security risk.[98] The concerns had enough credibility for politico-legal commentators to describe the prosecution, while it was proceeding, as a 'persecution'[99] and 'a legal fiasco of the first order'[100] that undermines 'the integrity of our democratic system'.[101] These perceptions persisted, and upon the resolution of the case, it was still described as a concern for 'civil liberty and rule of law',[102] 'unconscionable'[103] and 'unjust'.[104]

[95] Porter (n 14).

[96] S Zifcak, 'Why Bernard Collaery's Case is One of the Gravest Threats to Freedom of Expression' (2020) 69 *Law Society of NSW Journal* 88, 88–89; Zifcak, 'The Unconscionable Prosecution' (n 90) theconversation.com/the-unconscionable-prosecution-of-bernard-collaery-was-an-assault-on-the-values-australia-holds-dear-186560.

[97] *R v Collaery* [2019] ACTSC 278.

[98] C Fernandes, 'As Witness K Trial Opens, Questions Over How Much of Timor-Leste Spying Case to Keep Secret From Public' *The Conversation* (13 September 2018) www.theconversation.com/as-witness-k-trial-opens-questions-over-how-much-of-timor-leste-spying-case-to-keep-secret-from-public-103164.

[99] B Keane and C Fernandes, 'Government Goes All Out to Hide the Trial of K and Collaery From Public' *Crikey* (8 November 2018) www.crikey.com.au/2018/11/08/witness-k-trial-government-obstruction/.

[100] S Zifcak, 'Witness K and Bernard Collaery: An Unjust Prosecution Gets Even Worse' *Pearls and Irritations: John Menadue's Public Policy Journal* (12 October 2020) johnmenadue.com/spencer-zifcak-witness-k-and-bernard-collaery-an-unjust-prosecution-gets-even-worse/.

[101] M Miller, 'Why the Trial of "Witness K" and Bernard Collaery Should Concern All Australians' (newmatilda.com, 21 September 2018) *The New Matilda* newmatilda.com/2018/09/21/trial-witness-k-bernard-collaery-concern-australians/.

[102] R Payne, 'Witness K and Bernard Collaery: Civil Liberty and Rule of Law Concerns' (New South Wales Council for Civil Liberties, 14 October 2021) www.nswccl.org.au/witness_k_and_bernard_collaery.

[103] Zifcak, 'The Unconscionable Prosecution' (n 90).

[104] B Haigh, 'Labor's Mark Dreyfus Undoes Unjust Prosecution of Bernard Collaery' *Independent Australia* (9 July 2022) independentaustralia.net/politics/politics-display/labors-mark-dreyfus-undoes-unjust-prosecution-of-bernard-collaery-,16543.

The factors that legitimated the Attorney General's consent also justified him invoking the relevant statutory power to initiate the prosecution himself.[105] The initiation of the prosecution by the DPP has, therefore, been interpreted not as the independent exercise of the DPP's discretion, but as a deliberate strategy to distance the Attorney General and the government from decisions they actually made. Tasmanian Senator for the Australian Greens, Nick McKim, alleged openly that the Attorney General 'attempted to pass responsibility for it to the DPP, but ultimately this was a political decision made at the political level by the Attorney General'.[106] Senator McKim's allegations need to be treated with some scepticism. Larkin and Mulgan both argue that in modern parliaments 'the heavy lifting of ministerial accountability'[107] is undertaken by opposition parties seeking 'weapons' to 'hold the government accountable and thus improve their own electoral prospects'.[108] However, the civil rights activist Professor Spencer Zifcak agreed with McKim that

> two people who acted in the national interest by disclosing unlawful activity undertaken by Australia's overseas intelligence service in bugging East Timor's Cabinet were the defendants in the criminal case. Those in government who initiated the unlawful, covert operation, through their successors in government, had become the prosecutors. Something had gone very wrong.[109]

The prosecutions of Witness K and his lawyer may not actually have been improperly motivated. Even upon taking responsibility for discontinuing the prosecution, the new Labor Attorney General, Mark Dreyfus, did not allege impropriety on the part of the previous government or Attorney General, or question the judgement of the DPP. He actually impliedly seemed to support the original decision to prosecute by reflecting that

> prosecutions involve a balancing of interests. The balance of interests can change over time … Today I have determined that this prosecution should end. My decision was informed by the Government's commitment to Australia's national security and our relations with our neighbours. This is an exceptional case. Governments must protect secrets, and this government remains steadfast in our commitment to keep Australians safe by keeping secrets out of the wrong hands. The long-standing practice of government has been to neither confirm nor deny claims made about intelligence matters. And I will strictly adhere to that practice.[110]

However, the prosecutions are open to the interpretation of political motivation. This possibility demonstrates that the ODPP system does not simply enable the type of political influence on prosecutions the ODPPs were intended to eliminate. The establishment of independent statutory offices that deliberately

[105] DPP Act (Cth) (n 40) s 10(1)(a).
[106] Commonwealth of Australia, *Parliamentary Debates*, Senate, 16 August 2018, 4992 (Nicholas McKim).
[107] Larkin (n 8) 98.
[108] Mulgan, 'Ministerial Responsibility' (n 12) 190.
[109] Zifcak, 'The Unconscionable Prosecution' (n 90).
[110] M Dreyfus, 'Press Conference on Bernard Collaery', Press Conference, 7 July 2022.

keep the decision to prosecute at 'arm's length' from Attorneys General enables politically motivated decisions to be made 'behind the scenes'. Attorneys General are able to avoid accounting for the exercise of their powers in an open manner, by attributing the decision to the 'independent' ODPPs. The manifest possibility of this conduct, if not its demonstrated occurrence, undermines the accountability of the prosecutorial system.

III. Conclusions

The adoption of parliamentary accountability as the key form of prosecutorial accountability in a system based on prosecutorial independence creates practical difficulties. The accountability of the ODPPs is dependent on effective oversight by Parliament, through the Attorney General. However, the emergence of the 'new' administrative law, broadly contemporaneously with the establishment of the ODPPs, reflected the limited effectiveness of Parliament's control over the Attorney General. The Attorney General's statutory prosecutorial powers technically enable them to ensure prosecutorial decisions are accountable. However, the commitment to independence from political interference limits, in a practical sense, the level of involvement in the exercise of the prosecutorial discretion possible by the Attorney General.

The tension inherent in upholding both independence and accountability can be manipulated by Attorneys General. They can use the existence of statutory offices as a 'shield' that enables them to engage in the politically motivated exercise of their prosecutorial discretion. The expectation that ODPPs are independent masks the involvement of the Attorneys General, and weak parliamentary oversight prevents additional scrutiny of their actions. This situation enables them to avoid accounting to Parliament for any prosecutorial action they do take, which renders parliamentary accountability ineffective over the Attorney General and so compromises the accountability of the prosecutorial process.

The concurrent commitment to prosecutorial independence and parliamentary accountability compromises the accountability of the Attorney General just as it compromises the independence of the DPP. However, the accountability of the prosecutorial process also depends on the accountability of the DPP.

10

Accountability and the DPP

The ineffectiveness of traditional processes for achieving the Attorney General's accountability to Parliament means that the accountability of the prosecutorial process relies heavily on the accountability of the Director of Public Prosecutions (DPP). The investigation of the prosecution of Bruce Lehrmann for the rape illustrates a broad range of factors that can improperly influence the DPP's decision to prosecute in a particular case, and can jeopardise the rights of a defendant and the reputation of the criminal justice system. However, the courts prevent administrative law mechanisms from holding the DPP to account and achieving prosecutorial accountability. They deny the need for the adoption of accountability mechanisms under the 'new' administrative law without considering the applicability to prosecutions of mechanisms such as merits review by administrative tribunals, a specialist Ombudsman or a requirement to provide public reasons for decisions. DPP decisions are non-justiciable because prosecutorial discretion was once part of the prerogative power. Modern courts resist the application of judicial review of the decision to prosecute out of both concern that it would undermine the separation of powers doctrine and the belief that parliamentary accountability adequately holds DPPs to account. However, this judicial confidence in parliamentary accountability is misguided and discourages the adoption of external accountability mechanisms, leaving the Offices of Director of Public Prosecutions (ODPPs) accountable largely through self-regulating, internal accountability mechanisms.

I. The Lehrmann Prosecution

As discussed in chapter eight, Bruce Lehrmann faced trial in 2022 for the rape of Brittany Higgins in Parliament House in 2019. Prior to the trial, the DPP, Shane Drumgold, alleged wrongdoing on the part of the investigating police. He subsequently resiled from the allegations, but not before a Board of Inquiry into the Criminal Justice System was established to investigate possible improper conduct on the part of the police, the ODPP or the Victims of Crime Commissioner.[1]

[1] W Sofronoff, *Australian Capital Territory, Board of Inquiry: Criminal Justice System, Final Report* (31 July 2023) 5, 152.

Ultimately, the Chair of the Inquiry, Walter Sofronoff KC, made findings of misconduct against the DPP. The findings were serious enough that Sofronoff invited Drumgold to make submissions as to why he should not recommend to the Attorney General that Drumgold was not a fit and proper person to hold the office of DPP, and his tenure should be terminated for misbehaviour.[2] Sofronoff only declined to take this action after accepting submissions from Drumgold's counsel that such a recommendation was beyond his terms of reference.[3] The DPP resigned his position in 2023 and so pre-empted the need for investigation of his continuation in the role.[4] He also commenced legal action in the Australian Capital Territory (ACT) Supreme Court. The court found that Sofronoff's extensive communication with a journalist from *The Australian* newspaper gave rise to a reasonable apprehension of bias, and that his criticisms of Drumgold's cross-examination of a senator were 'legally unreasonable'.[5] Despite the outcome of the legal challenge, the finding of the report illustrates the ways a DPP may act improperly in office, even if Drumgold did not act improperly. The following discussion illustrates how the type of conduct imputed to Drumgold, although not necessarily undertaken by him, can adversely affect the decision to prosecute.[6]

The investigation and prosecution of Lehrmann presented unique challenges. An allegation that a rape was committed in Parliament House inevitably attracted media attention that challenged the defendant's right to a fair trial. The public exposure and its effects were heightened because Higgins gave interviews about the allegations to several journalists throughout 2021, including after Lehrmann had been charged and appeared in court. The publicity surrounding the interviews 'sparked enormous media and public interest', protests against the perceived lack of response by the Federal government[7] and a public apology from the Prime Minister,[8] all of which explicitly or implicitly accepted the truth of the allegations and, therefore, Lehrmann's guilt. The media attention placed considerable pressure on all those involved in the investigation and prosecution. One of the investigating officers explained:

> We had the Prime Minister commenting on it. We had senior government ministers making comment in the media on it. We had two government ministers who were witnesses within the investigation. There was also a significant movement at the time. The MeToo movement was gaining momentum. And the alleged victim in this case

[2] Notice of Proposed Adverse Comments from Walter Sofronoff KC, Chairperson, Board of Inquiry, to Neville Shane Drumgold SC DPP, 9 June 2023, 10.

[3] Sofronoff (n 1) 7.

[4] ACT Government, 'Joint Media Statement – Chief Minister and Attorney-General', Media Release, 7 August 2023.

[5] *Drumgold v Board of Inquiry – Criminal Justice System & Ors* – SC 347/23, Originating Application – Judicial Review (25 August 2023); *Drumgold v Board of Inquiry & Ors (No 3)* [2024] ACTSC (unreported) [399], [484].

[6] Sofronoff also found that Drumgold acted in a 'grossly unethical' way by putting to Senator Reynolds in cross-examination baseless allegations that implied she attempted to pervert the course of justice: Sofronoff (n 1) 136–37, 141–42; Notice of Proposed Adverse Comments (n 2) 6–7. However, this conduct does not relate to the decision to prosecute.

[7] *R v Lehrmann (No 2)* [2022] ACTSC 92 [7]–[9], [16]–[17].

[8] Commonwealth of Australia, *Parliamentary Debates*, House of Representatives, 8 February 2022, 1–2 (Scott Morrison, Prime Minister).

> became involved in that through very high profile journalists, which again created more of a media interest.[9]

However, even acknowledging the challenges of the prosecution, and agreeing with the decisions to proceed with, and then discontinue, the prosecution, Sofronoff was highly critical of Drumgold's conduct in making the decisions. His adverse findings related to Drumgold's dealings with police; interpretations of legal professional privilege and protected communications; treatment of colleagues; management of publicity; and public statements about the discontinuation of the case. As discussed below, these findings of the handling of the case all highlight the DPP's obligation to continually assess the veracity of the evidence and the reasonable prospects of conviction as the matter proceeds through and beyond trial.[10] The Director of the Centre for Public Integrity, Geoffrey Watson SC, assessed that the findings against Drumgold have 'no legal effect' given the outcome of judicial review. However, the issues themselves remain valuable for illustrating the type of issues that raise prosecutorial accountability.[11]

A. Investigation and Freedom of Information

Problems emerged early in the investigation, when Drumgold became frustrated with the investigators' doubts about the truthfulness of Higgins's allegations. He developed a suspicion that police were either actively undermining the prosecution or were so focused on the weaknesses in the evidence that their 'confirmation bias' limited the evidence-gathering process.[12] Instead of reporting his concerns to the National Anti-Corruption Commission or the AFP's Professional Standards Command to instigate a confidential investigation, Drumgold wrote to the Chief Police Officer calling for a public inquiry and impugning named police officers and Senator Linda Reynolds, in whose office the rape was alleged to have occurred. According to Sofronoff, this letter contained claims that were 'false' and 'defamatory', and had the potential to 'prejudice public confidence in the administration of criminal justice'[13] and aggravate Higgins's already fragile mental health.[14] The sending of the letter represented 'the path with the highest risk of his unsubstantiated claims entering the public domain'.[15] The letter was, indeed, subject to a freedom of information application from a journalist in 2021. Sofronoff found that Drumgold

[9] Sofronoff (n 1) 98.

[10] Director of Public Prosecutions, South Australia, *Statement of Prosecution Policy & Guidelines* (2014) 5; Memorandum from Nicholas Cowdery to Police Association of South Australia, 27 April 2015, 2.

[11] Patrick Bell, 'Contact between journalist and head of inquiry into Bruce Lehrmann's prosecution gave rise to an impression of bias, court rules' *ABC News* (8 March 2024) abc.net.au/news/2024-03-04/former-act-dpp-shane-drumgold-challenges-inquiry-findings/103542010.

[12] ibid 16–21, 24–26, 35, 49.

[13] Notice of Proposed Adverse Comments (n 2) 8–9.

[14] Sofronoff (n 1) 152.

[15] ibid 153.

not only hastily authorised the release of the letter, but when the police complained about the absence of the required consultation, he denied direct knowledge of the application and 'shamefully' and 'falsely' blamed the executive officer he had unambiguously advised to release it.[16]

B. Protected Communications

During the investigation, and with her permission, police obtained records of Higgins's sessions with a counsellor. These records constituted a 'protected confidence' that were erroneously disclosed as part of the police brief in 2021. When Lehrmann's barrister was advised of the wrongful disclosure, he returned the brief unread, but Drumgold held the view that the protection of confidence did not apply to his professional review of the notes, and he did read them.[17] Sofronoff found

> a disturbing lack of awareness in Mr Drumgold's understanding of his prosecutorial duties [and he] should not have read the notes because it placed him in position in which he may be thought to have significant information about the complainant that was denied to the defence.[18]

C. Disclosure and Privilege

Sofronoff criticised Drumgold for his interpretation and application of the obligation of disclosure over a number of items of evidence. During its investigation, police prepared several documents analysing inconsistencies and weaknesses in the prosecution evidence, particularly that of Higgins, and identifying further areas of investigation.[19] The defence applied for disclosure of the documents. Drumgold resisted disclosure on the grounds of legal professional privilege,[20] even though the police's legal representatives advised that the documents needed to be disclosed. Sofronoff found that Drumgold breached the obligation to disclose to defence all relevant material, noting the rule of thumb, 'if in doubt, disclose'.[21] Sofronoff further determined that Drumgold misrepresented the nature and purpose of the documents to the Chief Justice, to falsely claim legal professional privilege. Drumgold was found to have advanced this false claim by asking a junior lawyer to swear an affidavit that inaccurately suggested a source in ACT police advised the documents were subject to privilege, after a more senior lawyer had pointed out that such an action would breach relevant hearsay rules.[22] Overall, the finding was that the DPP deliberately advanced a false claim of legal

[16] ibid 163, 166–69.
[17] ibid 44–45, 54–57.
[18] ibid 61.
[19] ibid 67–69.
[20] Notice of Proposed Adverse Comments (n 2) 4–6.
[21] Sofronoff (n 1) 65.
[22] ibid 87–91.

professional privilege in court 'to thwart the defence from obtaining information that was potentially helpful in avoiding what might well have been a wrongful conviction' and that in so doing 'egregiously abused his authority and betrayed the trust of his young staff member to whom he owed a duty to be a mentor and role model'.[23]

A similar issue arose once the trial commenced. After Higgins's testimony was played in court, the Chief of Staff of the Minister in whose office the rape was alleged to have been committed emailed Drumgold to advise that Higgins's evidence included patently false statements regarding payment to go interstate during the election campaign and, possibly, not return to her position. As the evidence had the potential to significantly undermine Higgins's testimony, it should have been disclosed to defence, but was not.[24]

D. Media and a Fair Trial

In 2021, the television programme *The Project* aired an interview between Higgins and television presenter Lisa Wilkinson about the allegations of rape and the workplace culture in Parliament House. The segment received an award at the TV Week Logie Awards, which recognise achievement in Australian television. On receipt of the award, Wilkinson gave a speech that praised Higgins, and implied the guilt of Lehrmann. Wilkinson was strongly criticised for her speech in the media[25] and by the ACT Chief Justice, who vacated the trial date for the prosecution because of the speech's 'immediacy, its intensity and its capacity to obliterate the important distinction between an allegation that remains untested' and one that has been proven in court.[26] However, Wilkinson argued, and Sofronff accepted, that she had read the speech to Drumgold ahead of delivering it, and he had failed in his duty as a barrister and as DPP by not warning her that delivering the speech could jeopardise Lehrmann's right to a fair trial.[27]

Sofronoff found that Drumgold compounded this error in two significant and related ways. First, he misled the court by claiming that he had only heard the first line of the speech and had given an appropriate warning to Wilkinson. Secondly, during a defence application for adjournment in 2022, he referred in court to a document that he described as a contemporaneous note made by his instructing solicitor that supported his recollection of the meeting. In fact, the document by the junior colleague copied an email authored by Drumgold himself and conflicted with the colleague's own recollection of the meeting.[28]

[23] ibid 96.
[24] ibid 129–32; Notice of Proposed Adverse Comments (n 2) 7.
[25] 'Lisa's Logie Lashing' *Media Watch* (27 June 2022) www.abc.net.au/mediawatch/episodes/lisa/13948078.
[26] *R v Lehrmann* (No 3) [2022] ACTSC 145 [37]–[38].
[27] Notice of Proposed Adverse Comments (n 2) 3–4.
[28] Sofronoff (n 1) 110, 115; Notice of Proposed Adverse Comments (n 2) 2–3.

E. Public Statements on Discontinuation

Finally, Sofronoff criticised Drumgold for comments he made publicly explaining the decision not to reinstitute proceedings following the mistrial. Drumgold explained that he only discontinued the prosecution due to the public interest consideration of Higgins's mental health. He added that 'when I first examined the brief of evidence … I formed the clear view that there was a reasonable prospect of conviction. This is a view I still hold today.'[29] He also publicly commended Higgins for her 'bravery, grace and dignity'.[30] Sofronoff concluded that these statements, combined, implied that Drumgold accepted the truth of Higgins's complaint, and so 'undermined the presumption of innocence to which Mr Lehrmann was entitled'.[31] His supportive comments about Higgins are actually linked to the intense adverse publicity she faced in the light of the report and do not necessarily reflect a view about the truth of her allegations. However, in the context of the comments about the reasonable prospect of conviction, the comments could suggest an assertion of Lehrmann's guilt.

The discussion of the findings against Drumgold illustrates the power of the DPP in the decision to prosecute, the multiple ways in which that power could be abused, and the catastrophic effects of abuse for individuals involved in the prosecution and the integrity of the criminal justice system overall. The case illustrates the need for accountability measures to apply to the DPP and the risks associated with a deficit in these measures.

II. Judicial Review

The prosecutorial discretion that is now exercised in an independent, Australian statutory office was originally exercised as a prerogative power by the Attorney General for England and Wales. As successors of the Attorney General and contemporaries of other executive decision-makers, the ODDPs draw on two different traditions of accountability. The primary distinction between the two traditions is that, historically, prerogative decisions of the Attorney General were not subject to judicial review. The principle of the non-justiciability of the Attorney General's prosecutorial decisions is applied to decisions of the ODPPs, but without any apparent principled justification.

[29] ACT Director of Public Prosecutions, 'RE: DPP v Lehrmann SCC 264 o021', Media Release, 2 December 2022, 1–2.

[30] ibid.

[31] Notice of Proposed Adverse Comments (n 2) 9–10.

A. Statutory Offices

AV Dicey distilled precepts of executive accountability that became entrenched in the common law and constitutional law. According to Meyerson, part of Dicey's legacy is the view that the rule of law is only upheld if courts have the power to enforce the legal limits of executive power.[32] Administrative law reflects this legacy through the principle that individuals who are affected by an executive decision can 'require the executive government to submit its decision to scrutiny … by an independent judiciary'.[33] As a result, Burton Crawford argues that in common law countries, judicial review of executive decisions is an essential feature of the rule of law.[34] Modern Australian courts, therefore, check the power of most executive decision-makers through statutory and common law powers to review the legality, but not the merits, of executive decisions. The availability of judicial review protects the rights of individuals by preventing the executive from 'exceeding the powers and functions assigned to [it] by law',[35] and safeguards individuals against 'administrative tyranny'.[36]

The institution of a prosecution is an executive decision made within a statutory office. The decision has a profound effect on the life of a person charged with a criminal offence, on the experiences of victims of crime and on the reputation of the criminal justice system. However, through a line of cases that predates the establishment of most of the ODPPs, the High Court of Australia (HCA) has placed prosecutorial decisions outside the principle that 'every exercise of public power by Australian public officials is amenable to judicial review'.[37] Instead, it recognises the origin of the prosecutorial discretion in prerogative power, and applies the exemption from judicial review that applied to prerogative decisions.

B. The Attorney General and the Prerogative

In the 1980 case of *Barton*, the HCA considered an appeal against the New South Wales (NSW) Attorney General's issue of ex officio indictments under section 5 of the Australian Courts Act 1828 (Imp).[38] It evaluated nineteenth-century English

[32] D Meyerson, 'The Rule of Law and the Separation of Powers' (2004) 4 *Macquarie Law Journal* 1, 2.

[33] J Doyle, 'Accountability: Parliament, the Executive and the Judiciary' in S Kneebone (ed), *Administrative Law and the Rule of Law: Still Part of the Same Package?* (Canberra, Australian Institute of Administrative Law, 1999) 18, 26.

[34] L Burton Crawford, *The Rule of Law and the Australian Constitution* (Alexandria, Federation Press, 2017) 103.

[35] *Church of Scientology v Woodward* (1982) 154 CLR 25, 70.

[36] TRS Allan, 'Accountability to Law' in N Bamforth and P Leyland (eds), *Accountability in the Contemporary Constitution* (Oxford, Oxford University Press, 2013) 77, 79.

[37] B Walker and D Hume, 'Broadly Framed Powers and the Constitution' in N Williams (ed), *Key Issues in Public Law* (Alexandria, The Federation Press, 2018) 144, 149, 170–71.

[38] Ex officio indictments are issued without committal or other preliminary proceedings.

authorities, and found that prosecutorial discretion was originally a prerogative power. As such, prosecutorial decisions were subject to the general principles that 'prerogative power was not examinable by the courts', and the Attorney General was accountable only 'to Parliament for the manner in which he discharges his discretionary authority'.[39] The HCA's uncontroversial starting point in *Barton* was that the discretion of the Australian Attorney General was unreviewable by the courts because, as discussed in chapter three, section 5 conferred on the NSW Attorney General the same powers exercised by the Attorney General in England.[40]

In the 1989 case of *Brown*, three years after the establishment of the state's ODPP, the NSW Court of Criminal Appeal (CCA) considered whether a judge had the power to stay proceedings until the DPP charged the defendant with a more serious offence. The two relevant findings in *Brown* were also uncontroversial. The CCA applied *Barton* to decide that the 'courts exercise no control over the Attorney-General's decision to commence criminal proceedings'. It then found that the DPP had the 'same function in relation to finding a bill of indictment as the Attorney-General'.[41] However, these findings became controversial, but highly influential, when the CCA in *Brown* bluntly combined them in the following chain of reasoning: the Attorney General's decision to prosecute is not reviewable by the courts (except in cases involving abuse of process); the DPP has the same powers to initiate prosecutions as the Attorney General; and the DPP's decision to prosecute is not reviewable by the courts except in cases involving abuse of process.[42] This reasoning, which still applies to prosecutorial decisions, ignores the fact that the reasons for the original exemption from judicial review do not apply to decisions made by the ODPPs.

Originally, the non-justiciability of the prerogative reflected a range of factors related to its source, subject matter and breadth. Prerogative powers originally covered matters such as declaring war, entering treaties, defence and national security, appointment of ministers and dissolving Parliament. Decisions on these subjects were considered both beyond the court's competence and adequately reviewed by Parliament.[43] Despite the recognised limits on the effectiveness of parliamentary accountability, prerogative powers exercised on these matters are still largely insusceptible to judicial review.

In addition, Coke's sixteenth-century *Institutes* and Blackstone's seventeenth-century *Commentaries* both refer to the maxim that the 'Crown could do

[39] *Barton v The Queen* (1980) 147 CLR 75, 90–91, referencing *Prosser* (1848) 11 Beav 50 ER 838; *Reg v Comptroller-General of Patents, Designs, and Trade Marks* [1899] 1 QB 909; *London County Council v Attorney-General* [1902] AC 165.

[40] *Barton* (n 39) 92.

[41] (1989) 17 NSWLR 472, 478.

[42] ibid 479. There is dispute about whether a judge has the power to stay criminal proceedings for an abuse of power in itself or only where such an abuse is unfair or oppressive to a defendent: *R v Brown* (1989) 17 NSWLR 472.

[43] F Wheeler, 'Judicial Review of Prerogative Power in Australia: Issues and Prospects' (1992) 14 *Sydney Law Review* 432, 434–35.

no wrong'.[44] As the prerogative power represented the residual powers of the sovereign, its exercise by the Attorney General was insusceptible to judicial review. However, as Joseph reasoned in 2016, the 'prerogative surrendered its royal heritage when cabinet government was established over 200 years ago'.[45] Consistent with this argument, the 1985 English case of *Council of Civil Service Unions v Minister for the Civil Service* found that the subject of a power, rather than its source, determined the appropriateness of judicial review.[46] This reasoning alone would justify the abolition of the immunity from judicial review for prosecutorial decisions in Australia.

In the mid-1990s, England abolished the immunity for prosecutorial decisions and made decisions of the Crown Prosecution Service (CPS) subject to judicial review.[47] This change of practice acknowledged that decisions about individual prosecutions are of a different character from decisions about war, defence and other matters traditionally covered by the prerogative. In any event, the decision to prosecute is now made pursuant to a statutory power in Australia, so neither the source nor the nature of the prosecutorial power meets the historical criteria for exemption from judicial review.

Finally, prerogative powers were non-justiciable because they lacked 'the limitations in scope, purpose and criteria which render so many statutory powers' judiciable.[48] The statutory authority for decisions made by ODPPs, like 'Most statutory restatements of power[,] come with definable contexts, purposes, procedural rules, and governing criteria, the whole point being to bring the powers into sharper focus so that their repositories will be more accountable'.[49] The grounds for decisions to be immune from judicial review now have very limited application, and those grounds do not extend to ODPP decisions.

Australian courts have expressed some support for the justiciability of prerogative decisions in general, and of prosecutorial decisions in particular. In 1987 in *Peko-Wallsend*, a mining company took legal action over the Federal Cabinet exercising prerogative power to nominate Kakadu National Park for World Heritage designation. In that case, Bowen CJ of the Federal Court found that Australian courts should not accept a 'complete immunity in respect of decisions made under the prerogative'.[50]

In 1996 in *Maxwell*, the HCA offered some support for the application of this proposition to DPP decisions. The defendant pleaded guilty to the manslaughter

[44] H Barry, 'The King Can Do No Wrong' (1925) 11 *Virginia Law Review* 349, 353–54.

[45] PA Joseph, 'False Dichotomies in Administrative Law: From There to Here' (2016) 1 *New Zealand Law Review* 127, 135.

[46] [1985] 1 AC 374.

[47] *R v DPP, exp C* [1995] 1 Cr App R 136; Evidence to Royal Commission into Institutional Responses into Child Sexual Abuse, Sydney, 29 April 2016, 18 (Alison Saunders) 21–23.

[48] Wheeler (n 43) 435.

[49] M Aronson et al, *Judicial Review of Administrative Action and Government Liability*, 6th rev edn (Pyrmont, Thomson Reuters, 2017) 126.

[50] *Minister for Arts, Heritage and Environment v Peko-Wallsend Ltd* (1987) 15 FCR 274, 278.

of his wife on account of his diminished responsibility. However, the judge was not satisfied that the defence was made out on the facts. After obtaining further psychiatric advice, he accepted the advice of the prosecution to reject the plea. In Maxwell's appeal, the HCA found that the prosecution can withdraw the acceptance of a plea and a trial judge can reject a plea accepted by the prosecution. In the course of their judgment, Gaudron and Gummow JJ accepted that certain aspects of the prosecutorial discretion were, by their nature, unsuitable for judicial review. However, they also observed that, historically, the prosecutorial 'discretion was seen as part of the prerogative of the Crown and, thus, as unreviewable by the courts. That approach may not pay sufficient regard to the statutory office of Director of Public Prosecutions which now exists.'[51]

Kirby J took a similar view in 1998, when the case of *DPP (SA) v B* raised the issue of a trial judge's ability to refuse to accept the prosecution's entry of a *nolle prosequi*. He found that it would be inappropriate to apply to DPP decisions 'all of the hitherto unreviewable prerogative rights of the Crown formerly enjoyed by the Attorney-General'.[52] However, *Maxwell*'s legacy does not include doubts about the non-justiciability of prosecutorial decisions. The prosecutorial guidelines for the ACT and Tasmania still explicitly cite *Maxwell* for the proposition, accepted across the country, that courts do not 'exercise control over the institution or continuation of criminal proceedings' except to prevent an abuse of process or ensure a fair trial.[53] Australian prosecutorial policy reflects the exemption of the decision to prosecute from a principle of accountability that is fundamental to other executive decisions.

However, the unavailability of judicial review does not necessarily create a significant deficit in prosecutorial accountability. As Burton Crawford argues, the availability of judicial review is 'reactive and contingent' upon a small number of people pursuing matters that affect them.[54] Similarly, Doyle CJ argued in 1999 that judicial review could not be an effective accountability measure because it only occurs 'sporadically', and executive decision-makers do not use court decisions as 'a benchmark for their conduct'.[55] His reasoning does not acknowledge that where judicial review is available, all decisions are made in the shadow of the law. However, it still recognises a core limitation of the effectiveness of judicial review.

Ultimately, as Ham and Hill observe, using judicial review 'to counteract the discretionary behaviour of officials' only results in decisions being considered in court by 'a further set of discretionary actors, the judges'.[56] Judicial review of

[51] *Maxwell v The Queen* (1996) 184 CLR 501, 534.

[52] (1998) 194 CLR 566, 599.

[53] Director of Public Prosecutions (Tasmania), *Prosecution Policy and Guidelines* (2022) 1 (*DPP Policy* (Tas)); Director of Public Prosecutions, *Prosecution Policy of the Australian Capital Territory* (2021) 1 (*DPP Policy* (ACT)).

[54] Burton Crawford (n 34) 189.

[55] Doyle (n 33) 27.

[56] C Ham and M Hill, *The Policy Process in the Modern Capitalist State*, 2nd rev edn (New York, Harvester Wheatsheaf, 1993) 162.

prosecutorial decisions in England is rarely sought and even more rarely granted,[57] so there is little evidence of its effectiveness as an accountability measure. However, after a study of Australian, Canadian and English prosecutorial accountability mechanisms, Colvin concluded that the introduction of judicial review in Australia could enhance prosecutorial accountability and public confidence in the criminal justice system. She argued that its effectiveness relied on 'clear, predictable standards so that its ongoing effect on prosecutorial decision-making can be understood and assessed'.[58] Her conclusion is consistent with Majone's finding that evidence in the USA suggests that 'procedural rationality can be greatly enhanced by judicial review'.[59] While the introduction of judicial review might improve prosecutorial accountability, its coexistence with the separation of powers doctrine would create a new problem.

III. Separation of Powers

The following discussion of separation of powers, as in chapter five, refers only to the principle that governmental functions should be divided into legislative, judicial and executive functions. McMillan argues that this interpretation of the separation of powers is the 'most important doctrine in analysing government legal accountability'.[60] It relies on the courts finding a balance between reviewing executive decisions to constrain government power and respecting the exercise of executive power to uphold 'the autonomy of the three branches of government'.[61] The decision to prosecute is made in the executive branch, but it determines which matters proceed to court. As Gleeson CJ observed in the Supreme Court of NSW in *Maxwell*, prosecutorial decisions 'arise at the margin between executive and judicial power'.[62] Its existence at this intersection creates tension between the key accountability mechanism of separation of powers and judicial review.

Flynn advocated that judicial review should prevail over the separation of powers because lack of accountability in the exercise of prosecutorial discretion 'is more problematic than a perception that the judiciary are overlooking or supervising' prosecutorial decisions.[63] However, Australian scholars and practitioners

[57] *R v DPP, exp C* (n 47); Evidence to Royal Commission (n 47) 29 April 2016, 21–23 (Alison Saunders).

[58] I Colvin, 'The Charging Decision: Accountability, Transparency, and Control of the Decision to Prosecute' (PhD Thesis, University of Queensland, 2016) 236.

[59] G Majone, 'Independence vs Accountability?: Non-majoritarian Institutions and Democratic Government in Europe' (European University Institute, 1994) Working Paper No 94/3, 26.

[60] J McMillan, 'Rethinking the Separation of Powers' (2010) 38 *Federal Law Review* 423, 423.

[61] *A-G (NSW) v Quin* (1990) 170 CLR 1, 38.

[62] (1994) 34 NSWLR 606, 608.

[63] A Flynn, 'We've Changed Our Minds: What Do You Do With a Failed Plea Bargain – A Reflection on *R v Nixon*' (2012) 32 *Windsor Review of Legal and Social Issues* 123, 126.

generally take the opposite stance, and give priority to the separation of powers. Professor Mark Aronson testified to the Royal Commission into Institutional Responses to Child Sexual Abuse (Royal Commission) that judicial review was a 'non-starter'[64] because 'there is a real separation of powers issue when a judge is saying "[y]ou are charging the wrong thing. I want you to charge this" or "[y]ou shouldn't let this person off, you should be charging X."'[65] The DPP for Western Australia (WA), Joseph McGrath, similarly explained that his concern with judicial review of prosecutorial decisions was 'obviously'

> the separation of powers, the need to have the appearance and the actual reality of that separation and impartiality. The courts ultimately would be deciding who is the litigant, who is brought before the courts and the forensic decisions that would be made.[66]

These submissions do not recognise that the court would only review the legality of the prosecutorial decision, not direct the prosecutor to take certain actions.

Australian courts express less concern than do Australian prosecutors about conflict between the separation of powers and judicial review. However, they have found that the independence of the judiciary would be undermined if it engaged in prosecutorial decision-making. In *Barton*, Wilson J recognised 'wisdom' in the English perspective that judges 'should not have or appear to have any responsibility for the institution of a prosecution', because if they can decline to hear cases they may appear to approve the cases they do hear.[67] Gaudron and Gummow CJ confirmed in *Maxwell* that 'certain decisions involved in the prosecution process are, of their nature, insusceptible of judicial review'. They found that the integrity of the judicial process 'would be compromised' if courts were involved in decisions to prosecute.[68]

The courts also implicitly, but strongly, recognise the 'relative competence of prosecutors and courts'.[69] In *Brown* in 1989, the CCA was concerned with the 'substantial practical limitations upon the power of courts to control the exercise by prosecuting authorities of the wide discretion which they undoubtedly enjoy'.[70] Three years later, Kirby J elaborated that judges are generally unaware of the evidence that determined the decision to prosecute. He argued that judges deciding that their '"experienced eye" has perceived something which has escaped the attention of everyone else' easily leads to error.[71] Dawson and McHugh JJ acknowledged in *Maxwell* that judges 'seldom have the knowledge of the strengths and

[64] Evidence to Royal Commission (n 47) 29 April 2016, 62 (Mark Aronson).
[65] ibid 60.
[66] ibid 79 (Joseph McGrath).
[67] *Barton* (n 39) 110, citing *R v Humphreys* [1977] AC 1.
[68] *Maxwell* (n 51) 534.
[69] A Bowen Poulin, 'Prosecutorial Discretion and Selective Prosecution: Enforcing Protection After United States v Armstrong' (1997) 34 *American Criminal Law Review* 1071, 1094; *United States v Armstrong* 116 S Ct 1480, 1486 (1996).
[70] *Brown* (n 42) 479.
[71] *Chow v Director of Public Prosecutions* (1992) 28 NSWLR 593, 607.

weaknesses' of particular cases, or understand the 'matters which have properly motivated the decision of the prosecuting authority'.[72]

According to Allan, 'Parliament and the common law courts have been juxtaposed as rival sources of authority and legitimacy'.[73] Edwards predicted in 1984 that the conflicting claims of Parliament and the courts would result in periodic 'outbursts of … jurisdictional tug-of-war'[74] over the decision to prosecute. Australian judges have actually shown no appetite for entering the prosecutorial arena. They have, rather, repeatedly identified reasons why prosecutorial decisions belong, 'by statute, tradition and the principled demarcation of the prosecutorial and judicial functions, not to the judiciary but to the prosecution'.[75] They maintain that the 'functions of prosecutors and of judges must not be blurred',[76] and that 'the prosecutor's mantle … ill-becomes' judges.[77]

The prevailing view, expressed in *Wayte v United States*, that the 'decision to prosecute is particularly ill-suited to judicial review'[78] does not reflect any principled resolution of jurisdictional boundaries between the executive and the judiciary. Courts routinely enforce the limits of executive action by reviewing the legality of discretionary decisions in complex, controversial and politically sensitive areas, including social security, immigration, employment, taxation and national security. They identify decisions as unlawful where they are unreasonable, take irrelevant matters into account or are made for an improper purpose or in the absence of procedural fairness.[79] In these cases, they do not substitute their judgement for that of the original decision-maker. However, courts continue to starkly differentiate prosecutorial decisions from other administrative decisions without apparent justification, and to the detriment of prosecutorial accountability.

The absence of judicial review alone would not critically undermine the accountability of the ODPPs, because the limits of modern executive power are also enforced by other mechanisms in 'the province of administrative law'.[80] However, the courts ignore the limitations of parliamentary accountability discussed in the previous chapter. They create the misapprehension that ODPPs do not need to adopt administrative law's 'network of principles and practices … which mediate between the exercise of powers by officials and the community'.[81]

[72] *Maxwell* (n 51) 513–14.

[73] Allan (n 36) 79.

[74] J Edwards, *The Attorney General, Politics and the Public Interest* (London, Sweet & Maxwell, 1984) 125.

[75] *Chow* (n 71) 605.

[76] *Barton* (n 39) 110, citing *Humphreys* (n 67).

[77] *Chow* (n 71) 606.

[78] 70 US 598, 607 (1985).

[79] C Finn, 'The Concept of "Justiciability" in Administrative Law' in M Groves and HP Lee (eds), *Australian Administrative Law: Fundamentals, Principles and Doctrines* (Cambridge, Cambridge University Press, 2007) 143, 151–57.

[80] M Groves and HP Lee, 'Australian Administrative Law: The Constitutional and Legal Matrix' in Groves and Lee (n 79) 1, 3.

[81] DJ Galligan, *Discretionary Powers: A Legal Study of Official Discretion* (Oxford, Oxford University Press, 1986) 4.

IV. The 'New' Administrative Law

A. Confidence in Parliamentary Accountability

Since the establishment of the ODPPs, judicial and extra-judicial commentary have expressed confidence in the accountability of the DPP to the Attorney General and Parliament. In *Brown* in 1989, the NSW CCA recognised its limited ability to 'control' the prosecutorial discretion, and concluded that 'in practice the most important sanctions in this regard are likely to be political rather than legal'.[82] This position was maintained, almost verbatim, by the HCA in *Maxwell* in 1996. In that case, Dawson and McHugh JJ held that 'the most important sanctions governing the proper performance of a prosecuting authority's functions are likely to be political rather than legal'.[83] Similarly, in 2015, the Chief Justice of South Australia (SA) rejected calls from the Law Society for external review of DPP decisions.[84] In an address to the local Press Club, he supported the orthodox position that 'the Attorney General is the only supervisory authority which is necessary and constitutionally appropriate. Importantly, the Attorney General is ultimately answerable to the people of South Australia through Parliament.'[85]

This judicial opinion has received some support from DPPs. In 1996, the first DPP of WA, John McKechnie, agreed that 'accountability to Parliament is a useful corrective to incipient notions of megalomania. Parliamentary questions … require responsibility from a DPP'.[86] Similarly, in 2005, the DPP for SA, Stephen Pallaras, told the Press Club that his office was '100 percent accountable to the Courts, the Parliament and the Attorney-General'.[87] The hyperbolic claim of 100 per cent accountability encapsulates the overconfidence in the accountability of the ODPP system through the Attorney General and Parliament. It ignores the fact that the Attorney General's accountability to Parliament is limited, and stifles consideration of the adoption of additional accountability mechanisms.

The normative purpose of non-judicial accountability mechanisms differs little from the purpose of parliamentary accountability. Harders argues that administrative law's 'interest in accountability is, as is the interest in independence, grounded in serving the public good'.[88] Barr agrees that accountability

[82] *Brown* (n 42) 479.

[83] *Maxwell* (n 51) 514.

[84] R Perrotta, 'Time for External Review of Prosecution' (*Points of Law*, 11 May 2015) www.lawsocietysa.asn.au/pdf/POL%20110515%20DPP.pdf.

[85] C Kourakis, Speech, SA Press Club, 14 May 2015, 2.

[86] J McKechnie, 'Directors of Public Prosecutions: Independent and Accountable' (1996) 26 *University of Western Australia Law Review* 266, 276.

[87] S Pallaras, Speech, SA Press Club, 6 May 2005, 4.

[88] RT Harders, 'Striking a Balance: Administrative Law Judge Independence and Accountability' (1999) 19 *Journal of the National Association of Administrative Law Judges* 1, 9.

'undergirds the democratic legitimacy of administrative agencies'.[89] According to Groves, accountability gives 'moral and political legitimacy to administrative officials' by ensuring that they 'act according to the values and standards that are generally accepted as applying to the exercise of public powers'.[90] Since the establishment of the ODPPs, accountability principles and practices have developed within administrative law. The administrative law mechanisms do not directly involve Parliament or the courts, but are still 'linked to a democratic form of government'.[91] Key administrative law external and internal accountability mechanisms could, but do not, apply to the ODPPs.

B. External Accountability Mechanisms

According to Mulgan, external accountability involves a process through which a 'superior authority' seeks 'answers and rectification while the other side, that being held accountable, responds and accepts sanctions'.[92] The report of the Commonwealth Administrative Review Committee (the Kerr Committee) exerted a 'powerful influence' on Australian administrative law by promoting the view that accountability must be achieved through an external body that can review and reverse administrative decisions.[93] However, this view has not been stringently applied to prosecutorial decisions.

(i) *Annual Reporting*

The ODPPs' annual reporting processes, discussed in the previous chapter, constitute an external accountability measure. While the annual reports address the Attorney General's prosecutorial activities, their primary focus is the DPP's operational, policy and strategic decisions.[94] In 1991, WA Attorney General Joseph Berinson explained that annual reports provided 'information to the Attorney General to enable Parliament to be informed and questions answered about the

[89] MS Barr, 'Comment: Accountability and Independence in Financial Regulation: Checks and Balances, Public Engagement, and Other Innovations' (2015) 78 *Law and Contemporary Problems* 119, 119.

[90] M Groves, 'Ombudsmen's Jurisdiction in Prisons' (2002) 28 *Monash University Law Review* 181, 184.

[91] P Booth, *Controlling Development: Certainty and Discretion in Europe, the USA and Hong Kong* (London, Routledge, 1996) 133.

[92] R Mulgan, '"Accountability": An Ever-Expanding Concept?' (2000) 78 *Public Administration* 555, 555.

[93] R Creyke, *Control of Government Action: Text, Cases and Commentary*, 5th rev edn (Chatswood, LexisNexis Butterworths, 2018) 35.

[94] Director of Public Prosecutions Act 1990 (NT), s 33(1); Director of Public Prosecutions Act 1991 (WA), s 32(1); Director of Public Prosecutions Act 1984 (Qld), s 16(1); Annual Reports (Government Agencies) Act 2004 (ACT), ss 7, 8; Director of Public Prosecutions Act 1991 (SA), s 12(1); Director of Public Prosecutions Act 1986 (NSW), s 34(1); Director of Public Prosecutions Act 1973 (Tas), s 15(1); Public Prosecutions Act 1994 (Vic), s 12(1).

functions of the director', which would achieve 'accountability to Parliament of the performance of the director's functions'.[95] Ryan et al argued in 2002 that there is little evidence of the effectiveness of the annual reports that are 'statutorily required as the primary medium of accountability' across Australian public sector agencies.[96] This observation confirmed the pessimistic projection of the South Australian Shadow Attorney General in 1991. Trevor Griffin predicted that annual reports would be 'an inadequate mechanism for achieving [DPP] accountability' because they 'may not be tabled for some 15 or 16 months' after decisions had been made.[97]

The delay in reporting does, indeed, restrict the ability of Parliament to address issues as they arise. More fundamentally, the reporting focuses on organisational management. For example, the 2021–22 annual report for the WA DPP covers: agency performance in relation to the number and type of cases handled (including conviction and acquittal rates, and numbers of appeals allowed and dismissed); staff recruitment and training activities; disclosures and legal compliance relating to expenditure; key effectiveness indicators relating to timeliness of filing indictments and conviction rates; and key efficiency indicators relating to costs per prosecution and assets confiscated.[98] Monitoring and reporting on these matters promotes public sector values and encourages DPPs to be

> more accountable for their activities, more efficient and effective in their use of resources, less discriminatory in their personnel management decisions, more participative in their decision making styles; and more customer–oriented in their service delivery.[99]

However, reporting of this type does not provide any insight into how the decision to prosecute is made in individual cases, or address the core issue of whether the assessment of the reasonable prospects of conviction or public interest tests uphold the public interest.

In 1991, WA Attorney General Berinson implicitly accepted the limitations of the annual reporting system as part of the continuing problem of achieving prosecutorial accountability in a system predicated on prosecutorial independence. He fatalistically explained that, despite its limitations, 'It is difficult to see that more can be done without impinging on the DPP's independence'.[100] The focus on independence over accountability that impaired the accountability of the Attorney

[95] Western Australia, *Parliamentary Debates*, Legislative Council, 28 March 1991, 702 (Joseph Berinson, Attorney General).

[96] C Ryan et al, 'The Value of Public Sector Annual Reports and Annual Reporting Awards in Organisational Legitimacy' (2002) 8 *Accounting, Accountability and Performance* 61, 62.

[97] South Australia, *Parliamentary Debates*, Legislative Council, 8 October 1991, 871 (K Trevor Griffin).

[98] Office of the Director of Public Prosecutions for Western Australia, *Annual Report 2021–2022* (29 September 2022) 13, 33, 80–87.

[99] A Chowdhury and N Chandra Shil, 'Public Sector Reforms and New Public Management: Exploratory Evidence from Australian Public Sector' (2017) 5 *Asian Development Policy Review* 1, 6.

[100] Western Australia, *Parliamentary Debates*, Legislative Council, 28 March 1991, 702 (Joseph Berinson, Attorney General).

General also undermined the effectiveness of the annual reporting requirements that were supposed to enhance the accountability of the DPPs.

(ii) Other External Accountability Mechanisms

Australian statutory bodies other than the ODPPs are subject to various external accountability mechanisms. These alternatives to parliamentary accountability include merits review by administrative tribunals, a specialist Ombudsman, a requirement to provide public reasons for decisions and independent commissions.[101] They reflect Stone's observation that 'standard Westminster accountability mechanisms [a]re inapplicable' to agencies with a 'high level of independence from executive government'.[102] However, these mechanisms rarely apply to the ODPPs. In 2016, Colvin found that no Australian jurisdiction has a standing body with a mandate to review prosecutorial decisions; that commissions of inquiry, coroners and anti-corruption bodies rarely exercise their power to review decisions to prosecute; and that Human Rights Commissions, like courts, are reluctant to interfere with the decision to prosecute.[103]

In addition, Australia has not adopted the equivalent of His Majesty's Crown Prosecution Service Inspectorate (HMCPSI), which was established in England in the 1990s (as Her Majesty's Crown Prosecution Service) to maintain quality and accountability across prosecuting agencies. The HMCPSI does not appraise particular cases, but provides occasional thematic review of units and processes,[104] including the Rape and Serious Sexual Offences Unit in 2016[105] and the Special Crime and Counter Terrorism Division in 2019.[106] The HMCPSI provides the Attorney General and the Solicitor General with annual reports based on 'reliable and independently assessed material', which are used to 'hold the CPS to account'.[107] The CPS publicly acknowledges where inspectors find that it has 'failed to deliver the improvements' required,[108] as well as where 'the quality of legal decision making … has improved'.[109] In 2020, the CPS responded to the

[101] Australian Government, Attorney-General's Department, 'Administrative Law: Law That Regulates Government Decision Making' (undated) www.ag.gov.au/legal-system/administrative-law.

[102] B Stone, 'Accountability and the Design of an Anticorruption Agency in a Parliamentary Democracy' (2015) 36 *Policy Studies* 157, 158.

[103] Colvin (n 58) 204–09.

[104] His Majesty's Crown Prosecution Service Inspectorate, 'About HMCPSI' (2021) www.justiceinspectorates.gov.uk/hmcpsi/about-hmcpsi/.

[105] His Majesty's Crown Prosecution Service Inspectorate, *Thematic Review of the CPS Rape and Serious Sexual Offences Units* (February 2016).

[106] His Majesty's Crown Prosecution Service Inspectorate, *The Inspection of CPS Special Crime and Counter Terrorism* (February 2019).

[107] Evidence to Royal Commission (n 47) 29 April 2016, 57 (Kevin McGinty).

[108] Crown Prosecution Service, 'CPS Response to HMCPSI Follow Up Inspection of the Victim Communication Liaison Scheme: Letters to Victims' (22 October 2020) cps.gov.uk/publication/cps-response-hmcpsi-follow-inspection-victim-communication-liaison-scheme-letters.

[109] Crown Prosecution Service, 'CPS Response to HMCPSI 2020 Charging Inspection: A Thematic Review of the Quality and Timeliness of Charging Decisions' (29 September 2020) www.cps.gov.uk/publication/cps-response-hmcpsi-2020-charging-inspection-thematic-review-quality-and-timeliness.

HMCPSI's recommendations by making changes in areas including: information management, quality and timeliness of charging decisions, serious youth crime, domestic abuse and handling of evidence.[110]

After the acquittal of Constable Hoy in 2015, the President of the SA Law Society called for the establishment of a prosecutorial ombudsman, or similar body, to uphold public confidence in prosecutions. Rocco Perrotta argued that 'external review of prosecutorial decision-making is long overdue', because 'prosecutors are not accountable for failing to correctly apply their Prosecution Policy'.[111] Several members of the local criminal bar[112] and a barrister from the ACT agreed. Jack Pappas argued that, across the country, 'decisions by directors are clogging up our criminal justice system and resulting in unfairness, significant irrecoverable expense and inestimable stress to ordinary members of the public who, when acquitted, have no comeback'.[113] In 2015, the Royal Commission agreed that because prosecutorial decisions were so critical to individual defendants and victims, and to the community as a whole, 'it is relevant to ask whether … absolute immunity from review of any decision, is appropriate. Experience suggests that an absence of review increases the risk of administrative failure.'[114]

The Royal Commission's claim that ODPPs have absolute immunity from review is almost as overstated as Pallaras's claims that they are 100 per cent accountable. However, it supports the argument that ODPPs are subject to very limited external accountability, and the findings from the ACT Board of Inquiry demonstrate the limited oversight has the potential to undermine the integrity of the prosecutorial system. The absence of external accountability mechanisms does not necessarily mean that DPPs are not accountable. The concept of accountability has evolved to accommodate not only external scrutiny, but also internal agency processes and professional responsibility obligations that are evident in the ODPPs.

(iii) *Internal Accountability Mechanisms*

The concept of accountability can 'contemplate a network of complementary and overlapping checking mechanisms instead of assuming that control is necessarily to be exercised from any fixed place in the system'.[115] The ODPPs have a complex set

[110] Crown Prosecution Service, 'Inspectorate Responses' (2021) www.cps.gov.uk/publication/inspectorate-responses.

[111] Perrotta (n 84) 1–2.

[112] K McGregor and S Fewster, 'SA Lawyers Say DPP Must Be Held Accountable for Its Decisions, Not Pursue Cases Doomed to Failure' *The Advertiser* (11 May 2015) www.adelaidenow.com.au/news/south-australia/sa-lawyers-say-dpp-must-be-held-accountable-for-its-decisions-not-pursue-cases-doomed-to-failure/news-story/aed2c28e0c66b0c02f39e6792c91f67f.

[113] J Pappas, 'Watchdog Needed for Prosecutors' (Civil Liberties Australia, 12 July 2015) www.cla.asn.au/News/watchdog-needed-for-prosecutors/#gsc.tab=0.

[114] Royal Commission into Institutional Responses into Child Sexual Abuse, *Report of Case Study No 15: Response of Swimming Institutions, the Queensland and NSW Offices of the DPP and the Queensland Commission for Children and Young People and Child Guardian to Allegations of Sexual Abuse by Swimming Coaches* (November 2015) 21.

[115] Majone (n 59) 22–23.

of organisational protocols that assist in achieving accountability through policy, office structures and cultural practice, as well as professional and legal obligations.

(a) Policy

The DPP for WA, Robert Owen, explains the importance of prosecutorial guidelines by reference to the role of the ODPP: a 'prosecution agency has the power to make decisions which affect fundamental human rights, particularly the right to personal liberty. It must meet, and be seen to meet, the highest standards of integrity, professionalism, transparency and accountability.'[116]

Prosecution policies, particularly the reasonable prospects of conviction and public interest tests, provide a benchmark for prosecutors to 'ensure transparency and maintain a consistency of approach' in the decision to prosecute.[117] According to Majone, these standards recognise that accountability depends on well-defined 'institutional objectives' serving as 'clear yardsticks for judging performance'.[118] These standards are required because discretionary power must be 'confined, structured, and checked' to prevent its arbitrary exercise.[119] The ODPP policies comply with the United Nations' *Guidelines on the Role of Prosecutors*, which require prosecutors 'vested with discretionary functions' to follow 'guidelines to enhance fairness and consistency of approach' in prosecutorial decisions'.[120] However, the limitations of the reasonable prospects of conviction and public interest tests were discussed in previous chapters. The following section considers more general difficulties involved in relying on policy to constrain discretion, secure compliance of decision-makers and achieve accountability.

While the ODPP policies seek to ensure that discretion is subject to adequate restraint, they also acknowledge that too many restrictions are neither desirable nor possible. Prosecutorial decisions cannot accommodate individual circumstances while adhering to what Edwards refers to as 'an infallible set of discretionary yardsticks'.[121] The ACT guidelines assert that while 'general principles may be articulated, it is not possible to reduce such an important discretion to a mere formula'.[122] The Tasmanian guidelines agree that the

> criteria for the exercise of this discretion cannot be reduced to something akin to a mathematical formula; indeed it would be undesirable to attempt to do so. The breadth

[116] Director of Public Prosecutions for Western Australia, *Statement of Prosecution Policy and Guidelines* (2022) 3 (*DPP Policy* (WA)).
[117] *DPP Policy* (Tas) (n 53) 2.
[118] Majone (n 59) 26.
[119] WR LaFave, 'The Prosecutor's Discretion in the United States' (1970) 18 *The American Journal of Comparative Law* 532, 536.
[120] United Nations, Human Rights, Office of the High Commissioner, *Guidelines on the Role of Prosecutors*, adopted by the Eighth United Nations Congress on the Prevention of Crime and the Treatment of Offenders (1990) Art 17.
[121] Edwards (n 74) 87.
[122] *DPP Policy* (ACT) (n 53) 3.

> of the factors to be considered in exercising this discretion indicates a candid recognition of the need to tailor general principles to individual cases.[123]

The resistance of the ODPPs to strictly prescribing the criteria for decision-making reflects Edwards's further observation that the 'very nature of discretionary authority requires resistance to any attempt to develop rigid rules'.[124] However, it also undermines accountability by relaxing the mechanisms that intend to reduce the arbitrary exercise of discretionary decision-making. The WA DPP acknowledges that, given the extent of the prosecutorial discretion, the public is 'entitled to know the general framework the DPP and the staff of the Office of the Director of Public Prosecutions operate under'.[125]

However, the guidelines do not explain how discretion is exercised in any particular case. All of the prosecutorial guidelines include requirements that, subject to restrictions based on privacy considerations and possible harms, prosecutors provide victims with reasons for decisions not to proceed with prosecutions.[126] However, reasons for particular decisions given to individual victims, usually in response to individual applications, do not increase the general understanding of the nature of prosecutorial decisions.

Even if policy provisions could balance the need for flexibility and constraint, the Australian prosecution policies, like those for prosecution policies internationally, are difficult to enforce. The ODPP policies, like prosecution policies internationally, do not create enforceable legal rights[127] or attract remedies for their breach,[128] and rarely result in professional disciplinary measures,[129] especially for non-malicious decisions.[130] Johnson found in the USA that these characteristics made prosecutorial guidelines 'dead letters'.[131] Flynn's research into Australian plea bargaining supports this conclusion. Prosecutors disclosed to her that while policies are 'official', few processes are employed to monitor

[123] *DPP Policy* (Tas) (n 53) 6.

[124] Edwards (n 74) 426.

[125] *DPP Policy* (WA) (n 116) 3.

[126] *DPP Policy* (Tas) (n 53) 15; Office of the Director of Public Prosecutions, New South Wales, *Prosecution Guidelines* (2021) 27; Department of Justice and Attorney-General (Queensland), *Director's Guidelines* (2016) 28; Director of Public Prosecutions (Victoria) *Discontinuance Review Framework* (undated) 3; Director of Public Prosecutions, South Australia, *Statement of Prosecution Policy & Guidelines* (2014) 41; *DPP Policy* (ACT) (n 53) 28; *Guidelines of the Director of Public Prosecutions* (Northern Territory) (2016) s 11.6. The Commonwealth guidelines do not require reasons for decisions to be provided to victims.

[127] D Boerner, 'Prosecution in Washington State' (2012) 41 *Crime and Justice: A Review of Research* 167, 187.

[128] ES Podger, 'Prosecution Guidelines in the United States' in E Luna and M Wade (eds), *The Prosecutor in Transnational Perspective* (Oxford, Oxford University Press, 2012) 9, 10.

[129] ML Miller and RF Wright, 'Reporting for Duty: The Universal Prosecutorial Accountability Puzzle and an Experimental Transparency Alternative' in Luna and Wade (n 128) 392, 401.

[130] For the difficulties of taking disciplinary action against lawyers, see, eg LC Levin, 'Building a Better Lawyer Discipline System: The Queensland Experience' (2006) 9 *Legal Ethics* 187; K Toole and S Le Mire, 'From Failure to Hope: Lawyer Regulation in South Australia' (2014) 39 *Alternative Law Journal* 63.

[131] DT Johnson, *The Japanese Way of Justice: Prosecuting Crime in Japan* (Oxford, Oxford University Press, 2002) 128.

compliance with them, and few penalties are imposed where non-compliance is identified. In practice, adherence to policy largely 'relies upon "trusting" prosecutors to do the right thing'.[132]

However, policy direction is not the only internal process for achieving the accountability of the ODPPs. The ODPPs have a number of characteristics that create an organisational culture and structure that is compatible with internal accountability.

(b) Organisational Culture and Structure

The Australian ODPPs are small compared to many international prosecutorial offices. For example, California is the largest jurisdiction in the USA and has 58 District Attorney's offices[133] and approximately 1000 prosecutors in the Los Angeles office alone.[134] Australia's largest jurisdiction, NSW, has one DPP, nine suburban and regional branch offices[135] and approximately 609 legal staff.[136] The limited staff numbers foster a hierarchical organisational culture. DPPs maintain a high level of oversight of prosecutors in their team, and are directly involved in case management.[137] The level and nature of each DPP's involvement in particular cases varies across jurisdictions. They may be involved in cases of a certain type or level of seriousness or complexity. For example, a DPP may personally authorise the initiation or withdrawal of all murder prosecutions undertaken in their office.

The DPP of WA, Joseph McGrath, testified before the Royal Commission in 2016 that 'one of the great benefits' of his office is that, despite being based in 'one of the biggest provinces in the world, there are nine floors in one building so I'm within 80 metres of any decision maker. The population of Perth is only 2 million, so we've got this great control.'[138] The Deputy DPP of the Northern Territory (NT), Paul Usher, gave evidence that 'the beauty' of being in an office with only 45 prosecutors is that he can have 'direct contact' with all prosecutors.[139] Even the relatively populous state of Victoria has just one main office and one small regional office.[140] The Victorian DPP, John Champion, testified that if he is

[132] A Flynn, 'Plea-Negotiations, Prosecutors and Discretion: An Argument for Legal Reform' (2016) 49 *Australian & New Zealand Journal of Criminology* 564, 569.

[133] American Civil Liberties Union Foundation (California), 'Meet Your DA' (2018) meetyourda.org/.

[134] Los Angeles District Attorney's Office, 'Office Overview' (2020) da.lacounty.gov/about/office-overview.

[135] Office of the Director of Public Prosecutions, New South Wales, 'Our Organisation' (2023) www.odpp.nsw.gov.au/our-organisation.

[136] New South Wales, Office of the Director of Public Prosecutions, *Annual Report 2021–2022* (14 October 2022) 53.

[137] For a more detailed comparison of the ODPP organisational culture with a range of international prosecution services, see K Toole, 'The Decision to Prosecute – Accountability of Australian Prosecutors' in V Colvin and P Stenning (eds), *The Evolving Role of the Public Prosecutor: Challenges and Innovations* (New York, Routledge, 2019) 232.

[138] Evidence to Royal Commission (n 47) 29 April 2016, 92 (Joseph McGrath).

[139] ibid 89–90 (Paul Usher).

[140] Victoria, Director of Public Prosecutions, *Annual Report 2021–2022* (21 November 2022) 117.

'in doubt about a case or I want some more information' he would assemble the relevant prosecutors 'and we'll talk about it amongst the team'.[141] Even in cases where the DPP is not personally involved, decisions on initiating and terminating proceedings are generally made only by prosecutors at a management level, and regular management meetings bring consistency to decision-making.[142] The combination of hierarchical organisation and collectivity in decision-making reduces the scope of individual discretion and helps achieve individual and institutional accountability.

(c) Internal Review

Originally, the ODPP policies did not include processes for formal internal review of decisions to prosecute. In recent years, there has been some replication of the victim review processes adopted in England in 2014.[143] For example, in 2017 in SA, a policy on *Victims Right to Review of Discretionary Prosecutorial Decisions* was adopted in order to 'affirm accountability and transparency in the decision making process'.[144] Victims are notified when and why prosecutions are not going to progress, and are invited to discuss the decision with the responsible prosecutor. Several levels of internal review are then available to any victim who wishes to pursue the matter further.[145] Similar procedures have also been introduced in WA[146] and NSW.[147] Victim-initiated review of prosecutorial decisions and the principles underpinning that review increase the transparency of prosecutorial decisions and can increase victim involvement in, and satisfaction with, the prosecutorial process. However, ultimately, the review process is conducted within the ODPP. The resolution of the review depends on the discretionary judgement of another prosecutor, and may still conflict with the views of the victim who sought the review.

(d) Professional Responsibilities

Since the 1940s, the concept of accountability has encompassed 'inner responsibility of the individual to his or her conscience or moral values'.[148] While

[141] Evidence to Royal Commission (n 47) 29 April 2016, 95 (John Champion).

[142] Royal Commission into Institutional Responses into Child Sexual Abuse, *Public Hearing – Criminal Justice DPP Complaints and Oversight Mechanisms* (29 April 2016) 34–36, 48.

[143] Crown Prosecution Service, *Victims' Right to Review – Policy and Guidance* (2020).

[144] Director of Public Prosecutions, South Australia, *Victims Right to Review of Discretionary Prosecutorial Decisions* (2017) 1.

[145] ibid 1–2.

[146] Director of Public Prosecutions for Western Australia, *Policy and Guidelines for Victims of Crime* (2022) 37–52.

[147] Office of the Director of Public Prosecutions, New South Wales, *Victims' Right of Review Policy* (2021) 5–8.

[148] Mulgan (n 92) 557. The decades of debate about internal accountability are outside the scope of this book, but see, eg H Finer, 'Administrative Responsibility in Democratic Government' (1941) 1 *Public Administration Review* 335; CJ Friedrich, 'Public Policy and the Nature of Administrative Responsibility' in CJ Friedrich and ES Mason (eds), *Public Policy* (Cambridge, MA, Harvard University Press, 1940) 3.

'territorial jousting'[149] persists over the terms 'responsibility' and 'accountability', government agencies now routinely incorporate professional responsibility into their accountability regime.[150] The Australian Public Service, for example, 'extends the concept of accountability beyond the traditional idea of external scrutiny' to encompass 'the responsibility that individuals might have to their professional ethics and/or values'.[151] The assessment of the adequacy of ODPP accountability depends significantly on the level of confidence placed in these largely self-monitoring forms of internal accountability. Despite its increasing acceptance, this type of accountability is not amenable to objective determination, and still attracts scepticism.

Self-regulation of any profession can invite cynicism. Moliterno commented in 2012 that, at least in the USA, the legal profession was 'ponderous, backward looking, and self-preserving', and its history of 'self-regulation … is not a happy one'.[152] However, other international research has found that legal self-regulation is effective, and that lawyers are motivated to act ethically and professionally. As Majone suggests, 'for many purposes reliance upon qualities such as expertise, professionalism, consistency and independence has more importance than reliance upon direct political accountability'.[153]

In 2014, even the sceptical Molitano found that while the prospect of legal sanctions and disciplinary action did affect professional conduct, survey data disclosed that 'Overall, "doing the right thing" was the most powerful single motivator of conduct'.[154] This motivation has been found to be particularly strong in prosecutors, who have chosen to work in law enforcement rather than more lucrative fields[155] and lack the client direction and economic incentives that can exert negative pressures.[156]

Ultimately, the research leaves unanswered, and probably unanswerable, the question of the effectiveness of internal accountability mechanisms. However, a system is unlikely to satisfy the modern concept of prosecutorial accountability when it relies on the good will of prosecutors who are subject to limited external accountability mechanisms and have to satisfy complex and conflicting obligations according to discretionary interpretation of broad policies.[157]

[149] Mulgan (n 92) 558.

[150] R Creyke, 'Administrative Justice – Towards Integrity in Government' (2007) 31 *Melbourne University Law Review* 705, 707.

[151] Australian Government, Australian Public Service Commission, 'Delivering Performance and Accountability' (2018) legacy.apsc.gov.au/delivering-performance-and-accountability.

[152] JE Moliterno, 'The Trouble with Lawyer Regulation' (2012) 62 *Emory Law Journal* 885, 885–86.

[153] Majone (n 59) 22.

[154] J Moliterno and J Keyser, 'Why Lawyers Do What They Do (When Behaving Ethically)' (2014) 4 *St Mary's Journal on Legal Malpractice & Ethics* 2, 12.

[155] BA Green and FC Zacharias, 'Regulating Federal Prosecutors' Ethics' (2002) 55 *Vanderbilt Law Review* 381, 449; D Heilbroner, *Rough Justice: Days and Nights of a Young DA* (New York, Pantheon Books, 1990) 284; M Baker, *DA: Prosecutors in Their Own Words* (Simon & Schuster, 1999) 52.

[156] Green and Zacharias (n 155) 449–50.

[157] Industry self-regulation is an under-researched area, but for issues with self-regulation of corporations across industries, see J Sammeck (ed), *A New Institutional Economics Perspective on Industry Self-Regulation* (Wiesbaden, Springer Gabler, 2012).

V. Conclusions

The accountability of independent, statutory ODPPs cannot be achieved through the accountability regime that emerged from the historical, legal and political role of the Attorney General. When the ODPPs were established, concepts of government accountability were still evolving. The accountability mechanisms currently applied to the ODPPs have largely ignored decades of development in the area. Parliaments and courts have failed to recognise that the ODPPs present a significant challenge to the already limited effectiveness of parliamentary accountability, because their status as independent offices distances them from the reach of Parliament. Judges, in particular, maintain a confidence in the efficacy of parliamentary accountability over the ODPPs that has stymied the consideration of alternative or additional accountability mechanisms.

The unresolved tensions between the origins of the prosecutorial discretion and its exercise by the statutory ODPPs are evident in its accountability regime. They are also evident in the contrast between the accountability regimes of the ODPPs and other statutory offices. The tension results in critical deficits in traditional accountability processes to Parliament or the courts; a virtual absence of modern external accountability mechanisms appropriate to a statutory prosecutorial office under administrative law; and the presence of internal accountability mechanisms that are largely self-regulated and without enforcement mechanisms. This limited prosecutorial accountability framework falls short of the standards for public accountability necessary to guarantee public confidence in the system. As with the values of the public interest and independence, prosecutorial accountability is only partially upheld by the ODPPs.

11

Conclusions

The analysis of the tension between the core prosecutorial values of public interest, independence and accountability, and the ways in which the Office of Director of Public Prosecutions (ODPPs) navigates those tensions, helps us to understand one of the most fundamental state powers that is exercised against the individual. This study contributes to the understanding of the Australian criminal justice system, and adds the Australian experience to the emerging field of comparative study of prosecutions.

The application of administrative law theory and doctrine to the role of the prosecutor recognises that the ODPP is not just a criminal law institution, but an institution of the executive branch of government. Focusing on the ODPP as part of the executive branch provides a different dimension to research on the prosecutor as a major actor in the criminal justice system. It characterises prosecutors as executive decision-makers whose discretion is exercised in an environment saturated with political influences. This characterisation requires engagement with administrative law, which provides a broader perspective on the prosecutorial discretion, the implications of its exercise in the decision to prosecute, and the need for independence and accountability to protect the public interest.

The characterisation of the decision to prosecute as an expression of executive power heightens the importance of its interaction with prosecutorial values. Individual decisions concerning particular prosecutions have a profound impact on the experiences of defendants, victims and communities. Cumulative decisions concerning prosecutions affect the integrity and reputation of the criminal justice system, and the rule of law itself. This significance means that the values that underpin it must be open to scrutiny. The prosecutorial policies in each jurisdiction ostensibly provide the required transparency by articulating the prosecutorial values. However, this research has highlighted that a high level of subjectivity is involved in making the decision to prosecute, and personal judgement reduces the effectiveness of the mechanisms intended to uphold institutional expectations about the decision to prosecute.

Ultimately, the ODPPs solve the problem of actual or potential misuse of prosecutorial discretion, but create another, very similar, problem. The original problem the ODDPs were meant to solve was identified as arising from the exercise of prosecutorial discretion *by the Attorney General*. However, the real, but largely unacknowledged, problem was the *exercise of prosecutorial discretion* by the Attorney General: that is, the central problem was the prosecutorial discretion itself. It is far from an original insight that the exercise of discretion is inherently susceptible to misuse. That problem has been identified by scholars and politicians for centuries. However, the ODPPs provide a unique expression of the problem. The political role of the Attorney General created the possibility for misuse of prosecutorial discretion due to improper political interference. The independent status of the ODPPs creates the possibility of misuse of prosecutorial discretion due to lack of proper political oversight.

The ODPPs are ostensibly respectful of both their historical foundations and more recent administrative law principles and expectations. They were intended to constitute a coherent prosecutorial system that gives both the Attorney General and the DPP significant and compatible responsibilities that, together, uphold the public interest, independence and accountability. However, the ODPPs all uncomfortably combine a modern view of independence from political interference with a historical commitment to parliamentary accountability, which creates an inherent tension.

Independence was the driver for the ODPPs. However, while nine purportedly independent, statutory ODPPs have existed in Australia for several decades, the existing prosecutorial regime has not achieved real or perceived independence from political interference in criminal prosecutions. Rather, independence itself has not only been imperfectly implemented, but has been pursued at the expense of the other values the system professes to embody.

The expectation that the DPP's independent prosecutorial role could protect the public interest and secure parliamentary accountability represented an uneasy compromise between appropriate political oversight and inappropriate political influence. This compromise creates the problem that ODPPs do not properly reconcile the commitment to the independence of the DPP with the need for the accountability of the Attorney General. As a result, they all undermine the de facto independence of the DPP and, therefore, the ability of the prosecutorial system to uphold the public interest and accountability.

I now finish this book with some final observations that emerge from the study of the ODPPs but are relevant to other Australian executive decision-makers. The themes are: the enduring paradox of the role of politics in prosecutions; the debate about structural versus individual protection of accountability; and the role of the media.

I. Reflections on the Core Values

The values that underpin the ODPP system have proved remarkably enduring across centuries, continents and branches of law. They are as compatible with the demands of modern Australian administrative law as they are with the ancient office of Attorney General. However, as discussed throughout this book, the ODPPs have struggled with the perennial problem of achieving a balance between those values.

The ODPPs were intended to remove the risk of political interference in prosecutorial decisions by ensuring that they were made at arm's length from government. However, they gave elected political officials oversight of the process to maintain prosecutorial accountability. The extreme infrequency of political incursions into prosecutorial decisions can be interpreted as evidence of the independence of the prosecutorial system. However, the ODPP system provides a shield for the government to distance itself from difficult decisions when it is expedient to do so, but authority to exert political influence on prosecutions when it is expedient to do so. The extreme infrequency of political incursions speaks less to the independence of the prosecutorial system than to the mundanity of the majority of criminal prosecutions.

The bulk of prosecutorial work has always been undertaken without the reality or perception of political interference, but the risk of political involvement in a minority of cases justified the separation of the political and prosecutorial functions. A minority of controversial cases are now a similar indicator that complete freedom from improper political interference has not, and cannot, be achieved by the current system. The system allows the Attorney General to have power but avoid accountability. Attorneys General can keep themselves at 'arm's length' from unpopular prosecutions, but retain the ability to 'cherry pick' issues that could deliver political benefit. The questions remain whether the qualified independence of the DPP is appropriate or whether qualified independence is any independence at all.

II. Politics and Paradoxes

I have already identified a range of interrelated paradoxes that beset the establishment and operation of the ODPPs. The following key paradoxes all relate to the role of politics in prosecutions:

1. The independence of prosecutorial decisions needed to be secured through the separation of politics from the decision to prosecute, in a system where the public interest and accountability depended on those politics. This need for balance between prosecutorial values creates a dilemma. Prosecutors need sufficient independence to perform their role without political interference. They must be sufficiently accountable so that their discretion is exercised according to the standards of the communities they represent, but they must not be influenced by vagaries in popular opinion that lead to the 'path of persecution rather than prosecution'.[1]
2. An Attorney General can be distanced from the decision to prosecute and yet be accountable to Parliament for prosecutorial decisions. A DPP can be

[1] RK Daw, 'The "Public Interest" Criterion in the Decision to Prosecute' (1989) 53 *Journal of Criminal Law* 485, 490.

overseen by the Attorney General but keep the initiation and conduct of criminal prosecutions independent of political influence.

3. The DPP's independence is significantly tempered by having the Attorney General retain ultimate responsibility for prosecutions. The Attorney General's legal and practical ability to uphold prosecutorial accountability and the public interest is significantly tempered by the DPP's independence.
4. The discretion at the heart of prosecuting in the public interest has to be exercised at a distance from party political interests to ensure independence. The prosecutorial discretion must be constrained by legitimate public interest considerations to ensure accountability.

The ODPP system, and the public reaction to it, reveals a profound public ambivalence about modern politics. While there is sufficient cynicism to create discomfort about politics playing too much role in prosecutions, there is an equal concern about it having no role at all. The view that political involvement both threatens and protects the legitimacy of prosecutorial decisions entrenches a paradox that undermines the ability of the ODPP system to uphold the prosecutorial values.

A. Structural versus Individual Protection of Independence and Accountability

The other central paradox is that modern administrative law is based on processes for achieving accountability, yet research suggests that individual responsibility and professional ethics are the most effective protections of independence. In 1980, Edwards reviewed his two decades of research covering prosecutorial decision-making, and determined that 'no matter how entrenched constitutional safeguards may be', the 'strength of character and personal integrity of the holder of the offices … is of paramount importance'.[2]

In 2010, Stenning reflected on Edwards's observation and asked a salient question that applies to the ODPPs: 'if institutional and constitutional tinkering really make little difference, and the key lies in the "strength of character and personal integrity" of the relevant office holders, just how might the latter be guaranteed?'[3] In the same year, Condon applied an analogy from corporate law to both answer Stenning's question and undermine Edwards's proposition. She argued that the quality of corporate governance does not rest on 'the personal integrity of the Chief Executive Officer', but on 'mechanisms for information-sharing, up-the-line

[2] J Edwards, *Ministerial Responsibility for National Security as It Relates to the Offices of Prime Minister, Attorney General and Solicitor General of Canada* (Minister of Supply and Services Canada, 1980) 120–21.

[3] P Stenning, 'Prosecutions, Politics and the Public Interest: Some Recent Developments in the United Kingdom, Canada and Elsewhere' (2010) 55 *Criminal Law Quarterly* 449, 473–74.

reporting, codes for avoiding conflicts of interest, risk management processes and so on. In other words, the emphasis is on *processes for decision-making*.'[4]

Condon's argument might reasonably be interpreted as evidence of increasing commitment to accountability processes developing throughout the late twentieth and early twenty-first century. However, in 2016, Appleby's research on the independence of the Solicitor General supported the conclusion Edwards drew about the DPP nearly 40 years earlier. Appleby concluded from her interviews with current and former Australian Solicitors General and Attorneys General that, without

> internal fortitude, structural guarantees will not deliver independence. While statutory provisions can be important normative statements, may affect public perceptions and may create an environment in which internal capacity can be exercised, without individual integrity, statutory guarantees are easily undermined by subtle pressures and individual actions.[5]

She further concluded that the independence of the Solicitor General remains 'somewhat fragilely, protected by the probity of individuals, despite attempts to strengthen independence through the statutory framework'.[6] A powerful ethos among prosecutors may achieve independence without the accountability mechanisms used in the private commercial sector. However, as Appleby observes, that protection is fragile. It echoes the historical confidence that prosecutorial independence would be upheld if the Attorney General was an honourable person, even though loss of confidence in that safeguard drove the establishment of the ODPP system.

B. The Media

Finally, the effectiveness of parliamentary accountability depends, to a significant degree, on media attention alerting members of the public to prosecutorial decisions that raise public interest issues. However, the Australian media show only sporadic interest in prosecutorial decisions, and do not provide a balanced perspective on every reported case. Media reports tend to create oversimplified, oppositional caricatures of those involved in prosecutions. In the mainstream media, DPPs are frequently portrayed as bureaucrats who undermine the administration of criminal justice by initiating plea bargains to save themselves time and money. Their relative invisibility to the public is presented as evidence of lack of accountability and even integrity. On this view, the elected Attorney General has

[4] M Condon, 'Commentary on "Prosecutions, Politics and the Public Interest: Some Recent Developments in the United Kingdom, Canada and Elsewhere"' (2010) 55 *Criminal Law Quarterly* 479, 481 (emphasis in original).

[5] G Appleby, *The Role of the Solicitor-General: Negotiating Law, Politics and the Public Interest* (Oxford, Hart Publishing, 2016) 290.

[6] ibid 291.

to rescue the prosecutorial system by intervening in certain cases to ensure that decisions to prosecute reflect community standards.

On the other hand, political and legal commentators tend to portray DPPs as public officers untainted by political interests and resistant to hostile public and political opposition, who exercise their statutory powers independently to uphold the law. They are depicted as having to fight to fulfil their statutory role against the opportunistic interference of Attorneys General pandering to popular opinion in controversial cases and using 'tough on crime' politics for electoral advantage.

Resources, evidence and public interest considerations are all relevant factors in determining prosecutorial decisions. All these factors can be taken into account according to specified legal criteria, and all can be exploited cynically or opportunistically. The problem is that Attorneys General under the ODPP system have power on account of their legal role, but motivation to exercise power on account of their political role. The involvement of the Attorney General in a prosecution is not neatly divided into legal and political motivations, and political motivations are not necessarily sinister. However, the Attorney General may seek to use prosecutorial decisions for political gain, and any prosecutorial decision risks accusations of political impropriety.

III. Concluding Comments

Given the number and importance of the paradoxes within the ODPP system, it is appropriate that my final remarks are, themselves, a paradox. The ODPPs conduct the bulk of their work without attracting the interest of the Attorney General. There have been few ODPP decisions to prosecute that have been subject to unfavourable reviews by independent commissions or the courts, and there is no evidence of endemic problems with the initiation of prosecutions. There is reason to resist an assessment of the system based on instances like *Volkers*, which do raise genuine concerns about the exercise of the prosecutorial discretion.

However, there are limited opportunities for external review of prosecutorial decisions, and a scarcity of channels for complaint or expression of dissatisfaction with decisions to prosecute. The paucity of complaints about prosecutions cannot be taken as a conclusive sign of strength or success in the ODPP system, and can plausibly be interpreted as a sign of weakness reflecting the absence of accountability mechanisms.

The existence of so few cases of Attorneys General exercising concurrent powers and directing the DPPs shows that political intervention is not a consistent problem in criminal prosecutions. However, the number of cases that were persuasive of the need to remove the Attorney General from the direct prosecutorial role was also small, and the handling of exceptional criminal cases is critical in defining and upholding the values of a criminal justice system.

The potential for political interference is as concerning as its actual incidence. That potential is inherent in the Australian system, and creates an unresolved tension between the commitment to public interest, independence and accountability. The decision to achieve independence through separating the prosecutorial role from that of the Attorney General yet simultaneously achieving accountability through the oversight of that same Attorney General creates a tension that has rarely been identified and never addressed.

The structure of the ODPPs makes them unsuitable to completely uphold the core values of public interest, independence and accountability that underpinned their establishment and are central to their continuing operation. The system is formally protected by mechanisms that were introduced at a time when concepts of government accountability were just evolving. They are now out-of-date and fall short of general standards for public accountability. The faith in the role of the Attorney General overstates the actual role played by parliamentary accountability and stifles the adoption of administrative law accountability mechanisms.

However, the final paradox is that I also conclude that the organisational structure of the ODPPs constrains the exercise of prosecutorial discretion by individual prosecutors, and contains protective features that act as a bulwark against improper use of the discretion. Despite the formal lack of independence and accountability mechanisms, the bulk of decisions to prosecute seem to be made independently and in the public interest.

These counter findings invite further research on tensions and deficits within the ODPP system. A priority for future researchers could be empirical research involving interviews with current prosecutors, combined with comparative analysis of international prosecution services, to generate new knowledge on the practical exercise of discretion in individual cases. This proposed research could develop my descriptive conclusions into normative recommendations on the ODPP system. It could investigate whether it is possible to simultaneously achieve each of the prosecutorial values, or whether a certain level or type of imbalance is unavoidable. An acceptance of some imbalance would invite inquiry into whether the balance that is achieved in the ODPP system meets an acceptable standard or could be improved by adopting different standards. The resolution of these issues would provide the basis for conclusions about the robustness of the ODPP system, given my paradoxical conclusion that prosecutorial decisions are largely independent despite the lack of formal mechanisms to buttress independence.

BIBLIOGRAPHY

Articles/Books/Book Chapters

Abrams, N, 'Internal Policy: Guiding the Exercise of Prosecutorial Discretion' (1971) 19 *UCLA Law Review* 1.

Ackerman, JM, 'Understanding Independent Accountability Agencies' in S Rose-Ackerman and PL Lindseth (eds), *Comparative Administrative Law* (Cheltenham, Edward Elgar Publishing, 2010) 265.

Adekunle, A, 'Prosecutorial Independence and Effectiveness of the Nigerian Criminal Justice System' in V Colvin and P Stenning (eds), *The Evolving Role of the Public Prosecutor: Challenges and Innovations* (New York, Routledge, 2019) 220.

Airo-Farulla, G, 'Rationality and Judicial Review of Administrative Action' (2000) 24 *Melbourne University Law Review* 543.

Airo-Farulla, G, 'Reasonableness, Rationality and Proportionality' in M Groves and HP Lee (eds), *Australian Administrative Law: Fundamentals, Principles and Doctrines* (Cambridge, Cambridge University Press, 2007) 212.

Alexy, R, 'The Reasonableness of Law' in G Bongiovanni et al (eds), *Reasonableness and Law* (Dordrecht, Springer, 2009) 5.

Allan, TRS, 'Accountability to Law' in N Bamforth and P Leyland (eds), *Accountability in the Contemporary Constitution* (Oxford, Oxford University Press, 2013) 77.

Appleby, G, 'Imperfection and Inconvenience: Boilermakers' and the Separation of Judicial Power in Australia' (2012) 31 *University of Queensland Law Journal* 265.

Appleby, G, *The Role of the Solicitor-General: Negotiating Law, Politics and the Public Interest* (Oxford, Hart Publishing, 2016).

Appleby, G and Reilly, A, 'Unveiling the Public Interest: The Parameters of Executive Discretion in Australian Migration Legislation' (2017) 28 *Public Law Review* 293.

Archer, G, *Unmaking a Murder: The Mysterious Death of Anna-Jane Cheney* (Sydney, Penguin Random House Australia, 2017).

Aronson, M et al, *Judicial Review of Administrative Action and Government Liability* (Pyrmont, Thomson Reuters, 6th rev edn, 2017).

Atkinson, CL, 'Legitimacy in Public Administration' in A Farazmand (ed), *Global Encyclopedia of Public Administration, Public Policy, and Governance* (Cham, Springer Nature, 2018) 3781.

Ayling, J and Broadhurst, R, 'Organized Crime Control in Australia and New Zealand' in L Paoli (ed), *The Oxford Handbook of Organized Crime* (Oxford, Oxford University Press, 2013) 612.

Bacon, F, *The New Organon: Or True Directions Concerning the Interpretation of Nature* (1620) s XLVI, https://pages.uoregon.edu/kimball/Bacon.htm.

Baker, M, *DA: Prosecutors in Their Own Words* (New York, Simon & Schuster, 1999).

Balcetis, E and Dunning, D, 'See What You Want to See: Motivational Influences on Visual Perception' (2006) 91 *Journal of Personality and Social Psychology* 612.

Barnsley, K, 'Crony Capitalism or Corruption?: The Curious Case of British Tobacco and a Tasmanian Government' (2011) 58 *Tasmanian Historical Research Association* 173.

Barr, MS, 'Comment: Accountability and Independence in Financial Regulation: Checks and Balances, Public Engagement, and Other Innovations' (2015) 78 *Law and Contemporary Problems* 119.

Barry, H, 'The King Can Do No Wrong' (1925) 11 *Virginia Law Review* 349.

Barth, J, 'Criminal Prosecution in American History: Private or Public?' (2022) *South Dakota Law Review* 119.

Bayne, P, 'Prosecutorial Discretion and Administrative Law' in IL Potas (ed), *Prosecutorial Discretion*, Seminar Proceedings No 6 (Australian Institute of Criminology, 7–9 November 1984) 69.
Bentham, J, *Works*, vol 4 (London, William Tait, 1843).
Berliner, L, 'The Use of Expert Testimony in Child Sexual Abuse Cases' in SJ Ceci and H Hembrooke (eds), *Expert Witnesses in Child Abuse Cases: What Can and Should Be Said in Court* (Washington DC, American Psychological Association, 1998) 11.
Bibas, S, 'The Pitfalls of Professionalized Prosecution: A Response to Josh Bower's Legal Guilt, Normative Innocence, and the Equitable Decision Not to Prosecute' (2011) 111 *Columbia Law Review* 14.
Bibas, S, 'Transparency and Participation in Criminal Procedure' (2006) 81 *New York University Law Review* 911.
Bingham, EM, 'A Political Memoir' (2003) *Tasmanian Historical Research Association* 143.
Block, SD et al, 'Predictors of Prosecutorial Decisions in Reports of Child Sexual Abuse' (2023) 28 *Child Maltreatment* 488.
Blunt, D, 'Responsible Government: Ministerial Responsibility and Motions of "Censure"/ "No Confidence"'(2004) 19 *Australasian Parliamentary Review* 71.
Bobek, Ml, 'Reasonableness in Administrative Law: A Comparative Reflection on Functional Equivalence' in G Bongiovanni et al (eds), *Reasonableness and Law* (Dordrecht, Springer, 2009) 311.
Boerner, D, 'Prosecution in Washington State' (2012) 41 *Crime and Justice: A Review of Research* 167.
Booth, P, *Controlling Development: Certainty and Discretion in Europe, the USA and Hong Kong* (London, Routledge, 1996).
Bovens, M, 'Analysing and Assessing Accountability: A Conceptual Framework' (2007) 13 *European Law Journal* 447.
Bowers, J, 'Legal Guilt, Normative Innocence, and the Equitable Decision Not to Prosecute' (2010) 110 *Columbia Law Review* 1655.
Boyce, J, *Losing Streak: How Tasmania Was Gamed by the Gambling Industry* (Carlton, Redback, 2017).
Boyne, S, 'Is the Journey From the In-Box to the Out-Box a Straight Line? The Drive for Efficiency and the Prosecution of Low-Level Criminality in Germany' in E Luna and M Wade (eds), *The Prosecutor in Transnational Perspective* (Oxford, Oxford University Press, 2012).
Brady, PT, 'The Celluloid Advocate: The Evolution of the Twentieth Century Cinematic Lawyer' (2017) 27 *Southern California Interdisciplinary Law Journal* 165.
Brandon, GL et al, 'Open Prosecution' (2023) 75 *Stanford Law Review* 1365.
Bray, RS, 'Death Scene Jurisprudence – The Social Life of Coronial Facts' (2010) 19 *Griffith Law Review* 567.
Brenton, S, 'Ministers and Scandals' in K Dowding and C Lewis (eds), *Ministerial Careers and Accountability in the Australian Commonwealth Government* (Canberra, ANU Press, 2012) 135.
Bricker, B, '*Citizens United* and Political Accountability' in NS Lind and CE Rabe-Hemp (eds), *Corruption, Accountability and Discretion* (Bingley, Emerald Publishing, 2017).
Bronitt, SH and Stenning, P, 'Understanding Discretion in Modern Policing' (2011) 35 *Criminal Law Journal* 319.
Brown, DK, 'American Prosecutors' Powers and Obligations in the Era of Plea Bargaining' in E Luna and M Wade (eds), *The Prosecutor in Transnational Perspective* (Oxford, Oxford University Press, 2012) 200.
Burbank, SB, 'Judicial Independence, Judicial Accountability and Interbranch Relations' (2007) 95 *Georgetown Law Journal* 909.
Burton Crawford, L, *The Rule of Law and the Australian Constitution* (Alexandria, Federation Press, 2017).
Caianiello, M, 'The Italian Public Prosecutor: An Inquisitorial Figure in Adversarial Proceedings?' in E Luna and M Wade (eds), *Transnational Perspectives on Prosecutorial Power* (Oxford, Oxford University Press, 2011).
Carney, G, 'Comment – The Role of the Attorney-General' (1997) 9 *Bond Law Review* 1.
Carothers, T, 'The Rule of Law Revival' (1998) 77 *Foreign Affairs* 95.
Carroll, B, *Whitlam* (Kenthurst, Rosenberg Publishing, 2011).

Chin, D, 'Sentencing: A Role for Empathy' (2012) 160 *University of Pennsylvania Law Review* 1561.

Chohan, UW, 'Legislative Oversight of Bureaucracy' in A Farazmand (ed), *Global Encyclopedia of Public Administration, Public Policy, and Governance* (Cham, Springer Nature, 2018) 3762.

Chowdhury, A and Chandra, NS, 'Public Sector Reforms and New Public Management: Exploratory Evidence from Australian Public Sector' (2017) 5 *Asian Development Policy Review* 1.

Cocks, R, 'Dewigged, Bothered, and Bewildered: British Colonial Judges on Trial, 1800–1900' (2012) 33 *Journal of Legal History* 243.

Coldrey, J, 'The Office of the Director of Public Prosecutions: Independence Professionalism and Accountability' (1990).

Cole, M, *Democracy in Britain* (Edinburgh, Edinburgh University Press, 2006).

Condon, M, 'Commentary on "Prosecutions, Politics and the Public Interest: Some Recent Developments in the United Kingdom, Canada and Elsewhere"' (2010) 55 *Criminal Law Quarterly* 479.

Contini, F and Mohr, R, 'Reconciling Independence and Accountability in Judicial Systems' (2007) 3 *Utrecht Law Review* 26.

Corns, C, 'Police Summary Prosecutions in Australia and New Zealand: Some Comparisons' (2000) 19 *University of Tasmania Law Review* 280.

Corns, C, *Public Prosecutions in Australia: Law, Policy and Practice* (Pyrmont, Thomson Reuters, 2014).

Corns, C, 'The Politics of Prosecution' (1994) 68 *Law Institute Journal* 276.

Corrin, J and Douglas, H, 'Another Aboriginal Death in Custody: Uneasy Alliances and Tensions in the Mulrunji Case' (2008) 28 *Legal Studies* 531.

Cowdery, N, *Frank and Fearless* (Sydney, NewSouth Publishing, 2019).

Cox, RW III, 'Accountability and Responsibility in Organizations: The Ethics of Discretion' (2004) 13 *Viešoji Politika Ir Administravimas* 39.

Creyke, R, 'Administrative Justice – Towards Integrity in Government' (2007) 31 *Melbourne University Law Review* 705.

Creyke, R, *Control of Government Action: Text, Cases and Commentary*, 5th rev edn (Chatswood, LexisNexis Butterworths, 2018).

Custer, LB, 'The Origins of the Doctrine of Parens Patriae' (1978) 27 *Emory Law Journal* 195.

D'Amato, A, 'On the Connection Between Law and Justice' (1993) 26 *UC Davis Law Review* 527.

Daw, RK, 'The "Public Interest" Criterion in the Decision to Prosecute' (1989) 53 *Journal of Criminal Law* 485.

Di Federico, G, 'Prosecutorial Independence and the Democratic Requirement of Accountability in Italy: Analysis of a Deviant Case in a Comparative Perspective' (1998) 38 *British Journal of Criminology* 371.

Dicey, AV, *Introduction to the Study of the Law of the Constitution*, 8th rev edn (Carmel, Liberty Fund, 1915).

Dobinson, I and Houston, L, 'ICAC's Operation "Hale": A Low Point in the History of the Agency' (2017) 29 *Current Issues in Criminal Justice* 57.

Dowding, K and Lewis, C, 'Hiring, Firing, Roles and Responsibilities' in K Dowding and C Lewis (eds), *Ministerial Careers and Accountability in the Australian Commonwealth Government* (Canberra, ANU Press, 2012) 1.

Dowding, K et al, 'The Pattern of Forced Exits from the Ministry' in K Dowding and C Lewis (eds), *Ministerial Careers and Accountability in the Australian Commonwealth Government* (Canberra, ANU Press, 2012) 115.

Downs, A, 'The Public Interest: Its Meaning in a Democracy' (1962) 29 *Social Research: An International Quarterly* 1.

Doyle, J, 'Accountability: Parliament, the Executive and the Judiciary' in S Kneebone (ed), *Administrative Law and the Rule of Law: Still Part of the Same Package?* (Canberra, Australian Institute of Administrative Law, 1999) 18.

Duff, A, 'Discretion and Accountability in a Democratic Criminal Law' in M Langer and DA Sklansky (eds), *Prosecutors and Democracy: A Cross-National Study* (Cambridge, Cambridge University Press, 2017) 9.

Dunlea, RR, '"No Idea Whether He's Black, White, or Purple': Colorblindness and Cultural Scripting in Prosecution' (2022) 60 *Criminology* 237.

Dworkin, R, 'Hard Cases' (1975) 88 *Harvard Law Review* 1057.

Dworkin, R, 'No Right Answer' (1978) 53 *New York University Law Review* 1.

Dworkin, R, 'The Model of Rules' (1967) 35 *University of Chicago Law Review* 14.

East, P, 'Life as the Attorney-General: Being in the Right Place at the Right Time' (2017) 23 *Auckland University Law Review* 37.

Edwards, J, *The Attorney General, Politics and the Public Interest* (London, Sweet & Maxwell, 1984).

Edwards, J, *The Law Officers of the Crown: A Study of the Offices of Attorney-General and Solicitor-General of England, with an Account of the Office of the Director of Public Prosecutions of England* (London, Sweet & Maxwell, 1964).

Edwards, J, 'The Office of Attorney General – New Levels of Public Expectations and Accountability' in P Stenning (ed), *Accountability for Criminal Justice: Selected Essays* (Toronto, University of Toronto Press, 1995) 294.

Ehrlinger, J et al, 'Peering into the Bias Blind Spot: People's Assessments of Bias in Themselves and Others' (2005) 31 *Personality and Social Psychology Bulletin* 680.

Elrod, JW, 'W(h)ither the Jury? – The Diminishing Role of the Jury Trial in Our Legal System' (2011) 68 *Washington and Lee Law Review* 3.

Emy, HV, *The Politics of Australian Democracy: Fundamentals in Dispute*, 2nd rev edn (Melbourne, Macmillan, 1978).

Evans, G, 'The Discretion to Prosecute' in IL Potas (ed), *Prosecutorial Discretion*, Seminar Proceedings No 6 (Australian Institute of Criminology, 7–9 November 1984) 7.

Fabri, M, 'Clash of Visions: Regulating Judges and Prosecutors in Italy' in R Devlin and A Dodek (eds), *Regulating Judges: Beyond Independence and Accountability* (Cheltenham, Edward Elgar Publishing, 2016) 245.

Fawcett, P et al, 'Anti-Politics, Depoliticization, and Governance' in P Fawcett et al (eds), *Anti-Politics, Depoliticization, and Governance* (Oxford, Oxford Scholarship Online, 2017) 1.

Fewster, S, *City of Evil: The Truth About Adelaide's Strange and Violent Underbelly*, 2nd rev edn (Sydney, Hatchette Australia, 2011).

Finer, H, 'Administrative Responsibility in Democratic Government' (1941) 1 *Public Administration Review* 335.

Finn, C, 'The Concept of "Justiciability" in Administrative Law' in M Groves and HP Lee (eds), *Australian Administrative Law: Fundamentals, Principles and Doctrines* (Cambridge, Cambridge University Press, 2007) 143.

Flatman, G and Bagaric, M, 'Problems in Prosecuting Cases Involving Historical Child Sexual Abuse: The Victorian Experience' (1997–98) 4 *Deakin Law Review* 1.

Flynn, A, 'Plea-Negotiations, Prosecutors and Discretion: An Argument for Legal Reform' (2016) 49 *Australian & New Zealand Journal of Criminology* 564.

Flynn, A, 'We've Changed Our Minds: What Do You Do With a Failed Plea Bargain – A Reflection on *R v Nixon*' (2012) 32 *Windsor Review of Legal and Social Issues* 123.

Follingstad, DR et al, 'Decisions to Prosecute Battered Women's Homicide Cases: An Exploratory Study' (2015) 30 *Journal of Family Violence* 859.

Foote, SB, 'Independent Agencies Under Attack: A Skeptical View of the Importance of the Debate' (1988) *Duke Law Journal* 223.

Freckelton, I, 'The Evolving Institution of Coroner' (1999) 24 *Alternative Law Journal* 156.

French, R, 'Administrative Law in Australia: Themes and Values' in M Groves and HP Lee (eds), *Australian Administrative Law: Fundamentals, Principles and Doctrines* (Cambridge, Cambridge University Press, 2007) 15.

Friedrich, CJ, 'Public Policy and the Nature of Administrative Responsibility' in CJ Friedrich and ES Mason (eds), *Public Policy* (Cambridge, MA, Harvard University Press, 1940) 3.

Galligan, DJ, *Discretionary Powers: A Legal Study of Official Discretion* (Oxford, Oxford University Press, 1986).

Gardiner DG, 'Policy Review Reviewed: The Pubescent State of the New Administrative Law' (1988) 4 *Queensland University of Technology Law Journal* 123.
Gaudron, M, 'Some Reflections on the Boilermakers Case' (1995) *Journal of Industrial Relations* 306.
Givelber, DJ, 'The Application of Equal Protection Principles to Selective Enforcement of the Criminal Law' (1973) *University of Illinois Law Forum* 88.
Glaser, D, 'Treatment Issues in Child Sexual Abuse' (1991) 159 *British Journal of Psychiatry* 769.
Goethals, J et al, 'Preface to Special Issue: The Future of the Public Prosecutor's Office in the European Union (2000) 8 *European Journal of Crime, Criminal Law and Criminal Justice* 149.
Gold, RM, 'Promoting Democracy in Prosecution' (2011) 86 *Washington Law Review* 69.
Goldring, J, 'The Foundations of the "New Administrative Law" in Australia' (1981) 40 *Australian Journal of Public Administration* 79.
Goldring, J and Wettenhall, R, 'Three Perspectives on the Responsibility of Statutory Authorities' (1980) 15 *Politics* 136.
Gordon, S, *Controlling the State: Constitutionalism from Ancient Athens to Today* (Cambridge, MA, Harvard University Press, 1999).
Green, BA and Roiphe, R, 'A Fiduciary Theory of Progressive Prosecution' (2023) 60 *American Criminal Law Review* 1431.
Green, BA and Zacharias, FC, 'Regulating Federal Prosecutors' Ethics' (2002) 55 *Vanderbilt Law Review* 381.
Griffiths, J, 'Australian Administrative Law: Institutions, Reforms and Impact' (1985) 63 *Public Administration* 445.
Grosman, BA, *The Prosecutor: An Inquiry into the Exercise of Discretion* (Toronto, University of Toronto Press, 1969).
Groves, M, 'Ombudsmen's Jurisdiction in Prisons' (2002) 28 *Monash University Law Review* 181.
Groves, M and Lee, HP, 'Australian Administrative Law: The Constitutional and Legal Matrix' in M Groves and HP Lee (eds), *Australian Administrative Law: Fundamentals, Principles and Doctrines* (Cambridge, Cambridge University Press, 2007) 1.
Haines, CG, 'Effects of the Growth of Administrative Law Upon Traditional Anglo-American Legal Theories and Practices' (1932) 26 *American Political Science Review* 875.
Ham, C and Hill, M, *The Policy Process in the Modern Capitalist State*, 2nd rev edn (New York, Harvester Wheatsheaf, 1993).
Hamer, D, 'Keating v Morris; Leck v Morris: Politics and Procedure in the "Dr Death" Inquiry' (2006) 25 *University of Queensland Law Review* 131.
Hamer, D, 'The *Eastman* Case: Implications for an Australian Criminal Cases Review Commission' (2015) 17 *Flinders Law Journal* 433.
Hand, J, 'Primitive Justice: Private Prosecutions in Municipal Court Under New Jersey Rule 7: 4–4 (b)' (1991) 44 *Rutgers Law Review* 205.
Hanlon, F, 'Traditional Notions of the Attorney-General: Time for Some Justice' (2008) 33 *Alternative Law Journal* 15.
Harders, RT, 'Striking a Balance: Administrative Law Judge Independence and Accountability' (1999) 19 *Journal of the National Association of Administrative Law Judges* 1.
Hart, HLA, 'Discretion' (2013) 127 *Harvard Law Review* 652.
Hart, HLA, 'Positivism and the Separation of Law and Morals' (1958) 71 *Harvard Law Review* 593.
Hawkins, R and Briggs, F, 'The Institutionalised Abuse of Children in Australia: Past and Present' (1997) 133 *Early Child Development and Care* 41.
Heilbroner, D, *Rough Justice: Days and Nights of a Young DA* (New York, Pantheon Books, 1990).
Herrmann, J, 'The Rule of Compulsory Prosecution and the Scope of Prosecutorial Discretion in Germany' (1974) 41 *University of Chicago Law Review* 468.
SE Hobbs, 'Prosecutor's Bias, an Occupational Disease' (1949) 2 *Alabama Law Review* 40.
Hogan, TP, 'De-prosecution and Death: A Synthetic Control Analysis of the Impact of De-prosecution on Homicides' (2022) 21 *Criminology & Public Policy* 489.
Hollier, N, 'The Whitlam Project' (2002) 169 *Overland* 104.

Hourigan, B, 'Who Pays? Political Donations and Democratic Accountability' (2006) 58 *Institute of Public Affairs Review: A Quarterly Review of Politics and Public Affairs* 12.

Iontcheva, JT, 'Prosecutors and Bargaining in Weak Cases: A Comparative View' in E Luna and M Wade (eds), *The Prosecutor in Transnational Perspective* (Oxford, Oxford University Press, 2012) 102, 107.

Jackson, R, *Case for the Prosecution: A Biography of Sir Archibald Bodkin, Director of Public Prosecutions, 1920–1930* (London, Arthur Barker, 1962).

Johnson, DT, *The Japanese Way of Justice: Prosecuting Crime in Japan* (Oxford, Oxford University Press, 2002).

Johnston, M, 'A Brief History of Anticorruption Agencies' in A Schedler et al (eds), *The Self-Restraining State: Power & Accountability in New Democracies* (Boulder, CO, Lynne Reinner Publishers, 1999) 217.

Joseph, PA, 'False Dichotomies in Administrative Law: From There to Here' (2016) 1 *New Zealand Law Review* 127.

Kahan, DM et al, '"They Saw a Protest": Cognitive Illiberalism and the Speech–Conduct Distinction' (2012) 64 *Stanford Law Review* 851.

Kaplan, J, 'Prosecutorial Discretion – A Comment' (1965) 60 *North Western Law Review* 174.

Keating, M, 'Managing for Results in the Public Interest' (1990) 49 *Australian Journal of Public Administration* 387.

Keenan, S, 'A Blue Wristband View of History: The Death of Mulrunji Doomadgee and the Illusion of Postcolonial Australia' (2009) 34 *Alternative Law Journal* 248.

Kidston, RR, 'The Office of Crown Prosecutor (More Particularly in New South Wales)' (1958) 32 *Australian Law Journal* 148.

Kime, ZR, 'Aberrant Sexual Behavior, Violence, and Reproduction' (1992) 18 *Journal of Sex Education and Therapy* 231.

King, LJ, 'The Attorney General, Politics and the Judiciary' (2000) 29 *University of Western Australia Law Review* 155.

Kirby, M, 'Sir Isaac Isaacs – A Sesquicentenary Reflection' (2005) 29 *Melbourne University Law Review* 880.

Kovera, MB et al, 'Expert Testimony in Child Sexual Abuse Cases: Effects of Expert Evidence Type and Cross-Examination' (1994) 18 *Law and Human Behavior* 653.

Krasnostein, S, 'Too Much Individualisation, Not Enough Justice: Bugmy v The Queen' (2014) 39 *Alternative Law Journal* 12.

Lacey, N, *In Search of Criminal Responsibility: Ideas, Interests, and Institutions* (Oxford, Oxford University Press, 2016).

Lacey, N, 'The Path Not Taken: HLA Hart's Harvard Essay on Discretion' (2013) 127 *Harvard Law Review* 636.

LaFave, WR, 'The Prosecutor's Discretion in the United States' (1970) 18 *The American Journal of Comparative Law* 532.

Langbein, JH, 'Controlling Prosecutorial Discretion in Germany' (1974) 41 *University of Chicago Law Review* 439.

Langer, M and Sklansky, DA (eds), *Prosecutors and Democracy: A Cross-National Study* (Cambridge, Cambridge University Press, 2017).

Langevoort, DC, 'The Human Nature of Corporate Boards: Law, Norms, and the Unintended Consequences of Independence and Accountability' (2011) 89 *Georgetown Law Journal* 797.

Larkin, P, 'Ministerial Accountability to Parliament' in K Dowding and C Lewis (eds), *Ministerial Careers and Accountability in the Australian Commonwealth Government* (Canberra, ANU Press, 2012) 95.

Levin, LC, 'Building a Better Lawyer Discipline System: The Queensland Experience' (2006) 9 *Legal Ethics* 187.

Levin, RJ and van Berlo, W, 'Sexual Arousal and Orgasm in Subjects Who Experience Forced or Non-consensual Sexual Stimulation – A Review' (2004) 11 *Journal of Clinical Forensic Medicine* 82.

Lewis, T et al, 'Sentencing in Child Sexual Assault Cases: Factors Influencing Judicial Decision-making' (2014) *20 Journal of Sexual Aggression* 281.

Lezak, SI and Leonard, M, 'Prosecutor's Discretion: Out of the Closet – Not Out of Control' (1984) 63 *Oregon Law Review* 247.

Lino, D, 'The Rule of Law and the Rule of Empire: AV Dicey in Imperial Context' (2018) 81 *Modern Law Review* 739.

Lipson, L, 'The Two-Party System in British Politics' (1953) 47 *American Political Science Review* 337.

Luna, E and Wade, M, 'Adversarial and Inquisitorial Systems: Distinctive Aspects and Converging Trends' in E Luna and M Wade (eds), *The Prosecutor in Transnational Perspective* (Oxford, Oxford University Press, 2012) 177.

Luna, E and Wade, M, 'Looking Back and at the Challenges Ahead' in E Luna and M Wade (eds), *The Prosecutor in Transnational Perspective* (Oxford, Oxford University Press, 2012) 424.

MacFarlane, BA, 'Sunlight and Disinfectants: Prosecutorial Accountability and Independence Through Public Transparency' (2001) 45 *Criminal Law Quarterly* 272.

Mack, K and Anleu, SR, 'The Security of Tenure of Australian Magistrates' (2006) 30 *Melbourne University Law Review* 370.

Mackenzie, G et al, '"What Really Happened" Versus "What We Can Prove": Tension Between the Roles of Coroner and DPP in Queensland' (2006) 6 *Indigenous Law Bulletin* 6.

Madill, F, 'Love and Hate Under Hare Clark – Impact of Minority Government in Tasmania' (1997) 11 *Legislative Studies* 68.

Manes-Rossi, F, 'New Development: Alternative Reporting Formats: A Panacea for Accountability Dilemmas?' (2019) 39 *Public Money & Management* 528.

Mansfield, G and Peay, J, *The Director of Public Prosecutions: Principles and Practices for the Crown Prosecutor* (London, Tavistock Publications, 1987).

Marshall, G, 'The Evolving Practice of Parliamentary Accountability: Writing Down the Rules' (1991) 44 *Parliamentary Affairs* 460.

Mason, A, 'Administrative Review: The Experience of the First Twelve Years' (1989) 18 *Federal Law Review* 122.

Mason, K, 'The Office of Solicitor General for New South Wales' (1988) *Bar News* 22.

Mason, MA, 'A Judicial Dilemma: Expert Witness Testimony in Child Sex Abuse Cases' (1991) 19 *Journal of Psychiatry and Law* 185.

Mathews, B et al, 'Reports of Child Sexual Abuse of Boys and Girls: Longitudinal Trends Over a 20-Year Period in Victoria, Australia' (2017) 66 *Child Abuse & Neglect* 9.

Mathews, B and Collin-Vézina, D, 'Child Sexual Abuse: Raising Awareness and Empathy Is Essential to Promote New Public Health Responses' (2016) 37 *Journal of Public Health Policy* 304.

McCulloch, J, 'The Bongiorno Affair' (1995) 20 *Alternative Law Journal* 140.

McCulloch, J et al, 'Putting the Politics Back into Prosecution: The Kennett Government and the DPP' (1994) 19 *Alternative Law Journal* 78.

McHugh, M, 'Tensions Between the Executive and the Judiciary' (2002) 6 *The Judicial Review* 111.

McKechnie, J, 'Directors of Public Prosecutions: Independent and Accountable' (1996) 26 *University of Western Australia Law Review* 266.

McKibbin, R, 'A Brief Supremacy: The Fragmentation of the Two-Party System in British Politics, c 1950–2015' (2016) 27 *Twentieth Century British History* 450.

McMillan, J, 'Rethinking the Separation of Powers' (2010) 38 *Federal Law Review* 423.

Meldrum RC et al, 'Progressive and Traditional Orientations to Prosecution: An Empirical Assessment in Four Prosecutorial Offices' (2021) 48 *Criminal Justice and Behavior* 354.

Merrett, DT, 'Australian Banking Practice and the Crisis of 1893' (1989) 29 *Australian Economic History Review* 60.

Meston, CM, 'Sympathetic Nervous System Activity and Female Sexual Arousal' (2000) 86 *The American Journal of Cardiology* 30F.

Meyerson, D, 'The Rule of Law and the Separation of Powers' (2004) 4 *Macquarie Law Journal* 1.

Michel, V, 'The Role of Prosecutorial Independence and Prosecutorial Accountability in Domestic Human Rights Trials' (2016) *Journal of Human Rights* 1.

Miller, AS, 'The Public Interest Undefined' (1961) 10 *Journal of Public Law* 184.
Miller, GP, 'Independent Agencies' (1986) 1986 *Supreme Court Review* 41.
Miller, ML and Wright, RF, 'Reporting for Duty: The Universal Prosecutorial Accountability Puzzle and an Experimental Transparency Alternative' in E Luna and M Wade (eds), *The Prosecutor in Transnational Perspective* (Oxford, Oxford University Press, 2012) 392.
Misner, RL, 'Recasting Prosecutorial Discretion' (1996) 86 *Journal of Criminal Law and Criminology* 717.
Mizzi, P, 'Balancing Prosecution with the Right to a Fair Trial: The Child Sexual Abuse Reforms in NSW' (2019) 31 *Judicial Officers Bulletin* 11.
Moles, RN, *A State of Injustice* (South Melbourne, Robert N Moles, 2004).
Moley, R, *Politics and Criminal Prosecution* (New York, Minton, Balch & Company, 1929).
Moliterno, JE, 'The Trouble with Lawyer Regulation' (2012) 62 *Emory Law Journal* 885.
Moliterno, J and Keyser, J, 'Why Lawyers Do What They Do (When Behaving Ethically)' (2014) 4 *St Mary's Journal on Legal Malpractice and Ethics* 2.
Morgan, DF, 'The Public Interest' in TL Cooper (ed), *Handbook of Administrative Ethics*, 2nd rev edn (New York, Marcel Dekker, 2001).
Morgan, J, 'Securing the Administrative Appeals Tribunal's Independence: Tenure and Mechanisms of Appointment' (2018) 43 *Alternative Law Journal* 302.
Mulgan, R, '"Accountability": An Ever-Expanding Concept?' (2000) 78 *Public Administration* 555.
Mulgan, R, 'Assessing Ministerial Responsibility in Australia' in K Dowding and C Lewis (eds), *Ministerial Careers and Accountability in the Australian Commonwealth Government* (Canberra, ANU Press, 2012) 177.
Mulgan, R, 'The Extended Scope of Accountability in Public Administration' in *Oxford Research Encyclopedia, Politics* (Oxford, Oxford University Press, 2020) 1.
Murphy, J, 'Mercy and Legal Justice' (1986) 4 *Social Philosophy & Policy* 1.
Nehushtan, Y, 'The Non-Identical Twins in UK Public Law: Reasonableness and Proportionality' (2017) 50 *Israel Law Review* 69.
Newbury, M, 'Historical Child Sexual Abuse Investigations: A Case for Law Reform' (2014) 26 *Current Issues in Criminal Justice* 43.
Nickerson, RS, 'Confirmation Bias: A Ubiquitous Phenomenon in Many Guises' (1998) 2 *Review of General Psychology* 175.
Noone, MA, 'Challenges Facing the Australian Legal Aid System' in A Flynn and J Hodgson (eds), *Access to Justice and Legal Aid* (Oxford, Hart Publishing, 2017) 23.
Nunn, KB, 'The Trial as Text: Allegory, Myth and Symbol in the Adversarial Criminal Process – A Critique of the Role of the Public Defender and a Proposal for Reform' (1995) 32 *American Criminal Law Review* 743.
Oliver, D, 'Accountability and the Foundations of British Democracy – the Public Interest and Public Service Principles' in N Bamforth and P Leyland (eds), *Accountability in the Contemporary Constitution* (Oxford, Oxford University Press, 2013) 289.
Parry, JT, 'Culpability, Mistake, and Official Interpretations of Law' (1997) 25 *American Journal of Criminal Law* 1.
Pettit, P, 'Deliberative Democracy and the Case for Depoliticising Government' (2001) 24 *University of New South Wales Law Journal* 724.
Plater, D and de Vreeze, L, 'Is the "Golden Rule" of Full Prosecution Disclosure a Modern "Mission Impossible?"' (2012) 14 *Flinders Law Journal* 133.
Ploscowe, M, 'Purging Italian Criminal Justice of Fascism' (1945) 45 *Columbia Law Review* 240.
Podger, ES, 'Prosecution Guidelines in the United States' in E Luna and M Wade (eds), *The Prosecutor in Transnational Perspective* (Oxford, Oxford University Press, 2012) 9.
Pollard, C, 'Whitlam and Democracy' (2014) 133 *Arena Magazine* 5.
Poulin, AB, 'Prosecutorial Discretion and Selective Prosecution: Enforcing Protection after United States v Armstrong' (1997) 34 *American Criminal Law Review* 1071.
Pound, R, 'Discretion, Dispensation and Mitigation: The Problem of the Individual Special Case' (1960) 35 *New York Law Review* 925.

Pronin, E et al, 'Objectivity in the Eye of the Beholder: Divergent Perceptions of Bias in Self Versus Others' (2004) 111 *Psychological Review* 781.

Radan, P, 'Law, Politics, and the Attorney-General: The Context and Impact of *Gouriet v Union of Post Office Workers*' (2016) 16 *Macquarie Law Journal* 105.

Ramadan, HM, 'Reconstructing Reasonableness in Criminal Law: Moderate Jury Instructions Proposal' (2003) 29 *Journal of Legislation* 233.

Ramsey, CB, 'The Discretionary Power of "Public" Prosecutors in Historical Perspective' (2002) 39 *American Criminal Law Review* 1309.

Ransley, J and Johnstone, R, 'The Fitzgerald Symposium' (2009) 18 *Griffith Law Review* 531.

Raynor, P, 'Some Observations on Rehabilitation and Justice' (1997) 36 *The Howard Journal of Crime and Justice* 248.

Raz, J, *The Authority of Law: Essays on Law and Morality* (Oxford, Oxford Scholarship Online, 2012).

Read, RM, 'Prosecutorial Discretion in Victoria' in IL Potas (ed), *Prosecutorial Discretion*, Seminar Proceedings No 6 (Australian Institute of Criminology, 7–9 November 1984) 91.

Remington, FJ and Rosenblum, VG, 'The Criminal Law and the Legislative Process' (1960) *University of Illinois Law Forum* 481.

Richman, D, 'Accounting for Prosecutors' in M Langer and DA Sklansky (eds), *Prosecutors and Democracy: A Cross-National Study* (Cambridge, Cambridge University Press, 2017) 40.

Ripstein, A, 'Reasonable Persons in Private Law' in G Bongiovanni et al (eds), *Reasonableness and Law* (Dordrecht, Springer, 2009) 255.

Rowan, E, *Understanding Child Sexual Abuse* (Jackson, University of Mississippi Press, 2006).

Roy, MN and Saha, SS, *Statutory Auditors' Independence in Protecting Stakeholders' Interest: An Empirical Study* (Cham, Palgrave Macmillan, 2018).

Rozenberg, J, *The Case for the Crown: The Inside Story of the Director of Public Prosecutions* (Wellingborough, Equation, 1987).

Rozenberg, J, *Trial of Strength: The Battle Between Ministers and Judges Over Who Makes the Law* (London, Richard Cohen Books, 1997).

Ryan, C et al, 'The Value of Public Sector Annual Reports and Annual Reporting Awards in Organisational Legitimacy' (2002) 8 *Accounting, Accountability and Performance* 61.

Ryan, M, 'The Constitutional Reform and Governance Act 2010: The Evolution and Development of a Constitutional Act' (2014) 35 *Liverpool Law Review* 233.

Sarre, R, 'How I Would Spend $100 Million to Reduce Crime' (2017) 28 *Current Issues in Criminal Justice* 339.

Sarre, R, 'The Criminal Process' in M Marmo et al (eds), *Crime and Justice: A Guide to Criminology*, 4th rev edn (Pyrmont, Thomson Reuters, 2012).

Sarre, R, 'We Get the Crime We Deserve: Exploring the Disconnect in "Law and Order" Politics' (2011) 18 *James Cook University Law Review* 144.

Salzmann, VS and Dunwoody, PT, 'Prime-Time Lies: Do Portrayals of Lawyers Influence How People Think About the Legal Profession' (2005) 58 *SMU Law Review* 412.

Sammeck, J (ed), *A New Institutional Economics Perspective on Industry Self-Regulation* (Wiesbaden, Springer Gabler, 2012).

Sanders, A, 'Incorporating the "Public Interest" in the Decision to Prosecute' in J Williams (ed), *The Role of the Prosecutor: Report of the International Criminal Justice Seminar Held at the London School of Economics and Political Science in January 1987* (London, Dartmouth Publishing, 1988) 30.

Schmittat, SM et al, 'Alternative Stories and the Decision to Prosecute: An Applied Approach Against Confirmation Bias in Criminal Prosecution' (2022) 28 *Psychology, Crime & Law* 608.

Schubert, G, *The Public Interest: A Critique of the Theory of a Political Concept* (Glencoe, The Free Press, 1960).

Schuh, AM, 'Leadership in Organizations' in A Farazmand (ed), *Global Encyclopedia of Public Administration, Public Policy, and Governance* (Cham, Springer Nature, 2018) 3677.

Selway, B, 'The Different Role of an Australian Attorney-General' (2002) 13 *Public Law Review* 263.

Sexton, M, 'The Whitlam Government in Retrospect: Thirty Years On' (2006) 18 *The Sydney Papers* 133.
Sexton, M, 'Uncertain Justice: Inside Australia's Legal System' (2001) 33 *Australian Journal of Forensic Sciences* 51.
Shaw, GC, 'HLA Hart's Lost Essay: Discretion and the Legal Process School' (2013) 127 *Harvard Law Review* 666.
Shawcross, H, 'The Office of the Attorney-General' (1953) 7 *Parliamentary Affairs* 380.
Sheehy, E et al, 'Defending Battered Women on Trial: The Battered Woman Syndrome and Its Limitations' (1992) 16 *Criminal Law Journal* 369.
Shikibu, M, *The Tale of Genji* (c 1008).
Sossin, L and Smith, CW, 'The Politics of Transparency and Independence Before Administrative Boards' (2012) 75 *Saskatchewan Law Review* 13.
St George, S and Spohn, C, 'Liberating Discretion: The Effect of Rape Myth Factors on Prosecutors' Decisions to Charge Suspects in Penetrative and Non-Penetrative Sex Offenses' (2018) 35 *Justice Quarterly* 1280.
Stenning, PC, 'Discretion, Politics, and the Public Interest in High-Profile Criminal Investigations and Prosecutions' (2009) 24 *Canadian Journal of Law and Society* 337.
Stenning, PC, 'Prosecutions, Politics and the Public Interest: Some Recent Developments in the United Kingdom, Canada and Elsewhere' (2010) 55 *Criminal Law Quarterly* 449.
Stone, B, 'Accountability and the Design of an Anticorruption Agency in a Parliamentary Democracy' (2015) 36 *Policy Studies* 157.
Stoker, G, 'Embracing the Mixed Nature of Politics' in P Fawcett et al (eds), *Anti-Politics, Depoliticization, and Governance* (Oxford, Oxford Scholarship Online, 2017) 1.
Stuart, D, 'Prosecutorial Accountability in Canada' in P Stenning (ed), *Accountability for Criminal Justice: Selected Essays* (Toronto, University of Toronto Press, 1995) 330.
Stuntz, WJ, 'Self-Defeating Crimes' (2000) 86 *Virginia Law Review* 1871.
Stuntz, WJ, 'The Political Constitution of Criminal Justice' (2006) 119 *Harvard Law Review* 780.
Suchman, MC, 'Managing Legitimacy: Strategic and Institutional Approaches' (1995) 20 *The Academy of Management Review* 571.
Sweeny, PH, 'The Role of the Police Prosecutor in the Magistrates Court System' in IL Potas (ed), *Prosecutorial Discretion*, Seminar Proceedings No 6 (Australian Institute of Criminology, 7–9 November 1984) 135.
Sykes, EI, 'The "Rule of Law" in the Modern World: W Ivor Jennings, "The Law and the Constitution"' (1935) 1 *Res Judicatae* 56.
Tamanaha, BZ, *On the Rule of Law: History, Politics, Theory* (Cambridge, Cambridge University Press, 2004).
Tarling, R, 'Interdependence and the Crown Prosecution Service' in JEH Williams (ed), *The Role of the Prosecutor: Report of the International Criminal Justice Seminar Held at the London School of Economics and Political Science in January 1987* (London, Dartmouth Publishing, 1988) 43.
Temby, I, 'Prosecution Discretions and the Director of Public Prosecutions Act 1983' (1985) 59 *Australian Law Journal* 197.
Thatcher, M, 'Delegation to Independent Regulatory Agencies: Pressures, Functions and Contextual Mediation' (2002) 25 *West European Politics* 125.
Thompson, E, 'The Constitution and the Australian System of Limited Government, Responsible Government and Representative Democracy: Revisiting the Washminster Mutation' (2001) 24 *University of New South Wales Law Journal* 657.
Tombs, J, 'Prosecution – In the Public Interest?' in IL Potas (ed), *Prosecutorial Discretion*, Seminar Proceedings No 6 (Australian Institute of Criminology, 7–9 November 1984) 11.
Tonry, M, 'Preface' in M Tonry (ed), *Prosecutors and Politics: A Comparative Perspective* (Chicago, University of Chicago Press, 2013) vii.
Tonry, M, 'Prosecutors and Politics in Comparative Perspective' in M Tonry (ed), *Prosecutors and Politics: A Comparative Perspective* (Chicago, University of Chicago Press, 2012) 1.

Toole, K, 'The Decision to Prosecute – Accountability of Australian Prosecutors' in V Colvin and P Stenning (eds), *The Evolving Role of the Public Prosecutor: Challenges and Innovations* (New York, Routledge, 2019) 232.

Toole, K, 'The Making of Prosecutorial Decisions in Australia' (2014) 39 *Alternative Law Journal* 268.

Toole, K and Le Mire, S, 'From Failure to Hope?: Lawyer Regulation in South Australia' (2014) 39 *Alternative Law Journal* 63.

Trebilcock, MJ and Daniels, RJ, *Rule of Law Reform and Development: Charting the Fragile Path of Progress* (Cheltenham, Edward Elgar Publishing, 2009).

Ulliver, HR, 'The Neutral Prosecutor: The Obligation of Dispassion in a Passionate Dispute' (2000) 68 *Fordham Law Review* 1695.

Varuhas, J, 'The Public Interest Conception of Public Law: Its Procedural Origins and Substantive Implications' in J Bell et al (ed), *Public Law Adjudication in Common Law Systems: Process and Substance* (Oxford, Hart Publishing, 2016) 45.

Walker, B, 'Whitlam Oration: The Information that Democracy Needs' (2018) 47 *Law Society of NSW Journal* 76.

Walker B and Hume, D, 'Broadly Framed Powers and the Constitution' in N Williams (ed), *Key Issues in Public Law* (Alexandria, The Federation Press, 2018) 144.

Wanna, J, 'Queensland' (1997) 44 *Australian Journal of Politics and History* 261.

Weatherburn, D, 'Law and Order Blues' (2002) 35 *Australian & New Zealand Journal of Criminology* 127.

Weigend, T, 'A Judge by Another Name? Comparative Perspectives on the Role of the Public Prosecutor' in E Luna and M Wade (eds), *The Prosecutor in Transnational Perspective* (Oxford, Oxford University Press, 2012) 377.

Welling, LLM, 'Female Orgasm' in TK Shackelford and VA Weekes-Shackelford (eds), *Evolutionary Perspectives on Human Sexual Psychology and Behavior* (New York, Springer, 2014) 223.

Wheeler, C, 'The Public Interest Revisited – We Know It's Important but Do We Know What It Means?' (2013) 72 *Australian Institute of Administrative Law Forum* 34.

Wheeler, F, 'Judicial Review of Prerogative Power in Australia: Issues and Prospects' (1992) 14 *Sydney Law Review* 432.

Williams, JM, 'Bradley Maxwell Selway: A Personal Tribute' (2005) 33 *Federal Law Review* 181.

Williams, JM, 'Law and Order' in J Spoehr (ed), *State of South Australia: Trends and Issues* (Adelaide, Wakefield Press, 2005) 260.

Williams, R, 'Democracy, Development and Anti-Corruption Strategies: Learning from the Australian Experience' (1999) 37 *Journal of Commonwealth and Comparative Politics* 135.

Wilson, MD, 'The Common Prosecutor' (2022) 53 *Loyola University Chicago Law Journal* 325.

Winters, GM and Jeglic, EL, 'Stages of Sexual Grooming: Recognizing Potentially Predatory Behaviors of Child Molesters' (2017) 38 *Deviant Behavior* 724.

Woodhouse, D, 'The Attorney General' (1997) 50 *Parliamentary Affairs* 97.

Woodruff, P, 'Growing Toward Justice' in M LeBar (ed), *Justice* (Oxford, Oxford University Press, 2018) 13.

Worrall, JL et al, 'Modeling Prosecutors' Charging Decisions in Domestic Violence Cases' (2006) 52 *Crime & Delinquency* 472.

Yamahiro, H and Garzón-Montano, L, 'A Mirage Not a Movement: The Misguided Enterprise of Progressive Prosecution' (2022) *The Harbinger* 130.

Yang, K, 'Public Accountability of Public Prosecutions' (2013) 20 *Murdoch University Law Review* 28.

Zifcak, S, 'Why Bernard Collaery's Case Is One of the Gravest Threats to Freedom of Expression' (2020) 69 *Law Society of NSW Journal* 88.

Zifcak, S, 'Witness K and Bernard Collaery: An Unjust Prosecution Gets Even Worse', *Pearls and Irritations: John Menadue's Public Policy Journal* (12 October 2020) www.johnmenadue.com/spencer-zifcak-witness-k-and-bernard-collaery-an-unjust-prosecution-gets-even-worse/.

Reports/Briefing/Working Papers

Attorney-General's Office, *The Governance of Britain: A Consultation on the Role of the Attorney General* (26 July 2007).

Australian Communications and Media Authority, 'Seven News Broadcast on 21 March 2018' (18 July 2018) Investigation Report No BI-405.

Australian Law Reform Commission and NSW Law Reform Commission, *Family Violence – A National Legal Response* (Final Report, October 2010).

Champion, J, *Report of the Director of Public Prosecutions in Relation to Recommendation 12 of the Kellam Report* (2016).

Chilcot, J, *The Report of the Iraq Inquiry: Report of a Committee of Privy Counsellors* (House of Commons, 6 July 2016).

Clements, C, Office of the State Coroner, *Finding of Inquest: Inquest into the Death of Mulrunji* (27 September 2006).

Cole, T, *Report of the Inquiry into Certain Australian Companies in Relation to the UN Oil-for-Food Programme* (27 November 2006).

Commission on Criminal Law, *Eighth Report of Her Majesty's Commissioners on Criminal Law* (5 July 1845).

Comrie, N, *Victoria Police Human Source 3838: A Case Review* (2012).

Crime and Misconduct Commission (Queensland), *Seeking Justice: An Inquiry into How Sexual Offences Are Handled by the Queensland Criminal Justice System* (June 2003).

Crime and Misconduct Commission (Queensland), *The Volkers Case: Examining the Conduct of the Police and Prosecution* (March 2003).

Criminal Justice Commission (Queensland), *The Impact of the Connolly–Ryan Inquiry on the Criminal Justice Commission* (September 1997).

Department of the Parliamentary Library, Legislative Research Service, *Short Digest of Bill, Director of Public Prosecutions Bill 1983* (29 November 1983) 182.

Director of Public Prosecutions, Victoria, *The Pursuit of Justice: 25 Years of the DPP in Victoria* (Director of Public Prosecutions, 2008).

Edwards, J, *Ministerial Responsibility for National Security as It Relates to the Offices of Prime Minister, Attorney General and Solicitor General of Canada* (Minister of Supply and Services Canada, 1980).

Fitzgerald, GE, *Commission of Inquiry into Possible Illegal Activities and Associated Police Misconduct* (3 July 1989).

Ginwala, F, *Report of the Enquiry into the Fitness of Advocate VP Pikoli to Hold the Office of National Director of Public Prosecutions* (4 November 2008).

Grewal, BS, 'Australian Loan Council: Arrangements and Experience with Bailouts' (Latin American Research Network, 2000) Research Network Working Paper 397.

Hazlitt, G et al, *Sentencing Offenders Convicted of Child Sexual Assault: Judicial Commission of New South Wales*, Monograph Series 25 (September 2004).

His Majesty's Crown Prosecution Service Inspectorate, *Inspection of CPS Special Crime and Counter Terrorism Division* (February 2019).

His Majesty's Crown Prosecution Service Inspectorate, *Thematic Review of the CPS Rape and Serious Sexual Offences Units* (February 2016).

Hine, B, Office of the State Coroner, *Finding of Inquest: Inquest into the Death of Mulrunji* (14 May 2010).

House of Commons, Constitutional Affairs Committee, *Constitutional Role of the Attorney General* (Fifth Report of Session 2006–07, 17 July 2007).

Johns, R, 'Independence and Accountability of the Director of Public Prosecutions: A Comparative Survey' (July 2001) NSW Parliamentary Library Research Service Briefing Paper No 9/2001.

Kellam, M, *Report Concerning Victoria Police Handling of Human Source Code Name 3838* (2015).

Lamer, A, The *Lamer Commission of Inquiry Pertaining to the Cases of: Ronald Dalton, Gregory Parsons, Randy Druken: Report and Annexes* (St John's Government of Newfoundland and Labrador, 2006).

Law Commission, *Consents to Prosecution: Item 11 of the Sixth Programme of Law Reform Criminal Law* (19 October 1998).

Law Reform Commission of Canada, 'Controlling Criminal Prosecutions: The Attorney General and the Crown Prosecutor' (1990) Working Paper 62.

Law Reform Commission, *Sentencing of Federal Offenders: Interim* (Report No 15, Australian Government Publishing Service, 1980).

MacFarlane, BA and Cordner, SM, *Wrongful Convictions: The Effect of Tunnel Vision and Predisposing Circumstances in the Criminal Justice System* (Government of Ontario, 2008).

Majone, G, 'Independence vs Accountability?: Non-majoritarian Institutions and Democratic Government in Europe' (European University Institute, 1994) Working Paper No 94/3.

McMillan, J, 'Parliament and Administrative Law' (Department of the Parliamentary Library (7 November 2000) Research Paper No 13.

McMurdo, M, *Royal Commission into the Management of Police Informants: Final Report*, vol 1 (Victorian Government Printer, 2020).

McMurdo, M, *Royal Commission into the Management of Police Informants: Final Report*, vol 2 (Victorian Government Printer, 2020).

McMurdo, M, *Royal Commission into the Management of Police Informants: Summary and Recommendations* (Victorian Government Printer, 2020).

Ministry of Justice (New Zealand), *Examining the Prosecution Systems of England and Wales, Canada, Australia and Scotland: A Background Document to the Review of Public Prosecution Services in New Zealand* (September 2011).

National Committee on Law Observance and Law Enforcement, *Report on Prosecution* (Report No 4, 1931).

National Crime Authority, *Operation Hydra*, South Australian Reference No 2 (February 1991).

Nettle, G, *Special Report to Parliament* (20 June 2023).

New South Wales, Office of the Inspector of the Independent Commission against Corruption, *Report Pursuant to Section 77A Independent Commission Against Corruption Act 1988 Operation 'Hale': ICAC re Margaret Cunneen SC & Ors* (4 December 2015).

Parliament of the Commonwealth of Australia, Senate Standing Committee on Constitutional and Legal Affairs, *Report on the Freedom of Information Bill 1978, and Aspects of the Archives Bill 1978* (1979) Parliamentary Paper No 272/1979.

Parliament of Victoria, Legislative Council Privileges Committee, *Inquiry into Matters Relating to the Misuse of Electorate Office Staffing Entitlements* (Victorian Government Printer, August 2018).

Parliament of Western Australia, Legislative Council, *Report of Standing Committee on Legislation in Relation to the Director of Public Prosecutions Bill* (July 1990).

Parliamentary Committee for Electoral and Administrative Review, *Report on Review of Independence of the Attorney-General* (Legislative Assembly of Queensland, December 1993).

Parliamentary Committee for Electoral and Administrative Review, *The Independence of the Attorney-General, Review of an Electoral and Administrative Review Commission Report: Transcript of Proceedings* (Legislative Assembly of Queensland, 27 October 1993).

Royal Commission of Inquiry into Drug Trafficking: Final Report (Australian Government Publishing Service, February 1983).

Royal Commission on Criminal Procedure 1978–1981 (Command Report, 1981).

Royal Commission on the Activities of the Federated Ship Painters and Dockers Union, Interim Report, No 4, vol 1 (The Government of the Commonwealth of Australia and the Government of the State of Victoria, 1982).

Royal Commission on the Activities of the Federated Ship Painters and Dockers Union, Final Report (The Government of the Commonwealth of Australia and the Government of the State of Victoria, 1984).

Judd, K, *Response of Director of Public Prosecutions Kerri Judd KC to the Special Report of the Office of the Special Investigator* (1 December 2021).

Sofronoff, W, *Australian Capital Territory, Board of Inquiry: Criminal Justice System, Final Report* (31 July 2023).

Spencer, J, *Review of Public Prosecution Services (NZ)* (September 2011).

Victorian Ombudsman, *Investigation of a Matter Referred From the Legislative Council on 25 November 2015* (March 2018).
Vincent, F, *Report: Inquiry into the Circumstances that Led to the Conviction of Mr Farah Abdulkadir Jama* (Victorian Government Printer, May 2010).
Vinson, T et al, *Accountability and the Legal System: Drug Cases Terminating in the District Court 1980–1982* (Criminology Research Council, 1986).

Theses

Colvin, I, 'The Charging Decision: Accountability, Transparency, and Control of the Decision to Prosecute' (PhD Thesis, University of Queensland, 2016).
Hanlon, F, 'An Analysis of the Office of Attorney General in Australia and Directions for the Future' (PhD Thesis, University of Melbourne, 2007).
Kaib, D, 'The Mississippi Tobacco Case: Reform and the Boundaries of Law and Politics' (PhD Thesis, American University, 2011).
Plater, D, 'The Changing Role of the Modern Prosecutor: Has the Notion of the "Minister of Justice" Outlived its Usefulness?' (PhD Thesis, University of Tasmania, 2011).
Yang, K, 'Prosecutorial Discretion: A Balancing Act' (Honours Thesis, Murdoch University, 2012).

Parliamentary Debates

Australia

Australian Capital Territory, *Parliamentary Debates*, Legislative Assembly, 31 May 1990.
Commonwealth of Australia, *Parliamentary Debates*, Senate, 10 November 1983.
Commonwealth of Australia, *Parliamentary Debates*, Senate, 16 November 1983.
Commonwealth of Australia, *Parliamentary Debates*, Senate, 26 March 2015.
Commonwealth of Australia, *Parliamentary Debates*, Senate, 13 August 2015.
Commonwealth of Australia, *Parliamentary Debates*, Senate, 1 December 2015.
Commonwealth of Australia, *Parliamentary Debates*, Senate, 3 December 2015.
Commonwealth of Australia, *Parliamentary Debates*, Senate, 16 August 2018.
Commonwealth of Australia, *Parliamentary Debates*, House of Representatives, 6 September 1977.
Commonwealth of Australia, *Parliamentary Debates*, House of Representatives, 30 November 1983.
Commonwealth of Australia, *Parliamentary Debates*, House of Representatives, 17 February 1986.
Commonwealth of Australia, *Parliamentary Debates*, House of Representatives, 8 February 2022.
New South Wales, *Parliamentary Debates*, Legislative Assembly, 10 November 1983.
New South Wales, *Parliamentary Debates*, Legislative Assembly, 21 November 1985.
New South Wales, *Parliamentary Debates*, Legislative Assembly, 23 September 1986.
New South Wales, *Parliamentary Debates*, Legislative Assembly, 1 October 1986.
New South Wales, *Parliamentary Debates*, Legislative Assembly, 1 December 1986.
New South Wales, *Parliamentary Debates*, Legislative Council, 3 December 1986.
New South Wales, *Parliamentary Debates*, Legislative Council, 17 October 2007.
New South Wales, *Parliamentary Debates*, Legislative Assembly, 18 February 2016.
Northern Territory, *Parliamentary Debates*, Legislative Assembly, 28 February 1990.
Queensland, *Parliamentary Debates*, Legislative Assembly, 28 November 1984.
Queensland, *Parliamentary Debates*, Legislative Assembly, 7 March 2007.
South Australia, *Parliamentary Debates*, House of Assembly, 31 October 1991.
South Australia, *Parliamentary Debates*, House of Assembly, 17 September 2003.

South Australia, *Parliamentary Debates*, House of Assembly, 11 November 2003.
South Australia, *Parliamentary Debates*, House of Assembly, 16 February 2004.
South Australia, *Parliamentary Debates*, House of Assembly, 3 May 2004.
South Australia, *Parliamentary Debates*, House of Assembly, 6 May 2004.
South Australia, *Parliamentary Debates*, House of Assembly, 12 September 2005.
South Australia, *Parliamentary Debates*, House of Assembly, 20 September 2005.
South Australia, *Parliamentary Debates*, House of Assembly, 23 March 2016.
South Australia, *Parliamentary Debates*, House of Assembly, 17 May 2016.
South Australia, *Parliamentary Debates*, House of Assembly, 29 November 2017.
South Australia, *Parliamentary Debates*, Legislative Council, 12 August 1987.
South Australia, *Parliamentary Debates*, Legislative Council, 25 August 1988.
South Australia, *Parliamentary Debates*, Legislative Council, 21 August 1991.
South Australia, *Parliamentary Debates*, Legislative Council, 8 October 1991.
South Australia, *Parliamentary Debates*, Legislative Council, 9 October 1991.
Tasmania, *Parliamentary Debates*, Legislative Assembly, 17 September 2015.
Tasmania, *Parliamentary Debates*, Legislative Assembly, 24 September 2015.
Tasmania, *Parliamentary Debates*, Legislative Council, 15 March 2016.
Victoria, *Parliamentary Debates*, Legislative Assembly, 18 November 1982.
Victoria, *Parliamentary Debates*, Legislative Assembly, 9 December 1982.
Victoria, *Parliamentary Debates*, Legislative Assembly, 15 December 1982.
Victoria, *Parliamentary Debates*, Legislative Assembly, 10 November 1999.
Victoria, *Parliamentary Debates*, Legislative Assembly, 9 December 1999.
Victoria, *Parliamentary Debates*, Legislative Assembly, 13 December 2017.
Victoria, *Parliamentary Debates*, Legislative Assembly, 7 June 2018.
Victoria, *Parliamentary Debates*, Legislative Assembly, 8 August 2018.
Victoria, *Parliamentary Debates*, Legislative Council, 29 June 1982.
Victoria, *Parliamentary Debates*, Legislative Council, 14 December 1982.
Victoria, *Parliamentary Debates*, Legislative Council, 27 May 1994.
Victoria, *Parliamentary Debates*, Legislative Counsel, 15 December 1999.
Western Australia, *Parliamentary Debates*, Legislative Assembly, 15 June 1988.
Western Australia, *Parliamentary Debates*, Legislative Assembly, 4 April 1989.
Western Australia, *Parliamentary Debates*, Legislative Council, 19 October 1989.
Western Australia, *Parliamentary Debates*, Legislative Council, 24 October 1989.
Western Australia, *Parliamentary Debates*, Legislative Council, 23 November 1989.
Western Australia, *Parliamentary Debates*, Legislative Council, 28 November 1989.
Western Australia, *Parliamentary Debates*, Legislative Council, 7 June 1990.
Western Australia, *Parliamentary Debates*, Legislative Council, 28 March 1991.
Western Australia, *Parliamentary Debates*, Legislative Council, 30 April 1991.
Western Australia, *Parliamentary Debates*, Legislative Council, 14 May 1991.
Western Australia, *Parliamentary Debates*, Legislative Council, 7 June 1991.

United Kingdom

HC Deb 15 November 1979.
HC Deb 19 February 1903.
HC Deb 11 December 1924, vol 179, cols 354–55.
HC Deb 29 January 1951.
HL Deb 14 December 2006.
HL Deb 1 February 2007.

Australian Office of Director of Public Prosecutions Materials

Policy

Commonwealth Director of Public Prosecutions, *Prosecution Policy of the Commonwealth* (2021).
Commonwealth Director of Public Prosecutions, *Victims of Crime Policy* (undated).
Department of Justice and Attorney-General (Queensland), *Director's Guidelines* (2016).
Director of Public Prosecutions, *Prosecution Policy of the Australian Capital Territory* (2021).
Director of Public Prosecutions, South Australia, *Statement of Prosecution Policy & Guidelines* (2014).
Director of Public Prosecutions, South Australia, *Victims Right to Review of Discretionary Prosecutorial Decisions* (2017).
Director of Public Prosecutions (Tasmania), *Prosecution Policy and Guidelines* (2022).
Director of Public Prosecutions, Victoria, *Discontinuance Review Framework* (undated).
Guidelines of the Director of Public Prosecutions (Northern Territory) (2016).
Message from the Director of Public Prosecutions, Director of Public Prosecutions (Western Australia), *Statement of Prosecution Policy and Guidelines* (2018).
Office of the Director of Public Prosecutions, New South Wales, *Prosecution Guidelines* (2021).
Office of the Director of Public Prosecutions, New South Wales, *Victims' Right of Review Policy* (2021).
Office of the Director of Public Prosecutions (Western Australia), *Statement of Prosecution Policy and Guidelines* (2018).
Director of Public Prosecutions for Western Australia, *Policy and Guidelines for Victims of Crime* (2022).
Policy of the Director of Public Prosecutions for Victoria (2021).
Victims Services, New South Wales, Department of Communities and Justice, *Charter of Victims Rights* (2021).

Annual Reports

New South Wales, Office of the Director of Public Prosecutions, *Annual Report 2018–2019* (10 October 2019).
New South Wales, Office of the Director of Public Prosecutions, *Annual Report 2021–2022* (14 October 2022).
Office of the Director of Public Prosecutions for Western Australia, *Annual Report 2021–2022* (29 September 2022).
South Australia, Director of Public Prosecutions, *Annual Report 2019–2020* (30 September 2020).
Victoria, Director of Public Prosecutions, *Annual Report 2021–2022* (21 November 2022).

Royal Commission into Institutional Responses to Child Sexual Abuse Materials

Brennan, P, *Supreme Court of Queensland, Julie Therese Gilbert and Scott Alexander Volkers* (Expert Report, 31 October 2004).
Cashmore, J et al, *The Impact of Delayed Reporting on the Prosecution and Outcomes of Child Sexual Abuse Cases* (Report for the Royal Commission into Institutional Responses to Child Sexual Abuse, August 2016).

Evidence to Royal Commission into Institutional Responses into Child Sexual Abuse, 10 July 2014, 11 July 2014, 14 July 2014, 16 July 2014, 29 April 2016.

Freiberg, A et al, *Sentencing for Child Sexual Abuse in Institutional Contexts* (Report for the Royal Commission into Institutional Responses to Child Sexual Abuse, 2015).

Middleton, W, *Supreme Court of Queensland, Julie Therese Gilbert and Scott Alexander Volkers* (Expert Report, 15 October 2004).

Royal Commission into Institutional Responses into Child Sexual Abuse, *Final Report: Sport, Recreation, Arts, Culture, Community and Hobby Groups*, vol 14 (2017).

Royal Commission into Institutional Responses into Child Sexual Abuse, *Public Hearing – Criminal Justice DPP Complaints and Oversight Mechanisms* (29 April 2016).

Royal Commission into Institutional Responses into Child Sexual Abuse, *Report of Case Study No 15: Response of Swimming Institutions, the Queensland and NSW Offices of the DPP and the Queensland Commission for Children and Young People and Child Guardian to Allegations of Sexual Abuse by Swimming Coaches* (November 2015).

Royal Commission into Institutional Responses into Child Sexual Abuse, *Report of Case Study No 17: The Response of the Australian Indigenous Ministries, the Australian and NT Governments and the NT Police Force and Prosecuting Authorities to Allegations of Child Sexual Abuse Which Occurred at the Retta Dixon Home* (July 2015).

Royal Commission into Institutional Responses into Child Sexual Abuse, Statement of Anthony Moynihan, 14 July 2014.

Royal Commission into Institutional Responses into Child Sexual Abuse, Statement of Julie Gilbert, 23 May 2014.

Royal Commission into Institutional Responses into Child Sexual Abuse, Statement of Kylie Rogers, 6 July 2014.

Royal Commission into Institutional Responses into Child Sexual Abuse, Statement of Margaret Cunneen, 3 July 2014.

Royal Commission into Institutional Responses into Child Sexual Abuse, Statement of Nicholas Cowdery, 8 July 2014.

Royal Commission into Institutional Responses into Child Sexual Abuse, Statement of Simone Boyce, 4 July 2014.

Royal Commission into Institutional Responses to Child Sexual Abuse, Submissions of Counsel Assisting the Royal Commission (undated).

Royal Commission into Institutional Responses to Child Sexual Abuse, Submissions on Behalf of Julie Gilbert, Simone Boyce, Kylie Rogers, Sharyn Rogers and John Rogers as to the Effect of R v Wruck [2014] QCA 3, 14 July 2014.

Transcript of interview between Leanne Clare, Darren Brazier, Julie Gilbert, Shane Gilbert, Hetty Johnston and Mr Tolhurst, 11 May 2004.

Conference Presentations/Lectures/ Speeches/Press Conferences

Alvey, J, 'The Separation of Powers Between the Executive and the Judiciary', Conference Paper, Australasian Study of Parliament Conference, 27–29 September 2017.

Bugg, D, 'The Role of the DPP in the 20th Century', Speech, Judicial Conference of Australia, 13 November 1999.

De Vos, P, 'When Political and Prosecutorial Prerogatives Clash in a "Neo-Patrimonial" State: The Case of South Africa's National Prosecuting Authority', Conference Paper, The Evolving Role of the Prosecutor Domestically and Internationally, 28–29 July 2016.

Dreyfus, M, 'Press Conference on Bernard Collaery', Press Conference, 7 July 2022.

Flatman, G, 'Independence of the Prosecutor', Conference Paper, Australian Institute of Criminology, Prosecuting Justice Conference, 18–19 April 1996.
Kimber, A, '20 Years of the DPP: How Far Have We Come?', Speech, Justice Oration, 18 October 2012.
Kourakis, C, Speech, SA Press Club, 14 May 2015.
Krone, T, 'Police and Prosecution', Conference Paper, National Outlook Symposium on Crime in Australia: Mapping the Boundaries of Australia's Criminal Justice System, 22–23 March 1999.
Mason, A, 'The Kerr Report of 1971: Its Continuing Significance', Lecture, Council of Australasian Tribunals NSW Chapter, 19 September 2007.
Mathew, T, Address to the Law Society, 1952 cited in J Edwards, *The Law Officers of the Crown: A Study of the Offices of Attorney-General and Solicitor-General of England with an Account of the Office of the Director of Public Prosecutions of England* (London, Sweet & Maxwell, 1964) 390.
Mathew, T, Lecture, London University, 1950.
McClelland, R, 'Remarks at the Commonwealth Director of Public Prosecutions' 25th Anniversary Dinner', Speech, Old Parliament House, 5 March 2009.
Pallaras, S, Speech, SA Press Club, 6 May 2005.
Pepper, R, 'Celebrating 100 Years of the Commonwealth Solicitor-General: Closing Remarks', Speech, Banco Court, Sydney, 24 October 2016.
Selway, B, 'Nemer: Ethics and the DPP', Lecture, Selected Issues in Criminal Law & Procedure, University of Adelaide, 7 July 2004.
Warren, M, 'What Is Justice?', Speech, Newman Lecture Mannix College, 20 August 2014.

Published Correspondence

Letter from Colonial Secretary to Governor Darling, 1829.
Letter from Hartley Shawcross, *The Times*, 3 August 1977.
Letter from Leanne Clare to Nicholas Cowdery, 19 December 2003.
Letter from Leanne Clare to Woodgate Hughes Solicitors, 9 April 2003.
Letter from Michael J Byrne to Leanne Clare, 3 September 2002.
Letter from Nicholas Cowdery to Leanne Clare, 2 April 2004.
Letter from Paul Rutledge to Simone Boyce, 27 September 2002.
Letter from RV Hanson to Woodgate Hughes Solicitors, 20 February 2003.
Letter from RV Hanson to Woodgate Hughes Solicitors, 26 May 2004.
Letter from Tony Giugni to Nicholas Cowdery, 2 July 2014.
Letter from Woodgate Hughes Solicitors to Leanne Clare, 26 March 2003.
Memorandum of Justice Benjamin Boothby, 1862.
Memorandum of Margaret Cunneen to Nicholas Cowdery, 26 March 2004.
Memorandum of Nicholas Cowdery to Police Association of South Australia, 27 April 2015.
Memorandum of Thomas Hetherington to House of Commons Select Committee on Deaths in Police Custody, 1980.
Notice of Proposed Adverse Comments from Walter Sofronoff KC, Chairperson, Board of Inquiry, to Acting Assistant Commissioner Joanne Cameron, Australian Federal Police, 9 June 2023.
Notice of Proposed Adverse Comments from Walter Sofronoff KC, Chairperson, Board of Inquiry, to Commander Michael Chew, Australian Federal Police, 9 June 2023.
Notice of Proposed Adverse Comments from Walter Sofronoff KC, Chairperson, Board of Inquiry, to Detective Inspector Marcus Boorman, Australian Federal Police, 9 June 2023.
Notice of Proposed Adverse Comments from Walter Sofronoff KC, Chairperson, Board of Inquiry, to Detective Leading Senior Constable Trent Madders, Australian Federal Police, 9 June 2023.
Notice of Proposed Adverse Comments from Walter Sofronoff KC, Chairperson, Board of Inquiry, to Detective Sergeant Robert Rose, Australian Federal Police, 9 June 2023.

Notice of Proposed Adverse Comments from Walter Sofronoff KC, Chairperson, Board of Inquiry, to Detective Superintendent Scott Moller, Australian Federal Police, 9 June 2023.
Notice of Proposed Adverse Comments from Walter Sofronoff KC, Chairperson, Board of Inquiry, to Heidi Yates, Victims of Crime Commissioner, 9 June 2023.
Notice of Proposed Adverse Comments from Walter Sofronoff KC, Chairperson, Board of Inquiry, to Neville Shane Drumgold SC DPP, 9 June 2023.
Notice of Proposed Adverse Comments from Walter Sofronoff KC, Chairperson, Board of Inquiry, to Neville Shane Drumgold SC DPP, 9 July 2023.
Notice of Proposed Adverse Comments from Walter Sofronoff KC, Chairperson, Board of Inquiry, to Senior Constable Emma Frizzell, Australian Federal Police, 9 June 2023.
Notice of Proposed Adverse Comments from Walter Sofronoff KC, Chairperson, Board of Inquiry, to The Proper Officer, Australian Federal Police, 9 June 2023.

News Reports

Article in *Sun-Herald* (23 December 1993).
Comment of Premier Jeff Kennett reported in *The Age* (16 December 1993).
Lord Denman, *The Edinburgh Review* (1824) vol xl 191.
'Editorial' *The Times* (28 July 1977).
Hockley, C, 'Power of the People' *The Advertiser* (31 July 2003).
Rann, M, address to reporters in South Australia, 2003.
The Parliamentarian (July 1978).

Media Releases and Reasons for Decisions

ACT Director of Public Prosecutions, 'RE: DPP v Lehrmann SCC 264 o021', Media Release, 2 December 2022.
ACT Director of Public Prosecutions, 'Police v O – CC2019/3260 Charge of Aiding Suicide under Section 17(1) Crimes Act 1900', Statement of Reasons, 28 June 2019.
ACT Director of Public Prosecutions, 'RE: DPP v Lehrmann SCC 264 o021', Media Release, 2 December 2022.
ACT Government, 'Joint Media Statement – Chief Minister and Attorney-General', Media Release, 7 August 2023.
Attorney-General for Australia and Minister for Industrial Relations, 'Prosecution Matter', Media Release, 28 June 2018.
Crime and Misconduct Commission (Queensland), 'CMC Statement Regarding Palm Island Death in Custody', Media Release, 14 December 2006.
Director of Public Prosecutions, South Australia, '*R v Hoy*', Media Release, 4 February 2015.
Office of the Director of Public Prosecutions, Queensland, 'Hurley Not to Face Criminal Charges', Media Release, 14 December 2006.
Shine, K, 'Attorney-General's Report on Palm Island Death-in-Custody Prosecution', Media Release, 18 July 2007.
Victorian Premier, Attorney-General, Minister for Police and Emergency Services, Royal Commission into Management of Informants', Media Release, 3 December 2018.

International Materials

Seizure and Detention of Certain Documents and Data (Timor-Leste v Australia) (Provisional Measures Order) [2014] ICJ.
United Nations Declaration of Basic Principles of Justice for Victims of Crime and Abuse of Power, GA Res 40/34 (29 November 1985).
United Nations, Human Rights, Office of the High Commissioner, *Guidelines on the Role of Prosecutors*, adopted by the Eighth United Nations Congress on the Prevention of Crime and the Treatment of Offenders (1990).

Miscellaneous

British Cabinet Minutes, 6 August 1924.
Crown Prosecution Service, *Victims' Right to Review – Policy and Guidance* (2020).
Drumgold v Board of Inquiry – Criminal Justice System & Ors – SC 347/23, Originating Application – Judicial Review (25 August 2023).
Hetherington, T, written evidence submitted to the Royal Commission on Criminal Procedure, 1978.
Law Ministers' Meeting, Canada, Communique (August 1977).
Protocol between the Attorney General and the Prosecuting Departments (Attorney General's Office, Crown Prosecution Service, Serious Fraud Office, Revenue and Customs Prosecutions Office, July 2009).
Sentencing Remarks, *R v Nemer*, 25 July 2003 (Sulan J).
Transcript of Proceedings, *Nemer v Holloway and Others* [2004] HCATrans 24.

INDEX

Printed in the USA
CPSIA information can be obtained
at www.ICGtesting.com
LVHW080835070824
787367LV00015B/62

9 781509 973200